To all Mate...

with good wishes

love

Phil Gates

Nov 2002

A Soft Rebel Yell

From Grits to Gotham

Philomene A. Gates

Gridiron Publishers

To my family and friends whose stories I have told and whose lives have so enriched mine.

Also by Philomene A. Gates

Suddenly Alone, Harper & Row, 1990

Dedicated to:

My fabulous six granddaughters, Katie Wray Baughman, Hope Stearns Moeller, Bess Williamson, Leigh Stearns, Helen Howell Wray, Eleanor Fuqua Williamson, and fantastic six grandsons, Christopher Asher Wray, Owen Johnson Stearns, Samuel Gates Williamson, Edwin Williamson, Jr., Stephen Baughman, and Paul Moeller. These remarkable young people have added love and luster to my life and have, through their many accomplishments, made me proud. Now, through the content of these chapters they will know more about "where they came from," and about those who came before them in our families.

Acknowledgments

I would like to thank Michael Meatheringham, Marjorie Cline, Barbara Morgan, and Anna Menzies whose help was invaluable in bringing this memoir to fruition. The shelves of the Orlando, Florida library, the Archives of the state of North Carolina in Raleigh, and the rare document archives at Duke University, Durham, North Carolina, were sources of much I did not know from memory, and the articles of James Reston, Jr., and Eric Foner's books on the Reconstruction Period following the Civil War enlivened my research and provided much scholarship.

Table of Contents

Prologue

*People will not look forward to posterity who never look
backward to their ancestors.*

Reflections on the Revolution in France
— *Edmund Burke, 1729–1797*

I write these lines because after all these years I feel Southern. Southern is knowing where your people came from, how they got there, what they did with their lives, who married whom, and how it all turned out. This is my story as a proud granddaughter of Annie Elizabeth Powell Brown, born in Whiteville, North Carolina, in 1859. Her strong, sweet spirit helped us all swim through the tides of life and come out pretty well. Her unsmiling portrait hangs in the upstairs hallway of our country house in Long Island. Her face is framed, as it always was, by naturally curly chestnut hair, formally parted in the middle. No smidgen of makeup ever brushed across her silken, translucent skin, and it was unwrinkled until the day she died. She stares down at all my family members as they gallop by down the stairs, and I feel sure she would not approve of much of what she sees. The speed of my children, grandchildren, and soon great grandchildren passing her likeness depends entirely upon their ages, but no matter what the pace, "Miss Annie" would deem it too fast.

"Miss Annie" is what everyone called her, and to me, it perfectly fit the description often attributed to a true lady of the South, "a bulldozer . . . disguised as a powder puff . . . . She survived General Sherman's burning of Atlanta, she survived the Hari Krishnas taking over the plantations in Natchez."[1] She was a part of a breed which has endured in the South. She said, as Mary Norton Kratt wrote in her little book, "We treat people like they have money just because their granddaddy once did."[2]

She talked a lot about family so we all learned about our own history.

I never heard a word of complaint nor a whiny comment from her. God knows she had plenty to complain about. She had more patience than anyone I ever knew. Folks say that Southerners are more patient than people from other parts of the country because we have to sit through such long blessings before each meal, and we have to wait such a long time for the fish to bite.

Luckily for me and mine, she lived to be ninety-seven. She was keen of mind and never forgot details, whether they were attic smells, kitchen secrets, or the antics of her large brood. Nor did she ever forget to teach us values she thought important. Manners were almost a sacred heritage, such as calling colored people who were older "aunt" and "uncle." (Now those terms sound dated and condescending, but to her they were respectful.) She would occasionally call people "judges," even though they weren't, just because she thought they had acted fairly and in a dignified manner.

Her ancestors were Irish and Scottish and were ambitious, curious, and extremely hard working. I never remember anyone expressing rancor or acute resentment about the Yankee victory in the War between the States. What was more important than bitterness at losing was having the ability to make a living and keep what few assets they had left. After emancipation, they tried to hang on to what they could of their genteel way of life, acknowledging all the same, how essential slavery had been to their economy.

My North Carolina family spent many evenings after the sun had set on their fields, enjoying the literature of the day. Often gathering the whole household and any neighbors who cared to come, they read aloud about a world far away from their grief-filled days of war. They pored over Hawthorne, Longfellow, and Dickens and committed large portions to memory. Grandmother Annie remembered that whenever they read Scott's Waverly novels, they kept turning the pages well into the night, unwilling to put the vivid story down.

These gatherings were opportunities to share books and newspapers in the print-starved Confederate states. Since, by and large, most North Carolina families spent a good part of their days in manual labor, reading was a form of relaxation, self-education, and intellectual stimulation.

There were other gatherings—perhaps on a more regular schedule— for reading the Bible. Southerners have always seemed to me to be more familiar with the Bible than most northerners I knew who went to church out of habit, like brushing their teeth, not especially out of piety. Daddy used to say Mother's family talked about Jesus as if he were their next door neighbor!

Miss Annie often mused, "The postwar South is a failed empire, as well as a failed ideology. It is like a time bomb going tick-tock, tick-tock, waiting for things to explode." These are profound observations from one who had not finished high school. She was the Alpha and Omega to me, and I blindly adored her.

So this is my tale as Miss Annie's granddaughter, baptized Philomène for a French saint and a little Arcadian girl immortalized in a William Henry Drummond poem Daddy read to Mother when she was pregnant with me. He read it many times to me later, and I can still hear his melodious, dulcet Louisiana-accented speech. Although I was born in Daytona, Florida, in 1918, most of the first twenty years of my life were spent in Orlando.

These are the memories of a southern girl growing up in the "boom years" of the Roaring Twenties and the "bust years" of the Great Depression of the thirties. During those years we had a Model-T Ford, and as life went on to the nineties we had the moon landings and the Internet superhighway. I doubt that lifestyles have ever changed so dramatically in such a short period of time. I've surely tried to change with them, all the while clinging desperately to what I believe was good about the old times. Today I am probably politically correct—a woman lawyer, a woman undivorced (though widowed), and a past Southern Belle—at least that is the way I am frequently introduced to my extreme humiliation when I go home—home to the South.

I feel southern to the roots. I still remember, and repeat many family sayings and adages, and I've retained so many southern mannerisms. If I hear some member of my family criticize a relative, I am apt to say, "Its a base bird who defiles his own nest." After a particularly trying day I may describe my feeling as "death and destruction climbing up a collard stalk." Viewing an especially unpredictable member of our family, I might say, "she's flakier than mother's pie crust." Customs are also imbedded in my psyche, such as always carrying food to a family who has just lost a loved one. I was taught, "they may be grieving so hard they are not hungry and do not want to eat the food, but all the friends and relatives gathering around them have appetites."

I have rather lovingly nourished the sayings of my elders. When I resort to them, however, my progeny tend to look at me askance, and my married daughters, who grew up Yankees, tease me. They have even gone so far as to say that these old phrases are of a primitive society. Well, I guess the South I knew was, in its own way, a primitive society.

Family history, regional and geographical lore, Civil War memories— all were handed down by word of mouth through generations. Often the raconteur was a braggart. Never trust him or her, when he or she passes on a southern homily such as "if a chicken dips snuff, look under his wing for the can!" No one but southerners are familiar with snuff, and I heard that phrase time and again.

Cracker that I am, these words stay with me and are a part of who I am today. I'd like to "get them down" before they disappear from the scene. Today in many quarters honesty, kindness, reverence for family, and respect for older people are doing a fast disappearing act. Willingness to accept humble employment to further one's education is rarely encouraged. The love of learning, good taste, decency, the revulsion of obscene language and behavior is almost unknown, and people like me don't complain about so many lost or dying values for fear of being thought an "old fogey." I feel saddest about some of our young, so eager to "fulfill themselves" that they fail to consider the consequences of their conduct toward those who love them the most.

The idea slowly dawned on me that I might be able to describe my own charmed life and the extraordinary people I have known in a way which might catch the interest of today's reader. So many books I've read seem to dwell on dysfunctional families, on heroes and heroines who have been on psychoanalysts' couches and have all manner of dire goings on in their lives. Not that our family was without problems, eccentric relatives, and womanizing husbands, but we did seem to adjust, stay out of jail, earn a decent living, and contribute to our communities when we were needed. Is there no place for a story of a loving, lucky, loyal family? Do we have to wallow in erotic, violent X-rated behavior to catch the public interest? I hope not. Believe me there really is "a can of snuff under this old chicken's wing." Judge for yourself.

Notes

1. Marylyn Schwartz. *A Southern Belle's Primer: Or Why Princess Margaret Will Never be a Kappa Kappa Gamma.* (New York: Doubleday, 1991), x.

2. Mary Norton Kratt. *Southern Is....* (Atlanta: Peachtree Publishers Ltd., 1995), 6–7.

CHAPTER ONE

My Southern Heritage

The Greater Part of Our Happiness or Misery
Depends On Our Dispositions,
Not On Our Circumstances.
— *Martha Custis Washington, 1732–1802*

The Powells

My family history on Mother's side, as I know it, begins in the mid-eighteenth century in North Carolina. Whiteville, a small town less than fifty miles from the South Carolina border, is where Grandmother Annie Elizabeth Powell and Grandfather James Monroe Brown, lived, married, and raised their ten children, including my Mother, Mary Katherine. I hear their stories of my aunts and uncles—the banterings and reminiscences—ringing in my ears even today. Grandmother, a five-foot-two-inch lady, compact in body and mind, was always alert to the hustle and bustle that went on around her. In a flash she'd look up from her crocheting and comment on any bit of conversation one of her brood happened to make.

After my grandparents left their farm in Whiteville and retired to Maitland, Florida, the family chats continued for hours on end on the back screen porch. I remember joining these conversations when I was a small child. The words often painted a picture of a place both despised and blessed. They spoke of work never ceasing from the moment the light teased their sleepy eyes open until the sun crept below the ridge of the cottonwoods lining the meandering creek banks.

These are my people of the Old South who survived and raised a family on land they expected to pass on for generations. Yet in the terrible times to come, all that they held dear, down to the last smidgen of tea and the last uncracked family teacup, not crushed or stolen by invading Yankee troops, disappeared into oblivion.

If not for listening to these homey family conversations at Grandmother's knee, I might have never guessed that my roots had any reality in gentility and beauty. More important to me were the signs of genuine love that flowed back and forth between the people of color and our family members. When it came

Annie Elizabeth Powell

to the work, as Grandfather often said, "It didn't make no never mind what color we were. We all worked together."

Only once when I was seven years old did I visit the family farm in Whiteville and the large gray-shingled rambling home where Grandmother and Grandfather had lived. It was in my brief stays at Maitland in another gray-shingled home that I absorbed a sense of the God-fearing life they had led. These were people of conscience who practiced a work ethic just as precious as that of their Yankee counterparts. These were people who had to come to grips with the devastation of the War Between the States.

In April 1832, my relative, Thomas Powell, died and left his wife, Rachel, "all of his possessions except one sow, the pigs, and one-half of the swarms of bees which may have come this year." His will, as was the custom of that time, began, "In the name of God, *Amen*," showing his strong religious underpinnings. He added to the above provisions that "if she [Rachel] cannot manage the farm, she can sell all and have all of the monies arising from such sale. After her death, my grandsons, Duncan and McKay, can have it all." Both of those Scottish names persisted in our family for several generations. Another bequest passed on to "a negro named Fred" the following: "four suits of clothes, a blanket, a hat, three pairs of shoes and permission to call on medical facilities of our area."

Thomas Powell's nephew, my Great Great Grandfather Absalom

Powell, moved to Whiteville and started the Powell family farm in 1834. Whether he held an original Crown Grant or lands transferred to private hands after the American Revolution, I do not know, but his claims were authentic to his way of thinking.

Absalom's father, Jacob Powell, (my Great Great Great Grandfather) had bequeathed to him all of the "Negroes, cattle, hogs, and 2,500 acres of land with its furniture, horses, household accessories." The land and all that it produces and all that enables it to produce were in one big indivisible bundle. How could he even think of separating one of the essential elements that brought the land to life?

Absalom Powell, in his turn, attempted to care for the slaves who had worked on the farm. His will states, "The following Negroes came into my possession as the property of my immediately deceased ancestor, Jacob Powell." Absalom refers to those slaves who were minors. "For which," as he wrote, "I obtained the above notes for the hire of said Negroes. Their freedom had already been granted them at $550, namely Irwin, Alexander, Fred, Owen, Isabella, Elva, Caroline, Jim, Hannah, Daniel, Julia, and Frances." Absalom appointed George Pickett as the guardian of the minor children; all in his possession were free to live or die as best they could.

As I have looked through boxes and boxes of family records, I am amazed, and often saddened, to see how meticulously these farmers kept account of their meager assets. When Great Grandmother Francis Baldwin Powell died in 1870, the administrative judge, one Isaac Jackson, listed her estate on four pages. The possessions he itemized as part of the probate hardly seemed worth his time and effort: "Mug and cup 25 cents; 1 pair waffle irons 50 cents; an oven $2; a lard stand 70 cents; a churn 75 cents." Meat troughs, cleavers, warping bars and wheels, whatever they were, a cherry table for as little as $8.75. How sad!

Judge Jackson seemed to be a busy man as he parceled out the meager properties of others as well as of my ancestors. Horses, barrels, books, fodder, tools, cotton, as well as an ox cart or two went to the widow of James Smith. All she inherited, in addition to the above, was $736.05. These farming families and their descendants stayed on "the land between the RR and the Country Road, the land, 200 acres on Double Branch Creek, 100 acres in River Swamp." They "put one foot in front of the other" each day and survived. From all I ever could gather, they enjoyed good "family" times.

By 1860 South Carolina had seceded from the Union, outraged at Abraham Lincoln's presidential platform that opposed further extension of slavery and contained measures to strengthen and solidify the "Union." By mid-1861, North Carolina had followed. "States rights," Southerners said, caused the Civil War but no one denies that slavery and its abolition in states to be added to the "United States" was greatly encouraged by the secessionists revolt. Absalom, in face of the terrible trials that lay ahead for all concerned, had tried to assure the safety of his former slaves. These tragic times were to be different for master and former slave, but trials they most certainly were.

Grandmother Annie remembered when her Father, Eli Marvin Powell (my Great Grandfather), could no longer pay the $550 per year salary of his former slaves. She knew that only two of them had gone North and stayed. The rest came home, sad and bedraggled. They had followed that old "drinking gourd" to the land of milk and honey but soon became disillusioned with life in the North. There they endured nothing but unrelenting poverty and no familiar faces with whom to share their labor and sing the old songs as the sun set, and the last of the weeding and hoeing was done.

By 1862, soon after the first shots were fired in the War Between the States, North Carolina sent two regiments, the 7th and the 24th,[1] of its able men and bonny youth to join the Confederate forces fighting in Virginia. Great Grandfather Powell was among the first to go, leaving the Powell women to make a "life" in the dark, unlit country landscape. They were solely responsible for the care of the children, ill relatives, and the occasional disabled grown-up male relative. They were forced by necessity to plant and harvest the crops with their own hands and even breed the animals, the few the Yankee troops had let them keep for food. Their soft lily white hands soon became rough and calloused.

In the last two years of the war, there was no money at all for the use of the average Southern farm family. Only the occasional storekeeper, if he knew the family, would take "Confedericks," the worthless Confederate money. It required $50 (about $250 today) to buy a little yarn. Mary Chesnut,[2] in her famous diary, confirms that 16,000 Confederate dollars were exchanged for a warm coat. Southerners, even in the last days and months of the war, continued to buy Confederate bonds as well as their own state bonds, knowing full well that they were worthless paper. I played with Confederate money and bonds in Grandmother's attic, using that paper currency much like Monopoly money today.

Grandmother Annie never forgot the day at the end of March 1865 when General William Tecumseh Sherman's troops arrived in Whiteville.[3] The tale she spun told how her parents had received word of their movements through the "grapevine telegraph," a word-of-mouth communication network often carried on horseback through wooded trails. The Powells had hidden the family silver and other prized possessions in a swamp near a large shed where the tobacco was cured. On the day they heard that the Yankee troops were nearby, everyone on the farm, women and young boys, black and white, began a frenzied effort. They formed battalions to hide the good linens, preserved fruits, smoked hams, bags of potatoes, flour and rice and other vital foodstuffs.

While I sat wide-eyed as an owlet, Grandmother Annie told of the afternoon the Yankees galloped up the farm road stirring up so many whirls of dust that they spotted her pinafore. Horrified and helpless, she perched on the fence in front of the farmhouse, she watched Sherman's troops ransack their farm. Although they did not burn the buildings, they took all the foodstuff they could find, plus a year's supply of hand-dipped candles, which were quite dear because kerosene lamps and candles were all that were available for night lights.[4] She told me how a group of Yankee soldiers went through the house and even climbed the rickety ladder to the attic searching for treasure. They found only horsehair Victorian style sofas into which Confederate bonds were hidden. Within hours after their arrival, they had most of the edibles in their saddlebags, or in their stomachs. Grandmother never saw Sherman, himself, but she used to say that his troops looked very well fed compared to the South's soldiers who, by then, were straggling home all skin and bones.

Sherman's troops had burned Atlanta and Columbia to the ground, but they burned very few plantations in North Carolina as the general said he had already "punished the ones who started it." He was referring to South Carolina, of course. Only the really fine and elegant plantation homes owned by North Carolinians who had fled to escape the wrath of the Yankee army were burned and destroyed. Those families returned to find nothing standing save the lonely sentinel chimney guarding the ashes. Families who had fled too quickly to gather up their jewelry would never see these heirlooms again.

Savage reprisals and mutilations by the Yankee invaders, even though rare, terrified whole families. Racial violence was the ghost that refused to be laid to rest in the homes where women were left alone with the slaves. In North Carolina, however, one wife, who supported the Union, took comfort in the protection of "eighty-eight" negroes and had "not a sensation of fear."[5] Grandmother remembered often having her childhood sleep disturbed by the loud screams of children who had frequent nightmares after hearing stories their neighbors told. They sought safety and solace by climbing into the master bedroom's high canopy feather bed just to hug their mother or father, or instead they comforted themselves in the arms of a big sister or brother.

Great Grandfather Eli Marvin Powell was taken by the Yankees and did not come home from prison camps in New Jersey for several years, so my Great Grandmother Frances Baldwin Powell's bed had room for several sleepless frightened siblings. The North had its Andersonvilles, too.[6] Southern men in captivity died in even greater numbers than their Northern counterparts from infections, dysentery, and influenza because of the simple fact that they were not accustomed to the cold weather. Of the nearly 180,000 negro men who joined the Yankee troops, most never came home to the South again. There is no reliable record of their fate.[7]

We today forget that over 600,000 men died in that tragic war. Many in the North could pursue their trades and hire substitutes to take their draft calls. For the most part Southern men did not use substitutes because of their emotional devotion to "the cause" and to the disgrace they would face if they had. Both sides had their share of deserters, but in the fighting force, the South suffered more losses than the North.[8]

Grandmother Annie never forgot the day in July 1867 when her Father returned to the farm. She was then eight years old. "The Powell women and children," she said, "were picking cotton in 100 degree heat and humidity when they were startled by a man's hoarse rebel yell, a sound they had not heard in two years." The sound is described by historian Shelby Foote as, "wildcat screech, foxhunt yip, banshee squall," and he quotes a Tennessee veteran as saying that it was, "worse than folly to try to imitate it with a stomach full of food and a mouth full of false teeth."[9]

Since the war had ended in 1865, and no news had come to the Powell women about Great Grandfather, they had assumed that he was dead. So they were awestricken when they straightened their backs to see a naked red-bearded stranger limping up the dirt road to the house. He wore a glassy stare and an anxious and disoriented look. He had dumped his lice-infested prison clothes on the main road where the wagon had left him, for he did not want to bring such clothing into the home he had dreamed of since his departure in 1862.

Great Grandfather Powell was horrified at the sight of the dilapidated house, the surrounding fields disheveled, unweeded—the whole place unrecognizable. The beautiful women whom he had left behind when he marched off with his cousins now looked haggard, exhausted, ragged, and nervous. Like most Southern veterans he could never adjust to the life he found upon his return. The "Reaper," known as General Sherman, had not only changed Great Grandfather Powell's life but the lives, hopes, and dreams of Southern soldiers forever for they found many of their wives and mothers in a state of mental and physical exhaustion from "long pressures of anxiety and tension upon the nerves."[10]

From this point on, my family history sings a lament of loss. In 1869, when my Great Grandfather Powell died in his thirty-seventh year, part of his estate consisted of Confederate bonds in the amount of $2,200 and Confederate notes of $3,200 as well as stock in the Wilmington-Manchester Railroad. Obviously, that portion of the estate was then worthless. With currency and all other intangible assets obliterated in the ravages of the war and the period of Reconstruction that followed, the family's claim to real estate secured the faintest hope of survival.

It is hard for us to realize now what the loss of the war meant to the South. By Sherman's analysis, Southern cavalrymen, for the most part boys from farms, were better horsemen than their Northern counterparts. Using guerilla tactics, both northern and southern cavalrymen had bloody encounters for years after the surrender. Tensions remained extremely high. When Sherman informed Confederate General Joseph E. Johnston of the news that Lincoln had been assassinated, the Southerner proclaimed the act a disgrace to the age, and that the South had come to realize finally that Lincoln was their best friend. Sherman who must have been relieved to hear this, nevertheless told Johnston that, "One ill placed comment might infuriate his troops in Raleigh" and a "fate worse than that of Columbia would befall the place." Johnston tried to placate Sherman saying that he had fought hard and clean and he felt no army like Sherman's had existed since Caesar's time. A peace was finally signed between these two after Appomattox embracing all Confederate troops from the Potomac to the Rio Grande.[11] At the time of this meeting Johnston had 40,000 troops under his command, yet 100,000 Confederate soldiers were still under arms in Tennessee and central Alabama. None of these had been hemmed in as Lee's army in Virginia had been.

The troops who had raided my grandmother's parent's farm were roving around after these peace settlements foraging for sustenance and grabbing whatever they could for their long journey home.

The Browns

In 1885, Grandmother Annie married a neighbor, James Monroe Brown, my Grandfather. They worked diligently, loved each other, were indeed fruitful, and shared their hard-earned fortune with others, as was typical of the family. They produced ten children—and adopted two orphaned relatives. "Many hungry mouths make a happy table," as Grandmother said. And, Grandfather Brown would invariably add, those mouths were even happier when they sat down to a country meal prepared by "the best scratch biscuit maker in Albemarle County."

When folks said, "Miss Annie sets a mighty fine table," they didn't mean flat silver, linen, and a floral or fruit centerpiece. They meant mouth-watering hot breads and light-as-a-feather cakes. I can still close my eyes and breathe in the delicious aromas that billowed out of Grandmother's kitchen and, better still, remember the taste of chicken soup that had simmered all day on the top of her wood stove.

The Browns worked—one and all—from sun up to sun down, making the farm productive. They knew how to provide for almost all their own needs. They had bees to keep and honey to draw, but cotton and tobacco were the only two money crops. They also owned fifty dairy cows, a considerable herd in those days. This herd produced enough milk for the family, with some excess to sell to their neighbors. "Anyone who has not lived the life of a dairy farmer," she said, "can hardly imagine the wail of fifty cows whose udders are making ready to burst." Outside of the cotton, tobacco, and milk, I never heard of any other source of cash.

The Browns made their own clothes, knitted their socks and sweaters, and sewed their shirts, pants, and dresses. They had no need of nor could they have afforded Mall USA or even the modest wonders of the Sears Roebuck or later the L.L. Bean catalogues. Their earnings were no doubt about equal to those of the average North Carolinian farmer of their time, described as "scratch as scratch can." They managed to make do in what for them was a strange new world, without unpaid black labor to which their forebears had become accustomed. Survival made a sure-fire bonding agent in their family life and required perseverance of their studies and "Sunday School," as well.

Mother, Mary Katherine, one of Grandmother Annie's six daughters, spent her first nineteen years on the farm in Whiteville. She inherited her family's creativity and industry. She always bragged that she could milk faster and "weigh in" heavier than anyone else who worked in the cotton fields. She described grabbing a boll of cotton with each hand and going down the rows picking "lickety-split" with a bag tied on each shoulder. Only her younger brother, Clarence, tried to outdo her. Sadly, Clarence later developed a lingering case of hookworm disease, a common ailment for all the farm children, black and white. Mother always thought this childhood affliction accounted for his "lack of get up and go" as an adult.

In Mother's day, everyone—black and white, child or adult—had to work and work hard. The women kept busy canning and preserving fruits in jars or crocks, storing vegetables in root cellars, weaving warm blankets. Then there were candles to dip, and sweaters and socks to knit. Mother and Grandmother before her preached the gospel of "staying tied to the chores at hand." Busy hands are "unlikely to get into mischief." Waste time on self-examination? Self-pity? "Frankly," said Mother, "trouble was hard to come by." I remember the look on her face as she assured me that she never even considered the possibility of boredom. We tend to forget today what those people knew so well; a "shared task makes the day sweeter." One can imagine the hives of activity that surrounded Mother. She hated to be called "Kate" because of its association with *Taming of the Shrew* but tolerated "Cute," a description her brothers and sisters thought was apropos. To this day I cherish Mother's tales of her youth.

One of my favorite stories, told during another visit with Grandmother Annie in Maitland, was of little consequence except that it preserved an aspect the family history. When my Uncle Milton was fourteen years old, Grandfather gave him the task of "minding the tobacco curing," a chore that required him to sit on a round log where he could see the thermometer in the curing shed. If the temperature was allowed to rise too high, even for five minutes, the heat would ruin the leaves hanging from the shed's roof. I learned that Milton often had to sit so long on that round log that he fell asleep and rolled right off. Jolted awake, he would climb back up on the log and resume his tobacco vigil. If Mother saw him so awakened, she would scold him. At that point Milton's older brother Adrian would come to Milton's defense by calling Mother a "bossy little pest."

I loved hearing Grandmother tell me this story of my hapless uncle. She would always insist that Milton's chore, boring as it might be, was necessary because Rob MacLeod, Grandfather's cousin and a justice in the local court system, was "sickly" and often needed Grandfather "to ride his circuit" in his absence. She explained that Grandfather really hated farming and "jumped at any chance to get away." Besides, she added, the justice paid him "folding money" a scarce commodity on the farm.

In the end, the banterings over Milton's falling asleep and Mother's scolding amused everyone gathered on Grandmother's back porch and kept a chapter of family reminiscences alive for me.

One of the other constantly discussed subjects, spanning several decades at our family's North Carolina farm table was the Siamese twins who had been seen by some members of my family. They were known until their death in 1912 as Millie Christine under which name they had appeared in theaters and exhibitions for years beginning in the 1880s. Their billing was "Millie Christine the two headed girl." Above the waist they were two persons, below they were one. They spoke five languages and were exceptional singers and dancers. Two of my older uncles had heard them. They traveled to many parts of the country and played at the 8th Avenue Museum and Doris' Harlem Museum in New York the week of December 1, 1890, where they were billed as the "two headed Negress." The *New York Clipper* reported in January 1891 that, "Two weeks ago, Millie Christine made her first appearance here and succeeded in testing the capacity of the house, beating all records. People flocked from all the East Side to see her, and sometimes the crowd was so great that no one could move." They were "hot" properties in the theater world, were even abducted twice by persons wanting to exploit them, or keep others from profiting by their appearances.

I listened in awe when my relatives told me how the sisters were born in slavery on July 11, 1857, and were owned by their distant relative, Joseph Smith. He had received them in payment of a $200 debt. Smith's great granddaughter, Mrs. Kenneth Cribb, explained how the twins had come to Spartanburg, her home. "My great grandfather lived in North Carolina but moved to Spartanburg so his children could be educated at

Wofford College here. He brought his slaves with him, among whom were Millie Christine. The twins weighed seventeen pounds at birth." She apparently always referred to them as "she," a habit she said she picked up from her mother and grandmother. "My mother knew her well, as she had often sat in her lap. Of course she had to sit in a chair without arms. My mother had her to dinner after she became famous, after she had been to Europe and met all that royalty. Mother always said she was a real joy to talk to." "My aunt told me they walked crab fashion, both sideways. My aunt confirmed that they had a lovely soprano voice and an alto voice and they sang duets." Christine did all of the writing; the other, Millie, crocheted and dictated to Christine what to write." My great aunt Lucy apparently had one of the crocheted doilies Millie had made. Christine lived seventeen hours after Millie died.

Grandfather and Grandmother eked out a bare living, and by saving ten cents on the dollar, they were able to retire to Maitland, a tiny village in Orange County, Florida. Here the Brown family regrouped with their three sons, Adrian, Clarence, and Milton and daughter, Lucy, the youngest of their ten children. Carrie, the oldest daughter, had stayed in Whiteville to manage the farm. Mother was then married and resided in nearby Orlando.

Maitland's few streets were lined with stately live oaks that dripped majestically with Spanish Moss. No streets except the main one were paved, and things became dusty very quickly. My grandparents lived in a large, weathered, gray-shingled house, and while Grandmother ran the household, Grandfather lovingly tended the grounds and the house. Helping Grandmother were only "Aunt" Georganne and "Uncle" Matthew, who never wanted to leave the security of their "family," although they had been "freed." Their ten-year-old grandson helped around the house, but had plenty of time to play "cowboys and Indians" and "I Spy" with me. Aunt Georganne had peppery gray hair and a large comfortable bosom on which I could snuggle. She had a special treat hidden in an apron pocket for me—a cookie or a piece of dried fruit. She worked hard, but no harder than "Miss Annie." She and Uncle Matthew lived nearby, and after all these years, I still recall their neat, attractive cottage, its white organdy curtains, and the sweet piney aroma that permeated the rooms.

Uncle Matthew was a paradox; as old as the hills yet handsome as a speckled pup—a genuine Uncle Remus, sans beard. He was the epitome of style and grace. Uncle Matthew's father had been part and parcel in the home of Great Grandfather and Great Grandmother Powell. He was a man so good looking and genteel that the family asked him only to weave baskets for the household; he sat on the front porch in the summer and in the center hall when winter drove him inside—just weaving baskets.

When Aunt Lucy was a teenager, she attended high school in Winter Park, the home of Rollins College. Maitland was too small a town to afford a high school. Aunt Lucy was vivacious with a great bounce and zest, and her curiosity about life was infectious.

All four of Grandmother Annie's sons (mother's brothers) attended for a time Davidson College, founded in 1867 by the Presbyterian Church in Davidson, North Carolina. Her oldest son, Fletcher, went from there to the University of North Carolina Medical School at Chapel Hill and upon graduating joined the military service in World War I. By the time he finished his internship and residency, he had married and was desperate to get his practice started in order to support his family. Because he had no older doctor or patron to refer patients to him, he is said to have done "something which the Florida Medical Society considered advertising." Following this indiscretion, he was never allowed to be a member of the Florida Medical Society or the AMA—a restriction that broke his heart and almost ruined his life. His "mistake" was equivalent to advertising a law office, the latter, also illegal until recently. Although he never recovered from the devastating blow of the society's rejection, he went on to maintain a successful "caring" medical practice.

Uncle Fletcher was a tall, soft spoken, intelligent man, a dedicated doctor and a fine diagnostician. He had married an attractive society girl named Maud, lived in Jacksonville, and had an only son, Locke.

My other uncles ran the Maitland General Store, a glorious establishment that sold everything—dry goods, hardware, yarn, shoes, notions, and all manner of miscellaneous items. In one corner of the store was the town post office so I suppose Uncle Adrian earned the title of postmaster, as well as mayor.

Many of my cousins went to the University of North Carolina. This venerable, proud institution traces its history from 1795, when it first opened its doors to about one hundred students at its Chapel Hill campus. Governor David L. Swain, who was elected president of the university in 1835, popularized the institution during his term of office. He increased the coverage of its literary magazine, added law and modern languages, and agricultural chemistry so that it became a training school for public service.

By 1858, the university had a fine library and a soaring enrollment. In fact in 1858 it had the largest enrollment of any college or university in the United States except Yale. Swain tried unsuccessfully to spare the "seed corn," the younger students, from the Civil War draft as they became fired with the zeal of joining the "cause." The faculty also dwindled during the war, and those who remained accepted salary reductions, as the graduating class of 1862 was only 24, compared to 125 in 1859. There were dead heroes of the university in all of the war's major battles, and the campus and town were devastated. Swain, who was thrust forward in the surrender negotiations and the peacekeeping processes because of his opposition to the war, was not regarded highly by his southern contemporaries. He was part of the delegation that met with Federal commanders to obtain whatever concessions they could for the surrender of Richmond.

On his arrival at Union headquarters, Swain claimed not only General Sherman as a former correspondent, a fellow college president, but recognized two or three members of the Union staff whose parents and pedigrees he knew, and soon was at home amongst them. He was assured that the university buildings and property would be safeguarded. After the stars and stripes were hoisted over the state capital, Swain personally delivered the keys of the capital to General Sherman. The university and Raleigh were saved and on Easter Monday, April 17, General Smith B. Atkins, with a 4,000-man detachment of Union soldiers entered the campus and captured all its dignitaries without the use of force.

As a sentimental byproduct of this civility, the thirty-one-year-old General Atkins, called upon Swain at the university, where he was politely received by Swain and college officials. News of Lincoln's assassination had just arrived and everyone was nervous. To relieve the tension, Swain, a history buff, offered to show his military visitor General Cornwallis's order book, and asked his twenty-one year old daughter, Eleanor, to get it for him. She, according to William Snider's *Light on the Hill*, brought it out with a great deal of "hauteur," and was therefore introduced to General Atkins.

Apparently one thing led to another and soon came the earnest courtship of Eleanor Hope Swain and General Atkins. Every evening, the general would send the regimental band to play in President Swain's front yard. Atkins sent Swain a fine horse, and Miss Ellie a riding horse, with a gift note saying that "doubtless these animals had been swept from Southern stables." Many of Swain's acquaintances thought it was wrong to accept expensive gifts from one's conquerors.

As the occupying Union forces withdrew in May, Ellie handed her parents a note saying that she was engaged to Atkins and that nothing would change her mind. Bereft and agitated, they nevertheless could do nothing to dissuade the couple and the wedding was scheduled for August. It was said to have been a handsome affair, but though many were invited, few attended. It was reported that invitations were "spat upon in a few houses." No doubt fuel was added to the fire by the large cake presented to the couple "with the compliments of the colored people of Chapel Hill." They thought of Atkins as their deliverer. None of this helped Swain retain his popularity or power at Chapel Hill, and he later resigned from the university presidency.

Uncle Adrian, married a school teacher, Madeline Worley, my favorite aunt. It was not surprising that his younger brothers also chose school teachers for their wives since teaching in those days was one of the few respectable careers available to "proper young ladies." None of them was ever divorced and, so far as I know, the marriages were good, happy ones. They apparently believed in the adage, "If it ain't broke, don't fix it."

I treasured my moments with Grandmother Annie. Ever patient, she would insist during my visits that I sit very close to her. From that vantage point, I learned the fine points of tatting, crocheting, knitting, hemstitching, and how to make a picot edge—the finishing touch for her napkins and pillow cases. It was during those sessions that I not only learned valuable skills, but I got a double dose of history, Grandmother style. Even in her nineties, Grandmother enjoyed the gift of total recall.

I have only one bad memory of my visits to Grandmother's. It was a dark rainy afternoon when I visited Grandmother Annie with Mother. I was playing in the barn loft with my cousin Audrey, Aunt Mabel's son. He was a few years older than I and "got fresh," 1920s parlance for attempted rape, by pinning me down to the floor lifting my skirts and more. I tore myself loose from his steely grasp, bounded down the barn steps, and ran screaming to Mother, who was chatting gaily with Aunt Mabel and Grandmother Annie. This was, of course, a horrifying encounter—a trauma which makes me shudder today as it really never left me.

Imagine the reaction of the two sisters, Mother and Aunt Mabel. They were frantic and literally up in arms with one another. Grandmother tried to calm them to no avail. Red-haired, Scotch-tempered Mother took me home immediately in understandable indignation and did not speak to her sister for weeks. I never could look at that boy again without a sense of loathing.

After the War

The lives of my family—the Powells and the Browns—would be considered genteelly poor by today's standards. Any Southerner who had anything had been wiped out financially after the Civil War. The only exceptions were those who collaborated with the hated carpetbaggers, and they were "personae non grata" to their neighbors. Mother, in a rather brittle way, used to say the older Southeners should have died in the war for they were not unlike the post-revolution Russian aristocrats. They were never able to adjust to the upheaval of their ancestral lifestyles. They knew "who they were" and were proud of their lineage and landholdings. They could never, however, really accept living without domestics and slaves who "made it all work."

Yankees often wonder why many Southerners are still obsessed with Civil War history and are filled with resentments toward Reconstruction. The fact remained that the South, to a large extent, had been devastated by the war years and the period of Reconstruction. Even the victorious North showed its concern when the commanding general in Georgia asked General Sherman, "What is to be done with the freedmen?" This was the question that was frequently discussed at Grandmother Annie's supper table. Many former slaves felt that they had to relocate to know they were free. Some went to nearby cities; others went North and West. Still others had been moved by their masters during the war. A good number returned to their former homes in search of greater security and their friends and families.[12] The family talk turned to what was called the Bureau of Refugees, Freedmen, and Abandoned Lands. The War Department had authorized the bureau to assign to individual freedmen, "not more than forty acres and a mule" to help them make the difficult transition from slavery to freedom. According to Sherman's Order No. 15, the middle class southern planter was to give up 400,000 acres, thirty miles inland from Charleston to Jacksonville, to 40,000 freedmen. They were to rent the land for three years with an option to buy it at the end of that time.[13]

In addition to giving the freedmen land, the bureau declared that the negro must be given the vote before Rebel states would be restored to the

Union. Implemented in 1865 by the Reconstruction Act, this regulation prevailed only until 1877 when it was repealed. In forcing emancipation, the Union had not been able to guarantee the wellbeing of former slaves. For all its ills, in the hands of the good-hearted, the system, at the very least, did provide food, clothing, and marginal support for the welfare of the slave workers, adults as well as children. During Reconstruction, many former slaves had none of these basic provisions.

Many Southerners maintain a particularly heightened historical consciousness of both history and ancestry. Arnold Toynbee, an English historian who wrote his twelve-volume *A History of the World* for the Royal Institute of International Affairs pointed out "the vividness of historical impressions is apt to be proportionate to their violence and painfulness." He goes on to comment that "a child who had lived through the American Civil War in the territory of the Southern Confederacy would likely grow up more historical-minded than one who had lived through the same experience in the North."[14] Katherine Anne Porter, a Pulitzer Prize winning novelist, has written, "I am a grandchild of a lost war, and I have blood-knowledge of what life can be in a defeated country on the bare bones of privation."[15] As a great grandchild of such a background, I can still, even now, feel the pain and sorrow. There is an excerpt from *The Liberator*, a newspaper published by the abolitionist, William Lloyd Garrison, that captures the feelings of many during Reconstruction times: "When was it ever known that liberation from bondage was accompanied by a recognition of political equality? Chattels personal may be instantly translated from the auction-block into free men, but when were they ever taken at the same time to the ballot box, and invested with all political rights and immunities?" Indeed, Garrison continued that even if the president decreed it, he saw no permanent advantage in such an act.[16]

The above quote by one of the most famous abolitionists of the period echoed the prevailing attitude in the North. Perhaps this may make the emotions and actions of people like my great grandparents more readily understandable. The Southerners who had to survive those painful years did so by doing things that now seem unimaginable such as depending on Ku Klux Klanners for law and order. Certainly, both their actions and Mr. Garrison's words seem repugnant to me now. Most sensitive liberal thinking Southerners today try to wish them away. However, when I put myself in my ancestors' place, I understand.

The great black leader, William Edward Burghardt (W.E.B.) DuBois, contended that in 1861 "probably not one white American in a hundred believed that Negroes could become an integral part of American democracy," and concluded that even by 1868 "the country was not ready for Negro suffrage."[17] Yet it came very quickly in some parts of the South. Thaddeus Stevens, head of the Republican majority in the House and a leader in the Reconstruction period, was ready to confiscate great quantities of the Southerners' land and disenfranchise Southern whites in great numbers and stated, "Do not they deserve humiliation?" But even he, as well as his colleagues, William Lloyd Garrison, Horace Greeley, General Oliver O. Howard, and President Andrew Johnson, were not ready in the 1860s and 1870s to make an issue of enfranchisement in the North or the South. Stevens was quoted in December 1865, saying that "The conditions and laws of slavery . . . 'have prevented them from acquiring an education, understanding the commonest laws of contract, or managing the ordinary business of life.'" Stevens held that the states have the right, and always have had it, to fix the elective franchise within their own states and said in "four or five years hence, when the freedmen shall have been made free indeed," it would be reconsidered.[18]

Most of Grandmother's tales usually ended with the "Yankees just did not understand us, nor we them." I thought of that so often as I read *The Education of Henry Adams*, which partially inspired my effort to get down some of my forebears' past, as well as my own. Henry Adams returned in 1868 with his father and other family members to America after seven years abroad. When he had been back but a few months, he felt like a displaced person—so much had happened since he had left our shores. He moved to Washington and began his life as a journalist and a "genteel muckraker." In that city, then, as now, there were daily doses of wrongdoing and plenty to expose. Adams was kept very busy according to his own account in *The Education*, wondering when the scandals would finally reach their depths and stop destroying democracy. He said, "Grant's administration outraged every rule of ordinary decency"[19] and reported that he had researched everyone in all three branches of government and found "little but damaged reputation."[20]

There is no question that all of the lurid tales of the War Between the States (we were not allowed to call it the Civil War for some time) were exaggerated over the years, as have been all such histories from *Genesis*

Phil's grandmother, Annie Elizabeth Powell Brown, age 90, whose memories started the book. Shown here with Phil's uncles Fletcher, Clarence, and Milton.

onward. During my time, school textbooks still did not portray the situation with any kind of objectivity, but principally from the victor's point of view. As a "grown up" in 1940, I was horrified at what had gone on in the South, and ashamed that "my people" had been a part and party to it.

Yet over time, my view has become more balanced, more understanding of my southern ancestors. Indeed, after watching *Gone With the Wind* not long ago, I understand only too well that pre-1861 Southern life had indeed "gone with the wind."

Speaking of that famous film, *Gone With the Wind* still enjoys an annual revival in Atlanta movie houses. My late good friend, Fred Glass, happened to be there visiting his son and family. He and Fred Jr. took his three young grandsons to a performance. There were three sleepy little boys in the back seat of the car returning from the show when the eight-year-old asked his Father in a serious very Southern drawl, "Daddy, am I a Yankee?" Fred Jr. answered, "Well, son, I guess you are, you and your brothers were born in Darien, Connecticut." The little boy replied with a sigh, "Well, Daddy, I don't want to be." Surely not after seeing Margaret Mitchell's epic.

The farm women in my family reflected the hatred harbored by their

Phil's mother and her sisters at the Whiteville, North Carolina Farm: Mabel, center; seated are Phil's mother Mary Katherine, left, Lucy on Mabel's lap, and Carrie at right; and rear, kneeling are Beatrice and Clyde.

ancestors. They had struggled through an existence without the help of their men—gone forever or home ill and broken after the war—and nourished a paranoid hatred of Sherman. Perhaps they couldn't appreciate that Sherman's task was simply to keep the Union together, and so he had to crush his enemy, the Confederacy, once and for all. In his Civil War history, Charles Royster, said Sherman tried first and foremost to keep the two factions from remaining in a state of perpetual warfare, "Believing that American politics already had grown ridiculous, Sherman still wanted the United States to avoid 'the fate of Mexico,' which is eternal war."[21] According to Mr. Royster, after Sherman had left the South for the last time, he reminisced about his years there. He had found there an enviable social stability until its principal beneficiaries had thrown it all away.

Sherman had made many friends in the South and found their lifestyle congenial. He wrote in 1859, according to Royster, "I would not, if I could, abolish or modify slavery."[22] According to historian Yates Snowden, Sherman came to the Snowden plantation as a lieutenant bearing "balls and chains" to be put on two runaway slaves. He is reported to have said

Mary Katherine Brown as an RN in North Carolina.

that he would have resisted, even with arms, any attack on the Southerners' slavery rights if they had just agreed to stay in the Union. His postwar speeches explained that all of the half million dead and the devastation and ruin in the South resulted in great and lasting good. We, whose forebears suffered so much during the one hundred years after the war's end, have been biased, bitter, and belligerent —but in our heart of hearts, we know the result was best for all of us.

The climax of the war was the fall of Columbia, South Carolina, at least as far as Sherman could see after his "March." Sherman kept repeating that the Civil War had been "one of the most causeless, foolish wars ever devised by the brain of man," reports Royster.[23] Neither side could anticipate the scale of the force and passion of the other. "The Civil War demonstrated that we, its citizens, could defend the Government against the greatest of all enemies—OURSELVES."[24] Only through the awful violence did they come to know one another, mutually suffer so miserably, and require more than one-hundred years to effect a partial rapprochement socially and economically.

The anguish of those years is brought home to me most forcibly on Memorial Day. It is then that I reflect on the deaths of so many fine young men—both Yankee and Confederate. and it is a time when I wonder if our country appreciates the valor of those boys—as well as the absolute dependence today's Army has on southern boys. They volunteer in huge numbers like their ancestors to fight for what they believe in.

Jesse Jackson's recent brilliant autobiographical accounts in *The New Yorker* tear me apart. He is an eloquent witness to equally repressive "times" in Greenville, South Carolina, and Chicago. No one today doubts that it was everyone's fault that terrible consequences resulted in the slaves being traded by Europeans and African chiefs to the American and European colonies. It was known to Southern people at the time that European slave traders parked their ships in the waters outside African ports waiting for the African bigwigs to bring their own people to sell. As recently as December 1994, *The New York Times* reported that certain African nations are beginning to share the blame. Such people, including Cameroons, owned whole towns of slaves, whom their chiefs sold, to keep their institutions going and to maintain their own home establishments.

Caroline Alexander in an op-ed piece for *The New York Times* in July 1992 wrote, "The dirty job of raid and capture was done by free Africans working in organized tribal groups. Slave markets were held well out of reach of all but a few of the most intrepid . . . European explorers." Only then their "goods," gathered during raids of villages, were sold and ferried downstream by their new black owners to be traded to the coastal Orungu, who made the final sales to the Europeans moored offshore.[25]

Many European diaries substantiate all of this. So do oral accounts of the Africans, many of whom were often illiterate. "[T]he slave trade could not have existed without the voluntary participation of African tribes . . . . Are the descendants of East African slaves to compensate the descendants of slaves who ended up in Arab hands?"[26]

When I read such things written by a 1990s journalist, I cannot but feel resentful that our generation should be consistently blamed for the sins of African slave traders and their buyers over a hundred years ago. Slave labor was, however, the linchpin on which the southern agri-economy of the nineteenth century existed. Few plantations, large or small, could have prospered without it.

Keith Richburg, a journalist posted in Africa, has described his feelings about being called an African-American. They sound so like another friend who said, "I am not a French-American, nor is my sister-in-law an Australian-American. We have taken out citizenship papers and are AMERICANS."

Mr. Richburg describes seeing fellow blacks bloated and discolored, naked or just barely clothed, shackled, and missing limbs, or even heads finally being thrown into the waters below Rusumo Falls on the Tanzanian border. Thirty bodies an hour, seven hundred each day, as they were members of the Tutsi tribe and were genocide victims of the Hutu tribesmen of Rwanda. Mr. Richburg covered that area for the *Washington Post* for three years and saw inhumane killings in Liberia as well. As he watched this awful man's inhumanity to man, he confessed he kept thinking, there but for the grace of God go I.

Neither he, who felt like those being pushed over the cliff looked like him, nor I whose forebears owned African slaves in the South, ever want to defend slavery. But having condemned it doesn't mean we cannot feel that progress has been made in America toward helping good government emerge from that horrible evil. He feels that even though in the post-World War II era Japan and Germany became strong democracies, some good came out of the atrocities they committed. Africa seems to stay the same. Democracy was supposed to flourish in the decade of the 1990s, but the African continent seems to lie in ruins today. Elections are being stolen in Cameroon, rigged in Kenya, annulled in Nigeria, and mocked in Zaire. Richburg, therefore feels no connection with those countries, even though his ancestors came from there.[27]

As the understanding between races looms ever larger as a goal at the beginning of our new century, I find myself agonizing more and more on possible solutions to the growing rift between blacks and whites in America. Our sin in the past two centuries was letting slavery get hold of us. Shelby Foote thinks one of our sins was emancipation. He has said that in theory emancipation was supposed to be a magnificent milestone in our search for democracy. But the way it was implemented led to tragic events. Turning four million people loose with no jobs or trades or ability to read and write and then abandoning them by 1877 "for a few electoral votes," causing black and white citizens a lot of grief for which our republican form of government is still paying. Foote says, "it would be nice to talk to Lincoln. He'd really talk to you. Maybe run circles around you. Not like the others who you figure would be mostly rhetoric."[28] The National Portrait Gallery in Washington, one of my favorite places to visit and revisit, has the 1865 printmaker's version of the Emancipation Proclamation with a portrait of Lincoln screened through its texts.

Hurricanes and pestilence treat all people equally and force people to cooperate. Farmers throughout the world are always dependent upon the weather. They can be wiped out by cold, heat, rain, and drought. Never has this been more evident or true than in the cultivation of the Florida orange groves. Most city dwellers, certainly my own children and grandchildren, have never lived where one is dependent on the weather for one's livelihood. In Orlando, my hometown, the capital of Orange County, one good frost could ruin the citrus crop. Daddy's clients who, for the most part, were orange growers, would often be wiped out financially because of a single "freeze." When that occurred, he wouldn't get paid for his accounting, auditing and bookkeeping, income tax return preparation, or the other work he had done for them. For as long as I can remember, as soon as the temperature dropped, everyone went out to the groves, to place smudge pots among the trees so the fruit would not be frostbitten and the crop would be saved. The anxiety of citrus growers is shared by most farmers in every state of the Union.

Orange and grapefruit trees laden with beautiful fruit with their overpowering perfume make for exquisite living. How thankful I am to have come from a hardy, responsible farm family on Mother's side and the cultural and intellectual ancestry on Daddy's side. This is my family, my childhood mirror of America. This is my heritage.

Notes:

1. Colonel G.F.R. Henderson. *The Civil War: A Soldier's View. A Collection of Civil War Writings.* (Chicago, Illinois: University of Chicago Press, 1958).

2. Ben Ames Williams, ed. *A Diary from Dixie by Mary Boykin Chesnut.* (Cambridge, Massachusetts: Harvard University Press, 1980).

3. Shelby Foote, *The Civil War, A Narrative: Red River to Appomattox.* (New York: Random House, 1974) III, 825–38.

4. It was mid-twentieth century before the Rural Electrification Program provided rural Southern farms with electricity.

5. Drew Gilpin Faust. *Mother's of Invention: Women of the Slaveholding South in the American Civil War.* (Chapel Hill, North Carolina: University of North Carolina Press, 1996), 60.

6. Andersonville was a Confederate-run prisoner-of-war camp near Americus, Georgia, designed to hold 10,000 men. At one time it confined 33,000 and the total number imprisoned there was 49,485. The conditions were such that at one time the death rate was 150 per day. After the war Andersonville's superintendent, Captain Henry Wirz was convicted in a U.S. military court for murder and hanged. Andersonville is a national historical site.

7. Shelby Foote, 756.

8. Eric Foner. *Reconstruction: American's Unfinished Revolution, 1863–1877.* (New York: Harper and Row Publishers, 1986), 23, 125; Shelby Foote, 1040.

9. Shelby Foote, 1047.

10. Drew Gilpin Faust, 235.

11. All of the foregoing is in the fine articles in *The New York Times* by James Reston Jr. in January 1985.

12. Leon F. Litwack. *Been in the Storm So Long: The Aftermath of Slavery*. (New York: Alfred A. Knopf, 1979).

13. James M. McPherson. *Battle Cry of Freedom: The Civil War Era.* (New York: Ballatine Books, 1988), 841–843; *William Tecumseh Sherman: Memoirs of General W. T. Sherman*. (New York: The Library of America, 1990), 859-860.

14. Arnold J. Toynbee. *A Study of History*. (London: Oxford University Press, 1954), X, 3.

15. Katherine Anne Porter. "Portrait: Old South," *The Collected Essays and Occasional Writings of Katherine Anne Porter*. (Boston: Houghton Mifflin/Seymour Lawrence, 1970), 160.

16. James M. McPherson. *The Struggle for Equality: Abolitionists and the Negro in the Civil War and Reconstruction*. (Princeton: Princeton University Press, 1964), 294.

17. C. Vann Woodward. *The Burden of Southern History*. (Baton Rouge: Louisiana State University Press, 1960), 91.

18. *Ibid.*, 91-93.

19. Ernest Samuels, ed. *The Education of Henry Adams*. (Boston: Houghton Mifflin Company, 1974), 280.

20. *Ibid.*, 294.

21. Charles Royster. *The Destructive War: William Tecumseh Sherman, Stonewall Jackson, and the Americans*. (New York: Alfred Knopf, 1991), 126.

22. *Ibid.*, 126.

23. *Ibid.*, 383

24. *Ibid.*, 384.

25. Caroline Alexander. "Partners in the Slave Trade," *New York Times*, July 1992, A29.

26. *Ibid.*

27. Keith B. Richburg. "He's Not a Hyphenated American," *Reader's Digest*, October 1997, pp. 95-97.

28. Foote in his TV series.

CHAPTER TWO

Reconstruction Times for the Powell-Brown Family 1865-1877

She looked well to the ways of her household,
and eateth not the bread of idleness.
Her children arise up, and call her blessed.
— Proverbs 31:27-28

A little history is necessary to picture the political and economic climate of the reconstruction era. In the immediate postwar years, President Andrew Johnson appointed a man named William W. Holden "provisional governor" of North Carolina.[1] He had served as military governor of Tennessee during President Abraham Lincoln's administration. Holden loomed large enough that Grandmother never forgot his name. He came from poor parents. He had, however, married well, had become a Union sympathizer and, therefore, qualified as a member of Congress from North Carolina during the war.

One of Johnson's first acts was to offer a plan for reuniting the Confederate states with the Union. Foremost among the measures in his plan was his pardon to all Southerners who would swear allegiance to the United States, but his pardon excluded many in fourteen classes, among whom were high military officers, civilian officials, and anyone whose total net worth was over $20,000 (Lincoln's postwar plan had pardoned all but six classes). As a result, almost all former educated Southerners were disenfranchised.

In 1865, after considerable debate in the state convention, President Johnson "publicly required" the repudiation of North Carolina's war debt. This action wrought havoc for banks, colleges, and universities, as well as for many citizens who had bought North Carolina bonds right up to General Robert E. Lee's surrender of Confederate forces at Appomattox. The only people elected to the U.S. Congress in 1865 were Union men. One man, Jonathan Worth, a militant Unionist, defeated Holden for membership in the House of Representatives.[2]

The U.S. Congress, however, blocked President Johnson's conciliatory Reconstruction Plan[3] that would return the Southern states to the Union, by refusing to seat any Southerner either in the Senate or the House of Representatives until he had been pardoned by a two-thirds vote of the Congress. Punishment became the watchword, humiliation the objective. My older uncles often remarked how "beaten down" their grandparents and parents were, who apparently expected little status in the new Union. Eradication of state lines was threatened if the Southern states did not agree to all of Congress's conditions.

In 1866 the "Black Codes" defining the rights of Negroes passed the North Carolina Legislature. Hard fought for by the Unionists, they did not, however, give the Negroes very much, not even the right to vote or other equal civil rights with the whites in most areas. It did validate slave marriages and declared Negroes equal in equity and criminal law, except in cases of assault with intent to rape. It also purported to protect Negroes from fraud in the making of contracts resulting from their ignorance. Legally they had protection; but, in fact, for many years the Negroes suffered from unscrupulous tradesmen.[4]

Studying that era from today's vantage point, it is clear that in trying to put any kind of state government structure together, the "appointed" governor had to try to find people who had never been disloyal to the Union—an insurmountable task. General Daniel E. Sickles, commander of the military district occupying North Carolina, was unable to find any officials willing to serve. Reluctant to appoint illiterate blacks, he sought out North Carolinians who had served as Union soldiers, and these were naturally as scarce as hen's teeth.

In 1865 the first North Carolina Constitutional Convention marked the first concerted action by the new Negro leadership in the state. As a result, Republicans were in the majority.[5] Daniel Goodloe, editor of the

Union *Register* in Raleigh, a native-born Republican[6], totally free of the taint of being sympathetic to the South, wrote as follows concerning the make-up of the convention:

> As you may well suppose, with the former governing class of the people disenfranchised, the delegates are, for the most part, inferior in intelligence and character. Thirteen (actually fifteen) of them are persons of African descent—only one of whom, a Pennsylvanian, has any education worth speaking of. He is a Methodist preacher and seems to be a man of good character. Two others—natives—without much culture, show considerable talent for speaking. Others are barbers, and two or three, literally, are *field hands*. About twenty-seven of the delegates are recently from the North, and not of the most disinterested characteristics . . . .
>
> The difficulty about electing better Men is partly due—perhaps mainly due—to the disenfranchisement of the governing class, but also in great degree to the ignorance of the Negroes. They are the dupes of the lowest and meanest demagogues. The basest men are the most popular among the Negroes, because the basest men will bid the highest for their votes.[7]

How lucky we are that the convention ended up with a constitution better than expected. My North Carolina lawyer colleagues tell me that the constitution, as the basis for governing the state, remains fairly intact to the present date. Property qualifications for voting were abolished, and the constitution made the state more responsible to the needy. Ballot was granted to all white males, but not specifically denied to black males. An enlightened carpetbagger named Albion Tourgée, elected to North Carolina's Constitutional Convention in 1868, worked hard for humanitarian reforms. Tourgée's ability was recognized by all factions, especially during the years he served as a judge in defense of Negro rights.[8]

Economic and spiritual depression resulted from the withdrawal of the Federal Occupation Troops from North Carolina in 1870.[9]

The Ku Klux Klan, which began as a force to maintain order and protect farm families, became a terrorist organization. Their uniform of white robes and masks intimidated many decent people. It was well organized and its members, afraid of the blacks and their white sympathizers, were powerful. There were other groups also, as secret as they were illegal. These were called the Constitutional Union Guard and the White Brotherhood, smaller than the Klan but dedicated to the same aims of "keeping the Negro 'in his place.'" They rode horses, came calling mostly at night and frightened, assaulted, and killed blacks and the whites who befriended them. Many southern whites believed that only a dismal future for the land that they had fought for was in store for them.

We can see today that President Johnson was encircled by a (Union fundamentalist) radical control of the U.S. Congress. He was, in fact, a president without a party. The "Republican Party," an anti-Johnson party, was founded in 1866-67 in North Carolina with Holden at its head. It had as its principal membership poor white farmers, carpetbaggers, who had filtered down South to make a quick buck or establish themselves in a land vulnerable to exploitation. They carried on their backs in a "carpet bag" all of their worldly goods. Holden said to the populace: "Don't trust anyone who is not a Republican." The opponents of the Republicans, formerly well-to-do southern farmers, were badly organized, not united in policies, and therefore, ineffective. They were as irascible as their successors in present-day Scotland and Ireland!

The prewar Democrats and Whigs formed a Conservative Party and opposed the occupation of the Republican Party. This explains why the Democrats always won everything south of the Mason-Dixon Line until just before World War II. My mother and father would have never dreamed of voting other than the straight Democratic ticket—the true choice for political office was made in the Democratic primary. This was indeed the Solid South, Solidly Democratic.

For years, the Democratic primary decided the election. Not that the postwar Democratic Party resembled the Democratic Party of today in philosophy—it was very conservative. The majority of the members of the eastern counties of the North Carolina State Legislature were black for several decades after 1865. This resulted in a divisive, hostile atmosphere throughout North Carolina.

North Carolina was also blessed to have found, in the late 1800s, a public servant named Charles B. Aycock. His name was spoken of with much reverence by many generations of my family. His family, like almost everyone else, had lost everything in the War. He was born in 1859 and walked many miles to attend school. The repressive years of the Reconstruction and occupation periods bore down upon him and his family.

He often said, "the exploitation of the Reconstruction bosses ached in my bones." But Aycock would not allow the conditions of his life in the post-war period to defeat or embitter him. He studied law at the University of North Carolina and became obsessed with the desire to provide quality education for all.[11] The *Southwest Review* of 1933 said, "Advocates of white supremacy in the 1870s without at all knowing it or intending to, in plain truth, turned up an idealist." The Democratic Party wanted to disen-franchise the blacks, and Aycock wanted to educate them. He upgraded rural education by consolidating many of the country schools, which had only four-month terms. My own grandparents, aunts, and uncles had to learn everything they could in four months a year of schooling! So far as I have been able to discern, this strong Scotch-Irish stock thirsted pas-sionately after "learning" and were avid readers of what books were avail-able. Before the 1920s ended, North Carolina children attended public schools eight months a year.

By the time Grandmother was eighteen, in 1877, the state govern-ment had finally managed to squeak out some funds for normal or teacher training schools, one for young white men and one for young black men. Women were not to be offered this education until later. Schools, thus established, were conducted for the first time in Chapel Hill that year. It was the first summer school session of a university in the United States. Women were, a little later, admitted to this formerly all-male institution. Professor John Ladd of Vermont, a Brown University graduate, super-vised the famous "summer session." As young women, Grandmother and her contemporaries probably never questioned their exclusion, while many of their age group up North did. All readers of *Little Women* will remem-ber that Louisa May Alcott's Jo is furious that boys were offered fine prep school and university education, while girls were not. Southern women just never dreamed of having a better education. I remember Grand-mother telling me how lucky the family felt that some of their former slaves stayed on as long as they could pay them. That didn't last for too many months because her family ceased to have money for their own staples, such as flour, sugar, tea, much less salaries. And so it was inevi-table that one-by-one, the farm help left. Women and children of the fam-ily had to assume the farming chores. Sometimes whole weeks passed when the children could not attend school because the tobacco could not wait another day to be picked. The same situation was true of another crop. "Get in the cotton before the rain," for example, was frequently chanted around the barns.

Gossip reigned supreme in their part of the world—no radio, no regular newspapers, such as those that flourished in many parts of the North. About once a month a Whiteville paper was brought home when one of the men in the family took the horse and buggy to town for a loan, or a necessary purchase. People heard stories of atrocities committed by South Carolina or Georgia blacks who roamed the countryside, getting geographically closer and closer to the North and their new-found political and economic freedom.

Alas, a majority of the new freed men found things pretty bleak up North, too. No one blamed them for trying to find a better life in the North, but some planters resented the fact that they, who had treated their people well and started to free them, must suffer from a general exodus of their "hands." Eric Foner quotes a planter as saying, "Everyone of A.M. Dorman's Negroes quit him . . . . They have always been as free and as much indulged as his children."[12] Some of Mother's Powell family "people" left, only later to return disappointed in their treatment in the northern cities, where they had to pay for their own food and housing.

My Great Grandmother and my Grandmother, as female heads of families, always ran an in-house school for "readin' and writin'" for black and white children. Rudimentary education was not always available in the North to the children of some of those who had left their former homes for parts unknown. But there is no question that many former slaves who went North found education, much more freedom, and a better life than they had ever had before.

Grandmother also spoke of "church going." The Powells were Methodists. Their cousins, the MacLeods and Fergusons, were Presbyterians. She said most blacks worshipped together with them in the same church building, although from the balcony. Mr. Foner confirms that, "on the eve of the war, 42,000 black Methodists worshipped in biracial South Carolina churches and by the 1870s only 600 remained; Cleveland County, North Carolina, counted 200 black members of biracial Methodist churches in 1860, ten in 1867, and none five years later."[13]

The African Methodist Church, in the 1870-1890 period, so prominent in the South today, gained a lot of members, was strongly competitive and more satisfying for its members than the White rival church. Black authorities of the National African Methodist church sent South to "colonize" new chapters found that they had problems recruiting and maintaining members. Blacks wanted more rip-roaring (we called them holy-roller) services. They loved and preferred the spirited music and explosive energy, foot stamping and clapping of their own type of service.

Many Northern recruits, however, insisted upon the need for an educated ministry and demanded more sedate services than Southern blacks were accustomed to. "By the end of Reconstruction, black Baptists outnumbered all the other denominations combined; taken together, the Baptist churches formed the largest black organization ever created in this country."[14] The African Methodist Church began to come down to colonize and often found the Freedmen's religious practices excessively emotional. They were appalled by the anti-intellectualism of ex-slave preachers. "One sermon of the most famous 'old style' preacher, John Jasper, entitled: 'The Sun Do Move' disproved the heliocentric theory of astronomers."[15] Blacks loved Jasper, a well-known celebrity of the time, and hotly resented being deprived of his kind of preaching.

From all my family recollections, letters, and writings during that time, it was impossible to separate religion and politics. This is true today in many countries of the world. "Over 100 black ministers, hailing from North and South, from free and slave backgrounds, and from every black denomination from African Methodist Episcopal to Primitive Baptist, would be elected to legislative seats during Reconstruction."[16]

The strong linkage of politics and religion in the South continues into this century. My Mother once observed, "Several black minister friends in Maitland, Sanford, New Smyrna, and Tampa told me that they didn't want to be so politically active as they were, but their congregations made them get into politics." The pulpit, of course, was an excellent platform readily available for gifted orators, and it became an instrument to effect political change. As we know, it still is. Martin Luther King, Jr., Jesse Jackson, and many others now active in the political arena are products of their religious orientations and their great abilities as pulpiteers.

The economics of my family's livelihood was the overriding concern. My grandmother remembered how much small planters had to lose. They had been operating with minimum help **before** emancipation.

After the abolishment of slavery, awful things happened to the small planters as well as to everyone else in the South. Realistically, the South went through two depressions. All those years, they continued to blame the North for taking away the labor source of their agricultural economy. By the time I saw the farm, which had been sold to Aunt Carrie and her family, it was a dilapidated, messy place. The Smiths, my Aunt Carrie's family, had only eked out an existence on it. The farm was finally sold by one of Aunt Carrie's sons to an outsider in the 1950s.

Many families who had depended on agriculture for a living saw only a dismal future.[17] It was between the war's end and the beginning of the twentieth century that their outlook changed. Entrepreneurial Northerners came down with bags of money to fund projects. We can give credit to some remarkable native businessmen as well who did a great deal to industrialize their "New North Carolina." The Reynolds and Watts families in tobacco: the Cones, Tompkins, and Tanners in textiles; and the Dukes, Hanes, and Cannons were all from the South. Historian J. Carlyle Sitterson has shown that over 49.2 percent of the postwar business leaders between 1865-1900 were born into the Southern upper-economic class, and 37.5 percent were born into the middle-class, sons of planters or farmers.[18] Textile manufacturing came to the region, launched in the 1880s by a Cotton Mill Campaign. Northern factories often provided machinery in exchange for stock participation.

There had been a number of skilled cabinetmakers in North Carolina even before the war. Thomas Day, a free Negro in Milton, employed both white and black workers and made fine furniture. In the 1890s, Northeast furniture factories began to move South, lock, stock, and barrel. The first furniture company to use power machinery was begun in Mebane, North Carolina, in 1881 by the White brothers.

Before the turn of the century, a new market suddenly emerged. People were beginning to find a little "spending money" for updating their homes. The *Southern Lumberman* reported in 1901, when Mother was a toddler: "There are thousands of families in the Southern States that have not had a new bedstead, bureau, or set of chairs since the close of the War between the States."[19] High Point soon emerged as one of the centers of production. Still, in 1902, bedroom suites (bed, dresser, washstand) went for as little as $7.50.

These hard times lasted well into this century. When my daughter's South Carolina in-laws built a three-bedroom home on the beach at Pawley's Island, Sandy Cot, their first home right on the dunes was one of the few large original beach houses left after decades of hurricanes and lack of maintenance money. When I said to my daughter's mother-in-law,

"Sara, isn't it fun to have a new house like this with a modern kitchen?" She replied, "It sure is. We have never built anything except a barn." This was in 1968! Sara said she had absolutely no nostalgia for the "good old days." Her childhood years and early married life were spent in South Carolina homes with lots of traditions and history, but no modern conveniences and no heat! Both she and her husband had ancestors who signed the "Succession Papers." To them, Lincoln and Andrew Johnson were not very popular.

Many of us whose ancestors fought in the Civil War were brought up on family tales of underdog valor in the "War of Northern Aggression." An April 1995 *New York Times* article, reporting on the reenactment of Lee's retreat from Appomattox to Richmond, says we are showing signs of acceptance of defeat. That is surely a good omen for us all.

After 130 years, this celebration of Lee's retreat was replete with road markers along a 150-mile auto-trail from Appomattox to Richmond. On the auto-trail, soldiers clothed realistically in Union uniforms, depict the fall of the Confederacy. White women wearing old-fashioned hoopskirts and black spectators cried along the route of the retreat. The United Daughters of the Confederacy, whose meetings I attended with Mother, has had a drop in membership in the last forty years of about 10,000, even though the members of succeeding generations eligible for membership would have increased its roster.

Portraits of Lee, which I used to see displayed over the mantle and gracing the living or dining rooms of the southern homes I visited, are now less conspicuously hung, although statues of Lee astride his faithful horse "Traveler" are in every large and small southern town today. Historians write that the mystique of the "Lost Cause" filled a need that Southerners sought until World War I. Up to that time, we were the only Americans who had lost a war. We were for several decades after 1865, an economic colony, furnishing raw material for the industrialized North. Laying flowers on Confederate graves, even if they were not those of relatives, was a ritual we practiced at the Orlando Cemetery for years. We are "getting over it." As Americans drive the route across the hills of that gorgeous Virginia hilly countryside from the Appomattox Court House and see the exhibits explaining the surrender which took place there, they can rest at ease. Southerners are not filled with so much anger anymore. They no longer resemble the cartoon of a Rebel soldier brandishing his saber and growling "Forgive, Yes. Forget? Hell No!" The acrimony is waning and we all know that, as costly and horrible as the war was, the result was the maintenance of a strong and glorious United States of America.

It was Abraham Lincoln who did not cave in for a negotiated peace, but held out for a unified nation. All Southerners should still be grateful to him.

Notes:

1. Otto H. Olsen. *Carpetbagger's Crusade: The Life of Albion Winegar Tourgée.* (Baltimore: The Johns Hopkins Press, 1965), 27, 39.

2. Eric Foner. *Reconstruction: America's Unfinished Revolution, 1863-1877.* (New York: Harper & Row, 1988), 183-84, 189-194, 196; Eric Foner and Olivia Mahoney. *America's Reconstruction.* (New York: Harper Perennial, 1995), 73, 75.

3. Most of us believed the Johnson plan punitive, but conventional wisdom of modern historians judge it to be quite fair.

4. Olsen, 31-32.

5. Foner and Mahoney. *America's Reconstruction.* 75-79.

6. Olsen, 72.

7. William S. Powell. *North Carolina: A History.* (New York: W.W. Norton & Company, Inc., 1977),147-48. As reprinted from William A. Ross, Jr. "Radical Disenfranchment in North Carolina, 1867-1868," *North Carolina Historical Review,* 11 October 1934: 279.

8. Olsen, 97-98, 161-62, 168-69; Foner, *Reconstruction,* 430-31, 606.

9. Powell, 154.

10. *Ibid.,* 161-62.

11. *Ibid.,* 182-83.

12. Foner. *Reconstruction,* 80.

13. *Ibid.,* 91.

14. *Ibid.,* 92.

15. *Ibid.,* 101.

16. *Ibid.,* 93.

17. Powell, 164

18. *Ibid.,* 165.

19. *Ibid.,* 169.

CHAPTER THREE

Cammin to California

The lines have fallen unto me in pleasant places,
yea I have a goodly heritage.
— *Psalms* 16:6, The Holy Bible

The Ashers

While I consider myself a Cracker, only Mother's side of the family came from the South. Daddy's forbearers, the Ashers, came from Cammin, an old bishopric with a beautiful Romanesque cathedral, situated on the east side of the Oder River on the Polish-German border. The cathedral overlooks an extensive town plaza and marketplace. Up to the nineteenth century the city was protected from invaders by a fortress-like wall long since destroyed. Today about 6,000 inhabitants occupy Cammin, a small town, in one of the most scenic regions on the Baltic coast. It no longer is important as a thriving agricultural center that supported the people in the eighteenth century, but it has developed diversified industry and ship-building.

In the early 1800s, according to an Asher family historian, the Jewish families in Cammin lived close to the temple. Before the emancipation of the Jews—enslaved until 1810—they were forced to live in rooms in the houses of the Gentile community! As they became wealthier because of both intelligence and industry, they occupied larger and larger sections of the grander houses of the non-Jewish gentry, who were prevented by law to rent an entire home to Jews. Only after 1849 were they permitted to "register" as citizens so that their births, marriages, and deaths could be effectively recorded. It is a fine irony that the slaves of Mother's family and the Jews of Daddy's family were emancipated at about the same time. How clear it is that the struggle for freedom knows no boundaries and is limited to no particular country.

In 1776 a Mr. Asher lived in the back part of a Gentile's home and by 1778 the family occupied almost the entire building at the corner of Schule and Schützen Streets and paid three Taler, six Silbergroschen yearly for use of the cistern. One of the sons is reported to have written that his blind great grandmother let her silk dress trail over the ground to discern whether she was walking on gravel or ground. Marcus Asher, the first family patriarch on record, never could have married his beautiful rich wife, Ernestine, had he himself not come from a well-to-do family. His portraits reveal a very handsome man. He and Ernestine had nine sons and two daughters. History records that one of his nephews owned a bookshop in Berlin, and another lived in St. Petersburg with his family.

By 1803, the Asher family paid fourteen Silbergroschen in rent (I have no idea how much that might have been in U.S. dollars at that time). It seems from all historical documentation that a high standard of culture was maintained in their homes. They wrote poetry published in 1812, as noted in inscriptions found in a volume preserved today by their friends and neighbors, most of them Gentile.

Marcus Asher was reputed to have been very quick tempered and jealous of his young, beautiful wife, even to the extent of tying her up when he had to travel on business. She was a very young bride and her life with her husband must have been unbearable. Five of the sons went to a private boarding school in Stettin, a town dating from the twelfth century on the Oder River, now the largest port on the Baltic. As Marcus's business acumen was not as great as either his famous looks or temperament, Ernestine had to pawn most of her jewels to educate their children.

Ernestine never adjusted to the role of a humble, obedient wife instead of the beautiful sought-after-belle she once was. At one time she fled in a carriage to her father in Regenwalde, but Marcus went the next day and fetched her back home. Ultimately, she devoted herself to her eleven children and developed ties with them that proved to be stronger than those with which Marcus used to bind her. On one of their wedding anniversaries, most of the family was present, and a gift from the King of Prussia entitled "The Psalms of David" was sent to her. Great Grandfather Julius Asher, son of Isaac, arranged a festival for the occasion. Marcus died shortly thereafter due to complications brought on by a boil that was lanced too soon. However, Ernestine lived to be eighty-five and took an active interest in all of her grandchildren and great grandchildren who lived in Europe and Louisiana. The couple are buried next to one another in the cemetery on Schönhauser Allee in Cammin.

Another relative, Gustave Joseph, also married a famous beauty, Elise Berthold. In 1806 her grandfather had saved the crown and the scepter of Prussia from capture by Napoleon's French army by carrying them in a manure cart from Glogau to Königsberg! As a reward for his valor, he was permitted to start a shipping agency in Breslau.

Phillipe Asher, Phil's great grandfather.

According to family legend several of Marcus's sons suffered from their father's outbursts of temper. It is not clear why or how they decided to leave Cammin and to emigrate to America at an early age. It is possible that Great Grandfather Julius Asher was one of the first to arrive in the States. He was in Jackson, Mississippi, in 1860 when his son Philip was born. Julius served as quartermaster general of the Confederate army's installation in Alexandria, Louisiana, a key point west of the Mississippi River for the protection of the main waterway to the Gulf of Mexico.

Since Grandfather Philip was a small child at the beginning of the War Between the States, his generation of Ashers had scant memory of the family's participation in it. His knowledge comes from the records of his wife Cleona's father, Edouard Weil, whose naturalization papers in the Louisiana State Archives indicate that his petition for citizenship was filed in 1854 and finalized in 1855. His Certificate of Citizenship issued by the Parish of Rapides, Louisiana, states that Edouard Weil of the German Confederation of Bavaria renounced his allegiances and fidelities to a foreign power.

Seven years later, on December 1, 1862, Edouard enlisted in the Confederate Army in Alexandria, Louisiana. Thereafter he joined Company

Phil's grandfather and grandmother, Philip and Cleona Weil Asher.

K of Captain George Todd's Cavalry Regiment (Prairie Rangers) under General Richard Taylor. On April 20, 1863, General Nathaniel P. Banks with three Bay State regiments moved into Opelousas to rest after conducting raids and skirmishes in the Mississippi River delta in an effort to return this productive and strategic area to Union control. General Taylor, at that time stationed in Opelousas, did not challenge the Union occupation. He had under his command only three small Confederate cavalry regiments just arrived from Texas, and they soon withdrew. The Union soldiers then moved on to Vicksburg, obviously determined to finish their campaign and withdraw to New Orleans.[1]

Edouard was captured and placed on the roll of Prisoners of War of the Confederate States of America until he was released by the Union forces in June 1865.

On February 7, 1867, Edouard posted a surety bond of $1,000.00 for permission to marry Miss Fanny Beers. The terms of the bond goes on to say that if, after two years, it should appear that there existed at the time of granting the marriage license, any legal impediment to such marriage, then the obligation is null and void. I wonder whether he ever got his money back! The newlyweds could have found that amount useful.

After Grandfather Philip Asher married Cleona, daughter of Edouard and Fanny Weil, they had one daughter, Sylvia, and four sons, including Julius Benjamin (the eldest and my father), Hugo, Reginald, and Edward.

Grandfather Philip was a member of the Knights of Pythias, a secret fraternal order founded in 1864 in Washington, D.C., for philanthropic purposes. Newspaper accounts of his death were flowery with praise of his service to the community. In his fifty-first year he died, after suddenly collapsing while preparing to march in a great Elk's club procession to receive Colonel John P. Sullivan, the Grand Exalted Ruler of the order. In his obituary The New Orleans *Times Picayune*, July 21, 1911, described him as one of the best accountants in the country, a fine violinist, and a very gifted composer.

Julius Benjamin Asher married Mary Katherine Brown (my Father and Mother) in 1916 and lived in Orlando, Florida. Daddy did not say much about his ancestors except to tease Mother in her genealogical pursuits. He would joke, "When your forbears were fighting the War of 1812, mine were busy trying to keep Bismarck out of Alsace Lorraine." His dates were obviously incorrect, because my own research indicates that members of his family were in the United States prior to the 1860s, and fought for the Confederacy. While Daddy's southern roots may not be so deep as Mother's, they were still decidedly southern and helped to shape our family in so many ways.

Phil's father, Julius B. Asher, age 4, above, and as a college student at Louisiana State University.

Daddy, nonetheless, yearned to return to Opelousas, his home during his youth until college days. We made one memorable trip from Florida to Louisiana as a family when I was ten and my sister Cleona a toddler of two. We drove all the way from Orlando in a large, handsome, very comfortable Packard. Unfortunately, we suffered through fourteen, count them,

Phil's mother and father on their wedding day, 1916.

fourteen, flat tires on the way. Daddy changed all of them in 100 degree heat! It seemed that our car always followed every road-leveler-scraper-sander machine, which had just stirred up all the loose gravel on the surface of the roads, and with it numerous nails which pierced and punctured our tires. Lord, but it was terribly hot! I thought at the time the trip was not very much fun.

Daddy's spirits picked up when we stopped in New Orleans, where he introduced us to Creole Gumbo, a spicy American-Cajun type of bouillabaisse. Following Daddy's recipe, Mother always made it after Christmas or Thanksgiving with left-over turkey. I use that holiday recipe today starting with turkey stock and adding ham and bacon, tomatoes, okra, crab, oysters and shrimp, served over rice in a large bowl. It is a whole meal, and the aromas wafting from the boiling hot soup plate create paradise, indeed.

Sadly, I never knew either Grandmother or Grandfather Asher. Mother told me she had held Daddy's head in her arms trying to comfort him when his mother died. On her deathbed, he had promised he would care for two of his younger brothers, Hugo and Reginald, and his sister, Sylvia. I often wondered how Mother, a young wife still in her twenty-second year, ever adjusted to all that responsibility. Daddy's brothers and sister were, in reality, her step-children—teenagers—difficult and spendthrifts, but Daddy and Mother managed despite their meager means. Reginald, my uncle, was ten years older than I. He was the cutest, most vivacious young red-headed guy one could ever hope to meet. A born entertainer and stand-up comedian, a real "personality kid." He and his friend Mel taught me how to tap dance and how to ballroom dance. He took me to dance halls, perfectly respectable places, with terrific bands or jukeboxes filled with records of wonderful swing, big-band tunes. Boy, did we dance! We were truly a dancing generation.

Reginald would say, "Phil, you have to be a feather" every time I tightened up. Of course, his instruction has served me in good stead all of my life. No matter what my dancing partners have done with their feet, I think I have been able to follow their lead, right or wrong, all because of those dance halls, so vivid in my memories of my southern youth.

Memories of Daddy's younger brothers, Reginald and Hugo, remain with me in their white dinner jackets whirling girls around the dance floors. In those days, when it was not considered the "thing" for girls to do, the most beautiful and prominent young ladies in Orlando were constantly calling my uncles on the telephone. I am proud of my background. Mixed with the Powell-MacLeod Scotch-Irish stock, it has made me one of thousands of Americans enriched by European heritage—a melting pot product.

When I married Samuel Eugene Gates in 1941, we joined the French-German stock of the Ashers, the English-German stock of the Gates, with the Scotch-Irish stock of the Powells-MacLeods. As far as this melting pot goes, my own children are probably abysmally unaware of the rich ethnic traditions they have inherited.

The Gates

I know less about the history of the Gates family than I do about the Ashers. Around 1895, Sam's mother, Fanny Miller, was in Indiana teach-

Sam's mother, Fanny Miller Gates, shown here with her students from First Country School, Warren, Indiana, on October 1, 1893.

Sam's father and mother, the Reverend Frank and Fanny Miller Gates, posing for their wedding picture in 1900.

ing school. Photographs I have on the walls of my home in Westhampton show her pupils, all barefoot midwestern farmer's children. Granny Fanny taught all subjects to about four different grades in a one-room schoolhouse as well as giving piano lessons on the side. Her Pennsylvania Deutch family, then called Müller, migrated westward as so many Germans did to better their lives.

Frank Gates, Sam's father of English extraction, was one of several brothers, and one sister. His father died when he was about seven, causing the children to leave school to farm or to work at anything they could find to help their mother put food on the table. When Frank was seventeen, he rebelled because of his thirst for knowledge. He felt so deprived, not even knowing how to read or write, much less spell. He announced one evening at family supper that he was going back to school. One of his brothers yelled, "You will have to start in the first grade, 'cause that's when you left." Frank replied, "No, I won't, I'll start in the second grade. I know first grade stuff!"

Can you imagine the specter of Frank, a six-foot tall, young seventeen year-old going barefoot into the classroom with all of those seven-year-olds? (While, in the photographs, the students are wearing no shoes, I doubt that they thought of themselves as poor.) His desire to learn was so intense that he swallowed his pride and insecurity and made rapid strides. By the time he met Fanny Miller, he had graduated from DePauw University in Indiana and was on his way toward graduation from the Methodist Seminary to be a minister studying Sanskrit, Hebrew, Greek, and Latin. They had two sons, Samuel (my husband) and Mark.

Frank and Fanny began married life in Lagro, Indiana, where Sam was born in 1906. Granny Fanny, whom I adored, said the parsonage was furnished with all of the leftover chairs, sofas, lumpy mattresses, and raggedy rugs the parishioners could spare. For the first fifteen years of their married life, they never had a parsonage that didn't leak, nor one that had any decent furniture. That tested their dedication and endurance. They were moved from Lagro to Wymore, Nebraska, then to Moscow, Idaho, where Sam and his brother, Mark, spent their babyhood. Sam remembered being carried to first grade on top of his father's shoulders. Even at six feet above the ground he sometimes could not see over the snow drifts on either side of the shoveled passageway.

Fanny's brother, who owned a flour milling business in Oregon, became ill and called Frank to ask if he could possibly take over his busi-

Sam and his brother Mark.

ness for a few years, as he did not want to lose all he had worked for during his life, nor see the support for his family disappear. Fanny loved her brother and his family and could not bear to see them lose everything. She knew that Idaho was not Frank's favorite location and maybe he would like a change.

Had Frank Gates spent his life in commerce, he would have been a very successful, wealthy man. In his two years, 1911 to 1913, at the flour mill, he proved to be an excellent salesman and manager. On one of his regular trips, Frank happened to "hit Los Angeles," one day about 1914 when the annual Methodist Convention was to take place. He knew the presiding bishop, one of his former professors and paid him a visit. "What are you doing these days? We've missed you, Frank," the bishop began.

Frank told him that he was helping his brother-in-law out while he recovered from an illness, but he was rather miserable as a flour salesman and wanted to return to the ministry.

As Grandfather Gates told the story to me, he said, "I got up a lot of courage and blurted out, do you have any openings in a church for me?" The bishop said he really did not know, but asked, "Are you coming to the convention this afternoon, Frank?" While he knew he had important business calls to make, he replied, "I'll be there."

The bishop droned on and on in the assembly hall announcing the various church assignments, and then paused, looked up from his script and said, "Is Frank Gates in the hall?" Frank popped up and said, "Yes, Sir." The bishop yelled out, as he was in the very last row, "Will you take Springville?"

"Yes, Sir," was his reply although he said he had absolutely no idea in the world where Springville was. He felt that life had begun to "sing for him again" as he put it. He rushed to the Western Union office and dispatched a telegram to his wife, "Pack up everything and bring the boys on the train to Springville. We have a church there. I will meet your train." Whether he set a date for her arrival or whether he just met each train which came through, I do not know.

Granny Fanny quickly rounded up their clothing, their piano, and their few possessions, and made a reservation for herself, Sam, and Mark on the train to Springville, California. No one on the train had ever heard of their destination. About four hours into the third day, a man got on the train, and she ventured to ask, "Do you know where Springville is?"

"Why yes, lady," he said, "I go there ever so often; it's about three stops from here." That man's answer was heavenly music to her ears.

At the Springville stop Frank was standing along side two warm and friendly vestrymen or aldermen or whatever the Methodist church calls them. They all hugged and kissed her and the two little boys and made them feel welcome. The piano was finally loaded into a horse-drawn buggy, their luggage into another, and off they went into the glorious countryside filled with aromatic smells of eucalyptus.

The piano had been purchased with an accumulation of $2 marriage fees which Frank always handed over to Fanny each time he performed a marriage ceremony. She had finally amassed enough, along with her earnings as a piano teacher, to buy the piano before their move to Moscow, Idaho. She often said that playing the piano "for pay and for pleasure" had saved her sanity on many occasions. Frank Gates rode the circuit to preach and be pastor to his flock, located in three different areas of their parish. There was no school anywhere near, so Fanny, teacher that she was, sent off for correspondence course materials so that she could teach the boys at home through the fourth, fifth, and sixth grades. They continued to study piano with her.

Fanny's marriage was a very happy one which I observed over a long period of years, but she said those years in Springville were the happiest of all. She endured Frank's explosive, almost paranoic temper tantrums, which would show themselves for no reason at all. Perhaps a whole day would pass when he would not speak to anyone. His sons, Sam and Mark, both inherited the trait, although it was somewhat diluted in strength and less frequent by their generation. Fanny taught her daughters-in-law, Margaret and me, how to cope when the tantrums occurred. She would

Sam and Mark with their parents in Azusa, CA.

say, "Just close your eyes and lips and think of what wonderful men they are in every other respect. Intelligent, faithful, responsible, loving."

I once told her that I knew Grandfather Frank adored her, but he was surely not demonstrative. She confided that it had taken him ten years to say "I love you." I gasped in amazement when she told me, as Sam was quite good at expressing his love for me. Fanny said before they were married he would write her notes and even send her telegrams with only the words, "I do, do you?" When he finally said, "I love you," she thinks she said, "Well, now I really believe you!"

Why did Granny Fanny consider those years in the countryside at Springville the happiest of her life? Their friends were honest, loving people, neighbors in the truest sense. She had her family "all to herself." The fields were full of all manner of fruits, apricots, peaches, oranges, grapefruit, lemons, melons, plus vegetables and big, black olives. She was instructed by the wife of one of the aldermen how to "put up" olives. They were the big, black variety, and she put them in a large barrel on the back screened porch to soak in a brine solution for weeks. She would simply pick up a handful from the barrel every time she went in or out of the back door. In less than a year she had gained about twenty pounds. She attributed all of her added weight to the olives, as no one had told her how many calories were in them. Knowing what a master chef she was with pies, cakes, stews and all kinds of hot breads, I have never been completely satisfied that olives were the real culprit.

After a few years, Frank was called to a church in Azusa, California (named for A to Z USA!), where Fanny found two treasured allies. One was a violin and cello virtuoso. She agreed to give his daughters piano lessons in exchange for his teaching her sons violin and cello. Sam continued to study and play the cello until his graduation from University of Southern California, when he left to teach American political history at Long Beach Junior College. Her other mentor was a town tailor, an Aus-

Dr. and Mrs. E. F. Gates on their 50th anniversary, 1950.

trian by birth. Fanny taught his daughter piano in exchange for his teaching her how to tailor little boys' suits out of Frank's worn ministerial ones. In the upstairs hall of my country home, I have a picture of the two Gates boys holding their violin and cello and wearing suits tailored by their mother, fashioned out of their father's hand-me-downs.

When Frank was called to Santa Monica, he immediately loved the congregation and its community. He raised enough money to build a fine new Methodist Church there. Frank's flour sales adventure had created a small nest egg which he invested in what became Gates, Kingsley, and Gates, the local mortuary which his son, Mark, managed. Frank also invested in a number of real estate deals taking first mortgages from a variety of friends and acquaintances to whom the local bank would not give such agreeable interest rates or mortgage terms. When I met Sam in Washington, the Gateses, after all of the leaky parsonages, and hand-me down furniture, were able to build themselves a capacious, modern California-style home on the top of the hill in Santa Monica between two of its famous boulevards. From their living room and dining room they could see the Pacific Ocean and the Santa Monica mountains, breathtaking views at any hour, but especially at sunset.

After raising two sons and building two churches, they could afford to buy some authentic antiques, fine oriental rugs, and other furnishings their taste had demanded, but their pocketbooks had never before permitted. In 1950, when they celebrated their golden wedding anniversary in their new home, it was chock full of good friends and family. I had suggested to Sam, before the party that he and Mark should make a memorial gift of two stained glass windows which they could both help design and approve for their father's church. When Sam made this offer, Frank said, "Not on your life, you're going to build us a chapel!" After all, he was a past master at church fund raising, and his own sons were not going to get off that easily! So now proudly stands a Gates Chapel adjoining the First Methodist Church in Santa Monica. I visit it now and then, just to see the pictures and the plague commemorating Frank Gates's ministry, his contributions to the parish and the community, and his giving life. I always remember Granny Fanny when I pass the organ. She had played this instrument professionally for so many years. She always told me she was the cheapest organist in town as she was "non-Union." She willed her own prized piano to Kathe, her only grandchild who had studied, played, and loved music as much as she—the same piano bought with the $2 wedding fees. It is still in the Williamson's home in Georgetown.

Note:

1. Shelby Foote. *The Civil War: A Narrative, Fredericksburg and Meridian.* (New York: Random House, 1963), 391-93, 597; Joe Gray Taylor. *Louisiana, A History.* (New York: W. W. Norton & Company, 1984), 88, 94, 99.

CHAPTER FOUR

Florida Childhood

Bliss was it that dawn to be alive,
But to be young was very heaven!
— The Prelude, Book XI,
William Wordsworth, 1770-1850

It wasn't too long ago that central Florida of my childhood was a pine and lake-studded wilderness. It was there that Daddy and Mother first courted and spent twenty-five years together. Daddy had graduated from Louisiana State University as a civil engineer, but he soon abandoned his chosen profession. After four days of working in the Louisiana Bayou, where mosquitoes, snakes, and other life-threatening vermin infested the swamp land, he decided surveying was not a good way to earn a living. He again became dissatisfied while teaching chemistry and math to high school students in Alexandria, Louisiana, and then moved to Miami where he found employment with the National Cash Register Company.

An illness that confined him to a hospital soon became the luckiest event in his life because that is where he met Mother, who was employed there as a registered nurse. It is questionable as to who gave whom the larger dose of tender loving care. The next time Mother saw Daddy, she was attending a Sunday service at the Orlando Presbyterian Church—and lo and behold there he was in the choir, singing in a melodious tenor voice and looking even more handsome and irresistible to her than ever. Both were equally smitten and after a swift courtship, they were married (in 1916) and moved to Daytona, where I was born in 1918.

The adjustments Mother made to marriage were considerable. She had been reared in a God-fearing, rock-ribbed Methodist family who taught her to believe that playing cards and dancing on Sunday were sins. She

Phil with her nurse Louisa.

had been admonished from the pulpit to toe a very thin moral line. If she didn't, she would be headed for perdition—lost forever. How she resented those sermons! She told me that what she had liked best about going to church with her parents was the solidarity of their entrance, marching two by two down the aisle. All twelve Browns (parents and ten children) accompanied by uncles and aunts, sat together in pews, one behind the other. It must have been a colorful sight for most of them were red headed.

Daddy was from Alsatian/ German stock and had a Bohemian nature. Although his family was Jewish, he seldom went to temple except on Yom Kippur, and he lived the life of a cultivated European, albeit in a small-town Florida setting. He enjoyed the parish life at St. Lukes Cathedral in Orlando, and frequently cooked his famous spaghetti and Creole gumbo for their parish suppers. His Louisiana background led him to all manner of wine, good food, women, and gambling. The latter was to become his Achilles Heel.

Daddy was a devoted husband. In the last days of Mother's second pregnancy, he took her to the small maternity hospital in Daytona via horse and buggy. They bounced down the dusty, rutted road while Mother's labor pains worsened. Dr. Bohanan[1] had been alerted to meet them as soon as possible. Daddy held her hand through the ordeal of her labor and delivery. The doctor finally arrived—roaring drunk. The baby emerged, a beautiful little boy I was told later. Mother heard the nurse say: "Oh my God, doctor, you've killed the baby!" He had cut the umbilical cord either improperly or too soon, and the baby had died. After Daddy heard the nurse's exclamation, he lunged toward the doctor and threatened to kill him, but the hospital staff separated them just in time. Daddy was the most mild-mannered of men, but his outburst was understandable. Alas, my parents' only son never lived. His little grave is in the family plot in Opelousas.

These days, a malpractice suit would be filed, but such things were unheard of then. It would have been useless anyway. The doctor was poor, uninsured, and what could possibly compensate a couple for the loss of a child? Whenever we went to the cemetery, the three of us stood at the grave, weeping silently over this tragic and unnecessary death. My sister and I would have adored a brother and our parents, a son; but alas, it was not to be.

That was the only time I saw my paternal grandparents and I have little memory of the visit. After some months of unsuccessful job searches, our little family of three left Opelousas and moved back to Florida, this time to Orlando.

In the early 1920s, the decade of Florida's boom, migration to the state outstripped housing construction and thousands of newcomers were living in tents because they could not find a home. Daddy's fortune picked up with the boom that followed offering him a chance to move a long way from the backwoods bookkeeper working on a turpentine ranch. He bought a sedan convertible that cut quite a swath in Orlando's downtown area where, happily, most streets were paved.

Less than a century before our arrival, this part of central Florida had been occupied by moccasin-footed Seminole Indians. When the first U.S. settlers came from the North to live in Florida, they chose Orlando because of its abundant supply of fresh water and its habitable highlands. In 1823 three U.S. government representatives and thirty-two Seminoles signed the Treaty of Moultrie Creek which earmarked four million acres north of Charlotte Harbor and south of Ocala for an Indian reservation. In return the Seminoles relinquished their use of twenty-four million acres on which they had roamed for $6,000 worth of tools and livestock, $5,000 annually for twenty years to each tribe, plus meat, corn, and salt for a year.

Neamathla, one of the Seminole leaders, accepted the terms of the treaty saying, "We rely on your justice and humanity; we hope you will not send us south to a country where neither the hickory nut, the acorn, nor the persimmon grows. We depend much on these products of the forest for food. In the South, they are not to be found."[2]

All went well until 1835 when the settlers discovered that the Indians were harboring runaway slaves, while pillaging and stealing from them. To protect themselves from hostile Indians, the settlers had established troops at Fort Gatlin, and Orlando Reeves served as their "Sentinel." As the story goes, Trooper Reeves thought he saw a log floating across the lake. Unsure he sounded the alarm, but the "log" turned out to be an Indian sneaking up to his camp on what is now Lake Eola. The Indians summarily dispatched the unfortunate Reeves. A raging battle ensued between what is now Pine and Church streets, and the U.S. troops prevailed. Orlando Reeves was reverently buried on the lake shore, and the area was christened "Orlando's Grave." Later, "grave" was dropped and the area came to be known simply as Orlando. Today a stone, placed by Cherokee Junior High School students, marks the southeast corner of the lake where he was buried. The Indians moved south and west for hunting and farming, while the settlers established a series of forts or blockhouses principally for security.

Most of the descendants of families, who still live in Orlando, came from the North, long after the Civil War. Aaron and Isaac Jernigan, were the first to settle around Lake Holden.[3] They came with seven hundred head of cattle, two Negro men, and an elderly white man. Their grandsons and granddaughters called Overstreet, Guernsey, Bumby, Branch, Slemons, MacEwan, Howard, Giles, Way, Dickson, Lawton, Estes, and many others are now resident in the city.

By 1900, Orlando had a population of 2,481 hardy souls. Cattle had finally stopped roaming across Orange Avenue, and cowboys no longer came in on Saturday night to savor the night life in the saloons. Electric street lights had been introduced, supplanting Welsback gas burners. Surprisingly, Orlando's first newspaper was devoted entirely to black affairs and began publication as the *Florida Christian Record*. It thrived for fifteen years until its editor died, and no one could be found to take it over. The city's second newspaper, first published in 1885, was called the *South Florida Sentinel.*

History tells us that thousands of Englishmen had streamed into the Orlando area at the turn of the century. Many were young men who were not the firstborn of their families and, thus, did not inherit the family estate. They did not wish to go into the British army, navy, or the clergy, as was the English custom. They apparently lived on the income from small trust funds, insufficient to support a comfortable lifestyle in England, but ample for all manner of amenities in central Florida. Others were just plain laborers—but all sought a better life, climate, and working conditions.

From 1900 through the depression, many others drifted in from Scotland and Ireland, as well as more than a few "Yankees" who migrated from Maine, Massachusetts, Indiana, Pennsylvania, and Maryland. These newcomers were full of energy and anxious to make a new and better life. They were not exhausted by the Civil War and its seemingly endless, devastating reconstruction period. They were not, as many of my ancestors were, physically debilitated and financially downtrodden, as well as spiritually drained of entrepreneurial vim and vigor. The newcomers founded businesses, bought land, practiced law and medicine, and best of all they brought money.

An English army officer retired from the Dragoons named General Swindler conceived the Orlando polo team. Daddy, a member of the Polo Association, said he would have given anything to have played polo. He frequently recounted tales told to him by M. J. Daetwyler, a member of the 1912 Orlando polo team. The English, Mr. Daetwyler said, were homesick and imported their customs to Orlando. They even served tea after the Polo matches and built an Episcopal church.

In 1920, Joe Tinker, for whom Orlando's baseball field was later named, was shortstop for the Chicago Cubs. He was one-third of the famous "Tinker-to-Evers-to-Chance" double play combination—a household slogan at the time. There were occasions when Daddy sat glued to our first radio set listening to broadcasts of the baseball games even when the static was so loud he could not hear the commentator well. Two other friends, I remember, who came often to listen with him were Clyde McKinley and Wilbur Flower, who had a real estate and insurance business. In 1921 another developer, Walter Rose opened "Rosemont," the most successful real estate development in the area. Amazingly, it survived the entire depression. Mrs. Martha Lancaster, matron of the Orlando Day Nursery, on whose board of directors Mother served, frequently came to our house seeking her advice and help. Mrs. Lancaster was a "fixture" who contributed so much to Orlando's helpless and homeless children left in her care.

Daddy's two best friends in Orlando were the medical doctors, Gaston Edwards and J.S. "Johnny" MacEwan. They were partners on the golf course. In addition, they served as our family physicians, while Daddy was their family's and clinic's accountant/auditor. Neither ever submitted a bill! Professional courtesy ruled the day. The arrangement was beneficial to all parties, most particularly during the depression years when few "greenbacks" were circulating.

Those early Orlandoans never, well, almost never, forgot who they were. The city had one of the first Registers of Families and the people whose names graced the pages of the fine leather-bound volumes were proud. Although not many of them are left, those who remain hold onto their customs "as grimly as a fly upon a flivver" as it was sometimes expressed by the truly oldtimers.

In my early years, life was concentrated around my family, and a few near neighbors. One of the joys for me in this circle was going camping with Mother and Daddy in the woods near Orlando. There were fishing camps, hunting camps, and just plain camp camps all over the piney forests in Central Florida, where we went for an afternoon and early evening for a special treat. We built what seemed to me a huge bonfire and cooked fresh oysters on grills over the fire. We ate oysters until they were "coming out our ears." So delicious! With them we always had French bread, cut in half, and lathered with butter, something like a Hero sandwich.

On other occasions we visited Grandmother Annie and enjoyed a fabulous noon meal from Grandmother Annie's Maitland kitchen. It was the tastiest I can remember anywhere even today. She always had fresh oranges, grapefruit, satsumas, and kumquats from her own land or strawberries and occasionally figs from neighboring farms. Sunday dinner seemed to consist of fried chicken (home-grown) with cream gravy, or, perhaps, Country *Old* Ham, the Smithfield variety which was soaked overnight and served paper-thin, like American prosciutto, with sweet potatoes baked in their skins and kept hot on the side of a large wood cook stove until the rest of the meal was ready. We enjoyed coleslaw, or cold vegetable salad, and, of course, a variety of green vegetables, albeit cooked much too long, as was the custom. The meal ended with a variety of pies, cakes, and puddings. When I recall those menus that I looked forward to having as a child, I wonder why I did not blow up like a balloon. "Dieting" and "cholesterol" did not seem to be words in my family's vocabulary. In 1926, when my sister Cleona, named for Grandmother Asher, was born, I was eight years old. It was then that we began spending our summers at Daytona on one of the world's most famous beaches. At first we rented a cozy little cottage and later an apartment in a comfortable inn operated by Professor and Mrs. Ebsen, where many of the best families in Orlando also stayed. Their Orlando house/studio was an attractive and busy place with a ballroom for the Ebsen's dance academy. Their beach boarding house had a charming dining room for inn guests and served absolutely delicious meals. This was a convenient luxury, especially for Mother who did not have to cook.

I adored going to the inn because the Ebsens had two children about my Uncle Reggie's age, Buddy and Vilma. Buddy became a successful actor, still seen on TV (*Beverly Hillbillies* and *Barnaby Jones*).

Both our cottage and the Ebsen Inn were on the dunes. At low tide the shoreline was wide and the sand as hard as cement. This is where Sir Malcolm Campbell tried out his marvelous racing car called the "Blue Bird," well known for its speed records. At other times this is where the older boys and girls set up handball courts for neighborhood games. I did not mind climbing over the prickly shrubs that scratched my bare legs to watch the "Blue Bird" trial runs or to cheer my friends in their game.

Still ringing in my ears is the sound of the surf as it crashed down on the shore. Each morning I'd pull on my bathing suit and cap (always worn in those days) and race to the beach. I'd dash over the hot, powdery sand and through the salty spray that hit my face, and plunge into the sea. What an idyllic way to start a summer day!

Whenever I happened to have no playmates, which was often, I read three books a day borrowed from the local lending library. I drank lots of lemonade, ate tuna fish sandwiches, toasted marshmallows on saltines; all wonderful taste sensations I savor to this day. Daddy would occasionally come over in the middle of the week to see us and cool himself in the crystal clear ocean waters. He always spent the weekends with us. After all these years I still think fondly—and often—of those carefree summers at the shore.

The only summer pastime I now regret was hunting for turtle eggs. In the evening we would walk at the water's edge until we found the very stretch of sand where we remembered seeing female sea turtles lay their eggs a few days before. When we found several dozen of the small, round, ping-pong ball sized eggs, I would fill my bathing cap with all it could hold. Since the yolks were large and the whites tiny, Mother used them to make pound cake and sugar tea cookies, all gratefully devoured by my playmates almost before they cooled.

Perhaps I was not old enough to know better then but looking back on my participation in this activity makes me feel somewhat shamefaced. Environmentalists today are wiser. They have posted the dunes where the turtles lay their eggs to prevent people and vehicles from invading the areas. Now the eggs hatch in the warm sun, and the baby turtles escape to the safety of the sea.

Each fall we left Daytona Beach tanned and healthy and returned to Orlando. In our first year there, this meant kindergarten for me. The only class for pre-schoolers was in a nice lady's parlor, which had enough chairs for about seven children, but she squeezed in several more. We probably did not learn much except sharing toys,

Phil, age 3.

but we must have absorbed some reading readiness, for I read well at an early age. I shared a wing chair with Frank Jr. Guernsey. He still shoots his age playing golf with former President Bush, I hear.

In these days Mother and I went often to see Grandmother Annie and Grandfather Brown, whose house in Maitland was not far from ours. I always looked forward to these visits, except one time when Mother told me that Grandfather had died. His would be my first funeral.

He was laid out in state in the cool dark parlor, and I was pushed in to say goodbye to him, though I certainly had no desire to do so. Frankly, I was scared to death of the corpse. Four large candles were burning at the corners of his coffin—the parlor was darkened. The air was stuffy, and I was gasping for breath in that stifling atmosphere. It all seemed melodramatic and frightening. We went in cars to the cemetery for the service out in the Maitland brush, and we walked to the grave already dug in the back of the property. Just seeing that coffin being lowered into the ground, accompanied by the quiet sobs of children was an awesome first encounter with death for a seven-year-old. My chest throbbed, and I choked and sneezed—symptoms of chronic hayfever or asthma that troubled me.

I did manage to recover, however, and why? Because of the food we had after the funeral. The gusts of delicious aromas that billowed from Grandmother Annie's wood stove are with me forever. There was an everyday dish of grits, another of Virginia ham with redeye gravy, plus an assortment of casseroles filled with the very best delicacies brought by neighbors, friends, and family members in honor of Grandfather Brown.

In the family room there was, as always, a large contraption known as a stereopticon with which I had amused myself on other happier occasions. This gadget was made of oak, and beside it lay a large box of double-imaged, hardback postcards of scenes from all around the world. When I placed the postcard into a slot in the back of the stereopticon, I saw only one scene, merged so that it had depth, three-dimensional, as it were. What I saw gave me the effect of a still movie. I learned this effect was achieved by two plane mirrors set at an angle, allowing the twin pictures

Phil and her father, J.B. Asher, in Orlando, 1924.

to be seen as one. My favorite postcards were of Gainsborough's "Blue Boy," Canaletto's "Grand Canal" and other Venetian scenes, the "Baptistery" and "Duomo" in Florence, many cathedrals of Paris and London, as well as a few street settings of Old New York. Movies were really not a part of my world, so this had to do, and it did very well. I spent many hours oohing and aahing over the exciting world I thought I would never see in travel. This squeaky, magic lantern diverted me from the burial sobs, and I felt funerals were not so distressing as I had believed earlier in the day.

It was during this period, when I was five to eight years of age, that I was pressed into service to pass the refreshments at UDC (United Daughters of the Confederacy) meetings. Had Mother not been inspired by these meetings, she would not have persevered in her research on ancestral data, and I could not have written this book! Not only did students, who had won prizes for their writings, read their papers on an aspect of the Civil War theme but also members spoke about hand-me-down histories by grandchildren and great-grandchildren of the Reconstruction. Listening to these readings, even at my young age, was stimulating and inspiring.

Later, Mother and I became fascinated by the works of five historians of the period: Carl Sandburg's great multivolume works; James McPherson's *The Battle Cry of Freedom*, a Pulitzer Prize history; Clifford

Dowdey's *The Land They Fought For*, and also Bruce Cattons's *A Stillness at Appomattox*.[4] Shelby Foote's Civil War series[5] on public television was stirring and tear-jerking. At one time Mr. Foote was asked if he, today, were forced to make a choice about fighting for the Confederacy, "would he enlist?" He replied "Yes, they are my people, my homeland and my heritage. I don't necessarily think they should have won, but if I had been there, I would have served." Even in my generation, most of us were schooled in a sense of loyalty to and knowledge of "The Cause." Those feelings die very slowly. They were certainly very much alive as I now recall my childhood.

Notes:

1. Not his real name.

2. *Florida. A Guide to the Southernmost State*. Compiled and written by the Federal Writers' Project of the Work Projects Administration of the State of Florida. (New York, Oxford University Press, 1939), 222-24; James W. Covington. *The Seminoles of Florida*. (Gainesville, Florida: University Press of Florida, 1993), 52-54; James W. Covington, "Federal Relations with the Apalachicola Indians: 1823-1838."

3. Eve Bacon. *Orlando: A Centennial History*. (Chuluota, Florida: The Mickler House, Publishers, 1975), 3.

4. Carl Sandburg. *Abraham Lincoln, The War Years*. (New York: Harcourt, Brace & World, Inc., 1926), I-IV; James M. McPherson. *The Battle Cry of Freedom. The Civil War Era*. (New York: Oxford University Press, 1988); Clifford Dowdey. *The Land They Fought For; The Story of the South as the Confederacy*. (Garden City, New York: Doubleday, 1955); Bruce Catton. *A Stillness at Appomattox*. (New York: Anchor Books, 1990).

5. This series was based on a three volume history by Shelby Foote entitled *The Civil War: A Narrative*. (New York: Random House, 1963).

CHAPTER FIVE

Growing up on Dubsdread

There are all those early memories;
one cannot get another set; one has only those.

— Shadows on the Rock, *IV:2*
Willa Cather, 1876–1947

On a fine summer day in August 1928, Mother and I had returned from an afternoon swim at Daytona Beach and were sitting on the bed in the second floor of our apartment in Ebsen's Inn. Mother was holding a carton containing a mixture of frothy egg whites patting it on her very, very white skin to ease the pain of her sunburn. There were none of today's magic ointments with numbers from eight to thirty for blocking out the sun's rays. Mother found her homemade solution of raw egg whites soothing if she patted it on her arms and legs frequently. This was exactly what she was doing when Daddy, without knocking, burst into the room, whipped off his tie, shed his coat, and threw his bank book on the bed! "Cute, I'm a millionaire." (She hated being called "Kate" because of its association with the *Taming of the Shrew,* but tolerated "Cute," a name he had given her long before.)

I was only ten and did not know much about what he was up to, but it sounded like a good thing. I seem to recall Mother said, "I'm proud of you, Darling," or, "Isn't that wonderful, Darling,"— something to that effect. Mother was, in equal parts, vivacious and shy, even though she seemed unaware of her almost breathtaking auburn-haired beauty.

In the middle of the euphoric boom days in Florida (1926–1929), Daddy and his friend, Tim Otrich, an architect, and Carl Dann Jr., a golf pro, had invested in the Dubsdread Country Club and Development on

The Ashers in Dubsdread, 1929. Phil (far right) was 12 at the time.

the outskirts of Orlando where they started the Dubsdread Golf Club. These were Florida's halcyon days; days when Daddy and Mother decided to build a beautiful, large two-story Dutch Colonial home for us on a lot across from the second and seventh tees. Buyers for lots in this new suburb streamed through the sales office with their plans already in hand to build houses for themselves. To earn extra income from his investment, my father built an apartment house containing six three-bedroom apartments on the lot adjacent to our home. This multifamily unit was an immediate success, always fully rented in the winter and often year-round by tenants like the Lawtons, a gentle and loving couple from New York with two sons about my age, who had opened a jewelry shop on Orange Avenue.

Golf pros came from Scotland to give lessons and manage the golfing part of the enterprise at Dubsdread. They soon realized that the name of the club was appropriate— "dub" meaning someone who does not play golf well and "dread" referring to the challenging course. As Daddy was to find out later, the two syllables described the whole development.

We rocked along in comfort and good health while a rising tide of prosperity spread throughout the United States. Daddy played golf whenever he had time, sporting knickers ("plus fours") and looking as dashing as he was handsome. Mother, wearing large brimmed hats to protect her fair, mother-of-pearl complexion, played with him but with only mild enthusiasm. Her golf game was as slow and easy as was her speech. They often played the five holes "around the house," a good before-breakfast exercise. Florida was a "play" place, and they indeed "played." My problem was that they not only played golf and bridge but talked about golf or bridge all the time.

It was not that Daddy did not consider my pleasures too. He had a set of golf clubs made especially for me and had arranged for a Scottish golf pro, who rented one of the apartments next door, to give me lessons. Despite this attention to my needs, my golfing career never really took off. It is my

Phil's mother and grandmother in Dubsdread.

extreme regret now that I was not able to develop any skills or muscles in my youth that would have made my later golfing life less frustrating and self-flagellating.

I had no better luck with piano lessons, although I absolutely adored playing. Every time I started to practice Mother insisted that I stop at once. She said I was "waking up Cleona," who would, in fact, begin to cry. That ended my piano career for I did not want my baby sister to cry either. I really ached to play the piano, and I was devastated! Only much later in my junior year in college, when Daddy could again afford to pay for my lessons, did I resume them. Actually, as I think of it now, I did much better with piano than I did with golf.

A prosperous life for my parents was in full sway. Daddy owned a Packard sedan which he drove on most occasions. He also had a lavender Erskine convertible sports car for fun. When parties were at home, Mother would call the country club chef, who would bring over everything already prepared for guests—hors d'oeuvres, roasts, casseroles, and desserts. What a gay and happy life! Mother "became good at entertaining," as was the custom of Southern hostesses.

For immediate family needs, we had a cook and a maid, both black. Our cook, however, could not abide children around her when she worked. She was extremely bad-tempered and ran after me with a butcher knife whenever I went near her. Whenever "chicken" was on our menu, she would run around the backyard, catch a hen, wring its neck, and put it in boiling water to remove the feathers. I shuddered during this procedure, usually pulling my blouse over my head so as not to look.

Mother replaced this cook in her own way—impulsively. We were

The Asher's beloved housekeeper, Daisy Ashe, whom Phil's mother hired in a cotton field when passing through Swansea, South Carolina.

driving home from a short stay in New York, when she suddenly asked Daddy to stop by the side of the road near a town called Swansea, South Carolina. She leaped out of the car, promptly lifted her skirt, and bounded over a wooden fence into a cotton field. I watched her wondering what in heaven's name she was doing. She stopped at the first young black girl she came to, and I heard her say, "I need a housekeeper/nursemaid and I would like you to come to Florida to work for me." Daisy, the object of her inquiry, said, "I have a five-year-old boy and I cannot leave him."

Within a half hour Daisy and Carlie (we always assumed that his name was Carlyle although Daisy did not know how to spell it) were in our car and heading for Orlando. She was a wonderful human being and turned into a great cook, thanks to Mother's teaching. After a few weeks Daisy became an expert in making cottage cheese (Daddy called is smearkase) and served it with cold sliced potatoes and lots of dill, salt, and pepper, and sliced tomatoes. This was one of the tastiest all-time supper meals she ever made and it suited Daddy to a tee because of his Deutch taste buds. We never had "store-bought" mayonnaise. For breakfast she always prepared breads, light as a feather, hot enough to melt butter. A slice or two along with home-grown oranges, grapefruits, satsumas, and occasionally figs made the day start well.

Daisy was not only a wonderful housekeeper and cook, she was also a great companion. Sometimes when I had nothing else to do, I ventured outside to watch the rain making tiny iridescent bubbles, that would make our flowering shrubs glow until they suddenly burst. Daisy often came to the porch with me to enjoy Florida's late afternoon rains, and we would marvel together at the beautiful display. Despite the joy of the moment, I usually would have an asthma attack, and retreat to Daisy's kitchen to catch my breath.

This allergic sensitivity continued to be a trial to me at Dubsdread. I would often feel short of breath. All doctors did at that time was to administer intravenous shots of potassium hydrate, or adrenaline. Mother, depending upon her nursing knowledge, was not eager for me to resort to adrenaline. She told me, "You'll end up a cardiac case when you're only forty years old, wheezing for the rest of your life." Thanks to her wisdom, I did not suffer that fate.

What she prepared for me was an herbal powder in a red can called "Power's Asthma Relief." All she did was to put the powder in a metal dish, wreath my head under a cone or tent of newspapers, light a fire in the powder and let me breathe the fumes. Immediate relief was the result, although the preparation was time-consuming and cumbersome.

It is no wonder that during the first weeks or months my life as an eight-year old at Dubsdread was frighteningly quiet and isolated for I had no playmates. Although school absorbed every weekday, the weekends were painfully lonesome. Cleona was usually in Daisy's care and too small anyway, so I resorted to creating "playmates." Mother told me that she often put her ear to my bedroom door and thought I must have five friends inside. It was only me, talking to myself. My imaginary friends were answering. When I tired of this dual conversation, I resorted to reading and read voraciously—books written by Louisa May Alcott, Mary Roberts Rhinehart, and Rudyard Kipling.

Finally, in the fall of 1926, Mother put her arm around me during what seemed to me a particularly long day and said, "You know, Mr. Otrich, whom we see carrying his rolls of house designs everywhere, has just moved his family down from Indiana, and I understand they have a daughter just your age." She telephoned Mrs. Otrich immediately and said, "I have a little girl, eight years old, who is desperate for a playmate. I understand you have a little girl, too."

She replied, "I certainly do. Tell your daughter to come right over."

With some trepidation I walked slowly across the fairway to the Otrich house, which was designed very much like ours. A little girl named Sally Virginia Louise Otrich waited for me at the front door. We shook hands formally on the doorstep. Mrs. Otrich, looking like a John Singer Sargent painting of a Victorian lady with sparkling blue eyes, appeared immediately, and with some urgency in the tone of her low, modulated voice, she

Lucy, Lucinda, and Rosette—three Madame Alexander dolls that Phil and her friend Sally Virginia Louise Otrich played with as young girls.

asked, "Why don't you little girls sit on the sofa?" She meant, I believe, for us to "feel each other out."

After a while she brought us a book and dropped it on our laps, suggesting, "I think you girls might find it interesting." The huge, weighty volume, which took both of our laps to support, was John Milton's *Paradise Lost*. We turned the pages slowly and paused each time we came to a gory scene of men and women falling down into Hell, being tortured by huge diabolic, writhing serpents or ugly monsters. We spent the whole afternoon absorbed in the illustrations in this heavy book which I learned later was a very valuable second edition with engravings by a French artist named Paul Gustave Doré. I cannot imagine two eight-year-olds spending an afternoon like this today. By the end of our visit, thanks to lemonade, cookies, and *Paradise Lost* we had become friends.

After our first afternoon together, Sally and I saw each other very often. One of our favorite activities was playing with three Madame Alexander dolls—a blonde, a brunette, and a redhead named Lucy, Lucinda, and Rosette. They had been sent to Sally, along with three individual small wardrobe trunks full of the most exquisite hand-made doll clothes. These treasures were from Sally's aunt, Mrs. Otrich's sister, who lived somewhere in Indiana. She and the ladies in her bridge club had felt sorry for a little girl, now in the wilds of Florida, no doubt with few playmates. They decided that their Christmas project would be to send her some special dolls, each with its own wardrobe. It was obvious that these ladies had had a very good time collecting the materials, making the clothes, and sewing on designer labels, some Parisian, taken from their own garments. Remember this was "The Boom." Some of the cloaks had wisps of fur around the neck. There were silk stockings, lace brassieres, ski clothes, riding clothes—and all imaginable outfits. These dolls and clothes provided Sally and me with three years of wonderful play, casting Lucy, Lucinda, and Rosette in every possible role in a variety of dramas, original or adapted from our current reading. Not many years ago she sent me a photo of the three dolls and some wardrobe selections kept after sixty years.

On other occasions we climbed up to the Otrich attic to search through trunks full of Sally's grandmother's clothes. We created endless costumes, teetered around on the fairways in high-heeled shoes several sizes too large for us, sometimes pretending that we were sending our beaus off to the Civil War, never to see them again. No one could convince us that we were not destined for stardom.

It gives me such pleasure to think of the innocent, imaginative times that little girls enjoyed when I was young. We could concoct situations, conceive dramas, and amuse ourselves for days. We had no television and the radio was full of static. In the 1930s and even early 1940s movies were our principal spectator sport, and we often saw our favorites several times. I think we saw "Waterloo Bridge" with Kent Douglas and Mae Clarke five times and later the remake starring Robert Taylor and Vivian Leigh and cried just as heartbrokenly the last time as the first!

This was a busy time. The Florida land boom reached a crescendo in 1925, when I was seven years old. Daddy's development, Dubsdread, was a part of the prosperity which had grown out of sudden wealth. Thousands of people from all over the United States descended on Florida, particularly to Tampa, Palm Beach, and Miami to buy land, whether they would build on it immediately or not. They felt that land would never be cheaper (alas, not true) and savings and loan associations abounded to help them buy it.

Noted orators readily accepted invitations to "hawk" lots in the most "booming" areas such as Coral Gables. It is rumored that developers paid William Jennings Bryan, Clarence Darrow's opposing counsel in the famous Scopes/Evolution Monkey Trial, as much as $100,000 for his efforts, one-half in property and one-half in cash.

One day in 1926, after Cleona's birth, Mother confessed to me that she was feeling fat and dowdy. She, as well as Greta Garbo, had read of Dr. Gayelord Hauser's diet. She followed it for a month. Garbo also went on the diet, and it was rumored that she fell in love with the doctor! At the end of the thirty days, Mother had lost all of the "baby fat." She said, "I then bit my lip, closed my eyes and took the courageous step of having my long, luxuriant, auburn tresses 'bobbed.'" For her whole married life, she had been able to "sit" on her hair, literally. Daddy felt it was her crowning glory. He bounced into our Dubsdread living room one late afternoon right after she had returned from the beauty parlor. He let out one of his rare, loud shrieks and cried out, "My God, Cute, You've ruined yourself. You're not recognizable!" Naturally, she had wanted him to say, "Darling, you look fifteen years younger and so much prettier." Instead, he was devastated about the "flapper" bob.

Orlando held onto its boom days as long as possible. This was not without some perseverance. In 1926 a hurricane came roaring into South Florida leaving thousands temporarily homeless. Two years later a second, more serious storm swept through Miami and the Florida Keys laying waste much of area. This time the toll was 1,810 persons killed and about as many injured. The Florida East Coast Railway, operating a local rail service of great pride to all Floridians since the 1880s,[1] survived both storms but had to "give up the ghost" and surrender to its creditors in 1931. This was a forerunner to many other commercial enterprises that lost everything. Fortunately, Orlando had suffered only some bent trees from the storms' high winds.

Although times were "bad," Daddy, Tim Otrich, and Carl Dann Jr. continued to put Dubsdread together. They lured many sports greats to visit the golf course and play Pro-Am exhibition matches. Jack Dempsey, Gene Tunney, and Babe Ruth came, as did Bobby Jones.

Self-service supermarkets, already spread throughout the North, began to arrive when Orlando's population reached about 23,000. The city then had a business and shopping district that converged on Orange Avenue. We had always gone to a green grocer and then to a butcher, who knew exactly how to cut each type of meat for "madam." He knew everybody and everybody knew him. This first self-service market was called Handy Andy, soon to be replaced by Piggly-Wiggly. Today it is difficult to find a butcher or green grocer in an average town.

Nineteen thirty was the first time I ever saw slot machines. They had become popular, actually—a mania, even in the days when no one had any extra change. Judge Frank Smith issued a restraining order trying to keep these "one-armed bandits" in operation (if you can imagine that!) by preventing Mayor Giles from seizing and destroying them. It was a cause célèbre for weeks.

Another fad in the depression days, was the game of bridge, but it, more appropriately, was free. Mother and Father played duplicate bridge in tournaments several times a week, and they collected lots of silver trophies.

By the end of 1931, two years after "Black Thursday" (October 24, 1929), stock losses on the New York Stock Exchange reached the fifty billion dollar mark. Fifteen million people were out of work from a population of 125 million. Florida, by all accounts, was the hardest hit state in the Union. Gasoline prices dropped from 21 cents to 19 cents a gallon.

Our beloved Dubsdread Country Club and Development became a victim of the depression. In our family circle it was the end of Daddy's dream of becoming a millionaire. By 1932 Carl Dann, one of his partners, was offering lots for free to anyone who had seed and fertilizer to grow vegetables. Greens fees on the eighteen-hole golf course were $1.50.[2]

Orlandoans fought hard to recover, but many commented that recovery "was as slow as molasses in the winter." Daddy did not quit. He continued to audit his clients' accounts and prepared their tax returns, but few paid him. Rarely did he have enough cash on special occasions to buy hot tamales even though they were sold cheaply by a Cuban vendor in front of the post office, and he and I loved them. Instead we went to Morrisons Cafeteria where roast turkey and dressing with gravy was 23 cents a serving.

Daddy also continued to work for the citrus farmers, who gradually improved their methods of growing oranges and grapefruit, although they used hand laborers for harvesting until the 1970s. He acted as accountant for several cattle entrepreneurs who had begun importing Brahmin cattle from India. These animals crossed with English breeds flourished on Florida's burnt palmetto bushes and seemingly very dry unnourishing grass. As a consequence Florida became one of the largest cattle raising states in the Union and cattlemen became powerful as a group. For scores of years they were able to prevent the passage of a state law requiring grazing fields to be fenced. As a result cattle roamed arrogantly over the highways with more rights than motorists. The editor of one local newspaper suggested that the highways be renamed "Bullevards."

Frank Pounds, a friend of Daddy and Mother was another who did not quit. He built a house on Clifford Drive in Springlake Terrace near the Orlando Country Club and opened a "crate mill" in the 1930s providing jobs for sixty people. Arlie Pounds, his wife, was my Mother's close friend. To give support to her children, she disrupted her home by offering her living room and the screened porch adjacent to it to her son, Roger, and her daughter-in-law, Ruth, who were married right after graduation from high school. It was there that they taught ballroom dancing. Until the 1950s, it was a dance studio and a ballroom for Orlando's young socialites, called Pounds Studio.

Ruth says her classes started because Jane Maguire (a class or two below me and later the wife of Morris Abrams, a prominent New York attorney and president of Brandeis University) asked her to teach her to dance because she had an invitation she could not accept unless she knew how to dance. Jane brought two of her friends and Ruth quickly organized a class around the three of them.

Ruth had not, as had so many of us, taken lessons from Buddy Ebsen's father, Professor C. L. Ebsen, who ran the first dance school in Central Florida. She was just the "best dancer" and voted so in our high school yearbook.

For thirty-eight years after graduation from high school, teaching ballroom dancing was Ruth Pounds' principal activity, her love. She shaped the junior and senior high school students into respected members of what the *Orlando Morning Sentinel*, in an article praising her, called "The Country Club Set." She pounded (no pun intended) poise and grace into their dance movements as well as Terpsichorean dexterity, manners, and respect for elders. The Pounds' Dance Studio was, in fact, a Depression Finishing School. It offered a unique program to make "ladies and gentlemen" out of a motley crew of callow youths. Learning to dance the waltz, fox trot, and Samba was simply a bonus. Ruth placed the boys on one side of the room and the girls on the other, and one by one they would find a partner. She often said, "it was during the depression and there was literally no other place for the kids to go. There was many a crush born in that living room."

As I recall, the Victrola played all the danceable tunes of Benny Goodman, Bing Crosby, Johnny Mercer, Duke Ellington, Kay Kyser, and their crowd. Outside the mothers and fathers lined up in the Packards, Buicks, Essexes, and Reos to gather their sons and daughters when the dancing lesson was over.

Thus there began a waiting list for the Pounds's dancing class which would continue for many decades. When my eighty-five-year-old mother was languishing in a nursing home in Orlando, she said she had dozens of phone calls asking her, as an old Pounds' family friend, to call Ruth so that their child could be admitted.

If one is extremely quiet on balmy nights on Clifford Drive with the sweet smell of night blooming jasmine, one can still hear the swish swish of their dancing feet. Shadows on the wall glide and twirl like a traditional waltz, while branches rattle to the click click of the fox trots, the giggles, the thank-you's, the laughter and cries in the night are of another era or perhaps in the heart of the listener. Today's modern studio, moved to a larger location, still carries on many of the traditions started by Ruth Pounds and continued by her daughter. This was only one of the ways Orlando tried gallantly to survive the economic abyss in which it, like other towns, found itself. To many of us, the Pounds's studio was and always will be the very best.

On a national level, President Franklin Roosevelt, once inaugurated, closed all of the country's banks. This was on March 6, 1934. Bank withdrawals and our national loss of confidence finally began to abate. On March 7, the Secretary of Treasury, Henry Morgenthau Jr., allowed those banks to open which could satisfy certain standards. They formed an Emergency Relief Council, for there had been, indeed, a real emergency for five years. Earlier in 1933, ale and beer were legalized if they contained no more that 3.4 percent alcohol. Daddy bought an interest in a beer store on Church Street, probably by donating his accounting skills, but I was terribly ashamed of this and never mentioned it to my friends. How cruel it was of me to feel that way as it paid for many very necessary expenses of my teen years!

As a teenager I heard President Roosevelt give a campaign speech in a tent meeting in De Land, Florida, before the 1932 elections. I remember his remark, "I will either be the **best** president you have had in a very long time or the **last** one." In the Depression year, 1932, 90 percent of our country's wealth was owned by about 1 percent of the people. Roosevelt feared an armed uprising throughout the nation just as the World War I veterans had stormed Washington demanding the promised but unpaid bonus for their service in the Great War. They were shot at by troops commanded by MacArthur.

During those years, to a greater extent than today, children were protected, when possible, from the heartache of family financial misery. Parents always absorbed anxiety no matter how dire and "put up a good front." My parents did so valiantly. They belonged to several country clubs, which I am sure carried overdue accounts with undue patience. I will always remember, however, the fear that Mother felt on entering a retail store to make a purchase, never knowing whether the proprietor would accost her with, "Mrs. Asher, I have a little souvenir for you." The souvenir would be a check which she had issued to pay for her last purchase, but had reached the bank when there were insufficient funds in their joint account. We were actually living from day to day. Only in a small town, where store owners knew that we would "make good" on these debts and gave us time to do so, could this happen.

Daddy continued as the certified public accountant in Orlando, filed bankruptcies, and got paid very little for his work. Many clients, who had no greenbacks, would let him fill up his car at their company gas station or gave him a bag of grapefruit or oranges. More than a few of his clients lost their homes. When Daddy could not pay his taxes, tax liens caused foreclosure on our Dubsdread home, as well as his large interest in Orange Avenue's principal blocks although the properties were not mortgaged.

Daddy's luck had run out. It was a heartbreaking day for my parents when they had to leave Dubsdread. I felt their disappointment and sorrow then, and, with the passing of time, I have happy thoughts of the simple pleasures I enjoyed there. I treasure even more my memories of the care and nurturing devoted to me by Mother and Daddy in those early years of my life.

Notes:

1. *Florida. A Guide to the Southernmost State.* Compiled by and written by the Federal Writer's Project of the Work Projects Administration for the State of Florida. (New York: Oxford University Press, 1946), 71–72.

2. *Ibid.*, 222.

CHAPTER SIX

_____

School Days

Learning is but an adjunct to ourself.
— Love's Labour Lost, *IV, 3*
William Shakespeare, 1564–1616

Cathedral School: Grades One to Nine

In the fall of 1924, when I was six years old, my parents enrolled me in the first grade at the Cathedral School for Girls in a beautiful section of East Central Avenue on the edge of Lake Eola in Orlando. Although Florida had built many public schools by the 1900s, Mother chose for me a small, private, boarding-day school subsidized by the Episcopal Diocese of Central Florida. Mother's decision may have resulted from her feeling at that time that public school education or "free education was synonymous with pauper education."[1]

How I loved the Cathedral School! In 1897 the Episcopal Missionary Jurisdiction of South Florida had bought the home and grounds from W.R. O'Neal where the first Bishop of the Diocese and Mrs. William Crane Gray made their home while the school was constructed. Their home became the first dormitory for girls. Deaconess Harriett Parkhill was the first principal.[2]

In the mornings at 8 a.m. Daddy dropped me at the school just as the whole student body was lining up for inspection. The headmistress would pass along the line and stop at each girl to look inside her undergarments to see if she was wearing sufficient clothing to cover her scrawny undeveloped bosom. **Honest!** With inspection at last over, we would form up two by two and march for about a mile around Lake Eola, arms swinging

Phil (bottom right), at Cathedral School for Girls, Orlando, Florida, 1929.

rhythmically. This was my opportunity, as a day student, to have companionship with the girls who were boarding. It rarely rained on us, but if it did, we would walk more vigorously, but walk we did.

Our school day opened with Episcopal rituals, beginning with reciting verses of a morning prayer and singing of hymns, except on Friday, when we participated in the more formal Episcopal service in the school's chapel. The entire student body answered the ceremonious roll call by the Latin response "Ad Sum" instead of "here" or "present." Following these formalities, we separated into classrooms.

After a few weeks in the first grade, my teacher, who came from New York, reported to Mother: "This child has had such good training both in kindergarten and at home, that I cannot in all conscience keep her in the first grade. She will be bored to extinction and probably disruptive to the others." In effect, I really began school in the second grade. My studies were easy—a breeze—even in arithmetic, for Mother tutored me in addition and subtraction exercises at home.

As the following fall arrived and it was time to enter the third grade, my teacher repeated the same scenario. This time she instructed Mother to drill me on multiplication tables. When I completed these mathematical exercises, I moved up again, skipping the third grade, to the fourth. Since grades three and four occupied the same room, I did not have to move and continued to share a desk with Anna Tilden, a beautiful blonde with ringlets all over her head and now my classmate. Academically it was great and I was never bored. For all intents and purposes, I was privately tutored for the first six and the last seven weeks of school until the sixth grade, when I was only eight years old, as the children from the north arrived late and left early.

At Cathedral academic subjects were emphasized. Our classes were small—ten or twelve girls in a room—so we received a quantity of individual attention. In addition to reading, writing, and arithmetic, we were drilled in good manners, especially to stand up whenever anyone older than we walked into the room. We popped up automatically even if the janitor, making his regular rounds of classrooms, appeared, and we stood in ramrod posture until we were told to be "at ease." This custom remains with me today for Cathedral teachers, as well as our parents, made a special point of this kind of courtesy to our elders. I still shudder inwardly when I see young people today who do not "move a muscle" when an older person enters their room.

In addition to scheduled classes required for each grade, we had extra curricula opportunities about once a month. Our most frequent guest was Dr. Hamilton Holt, then president of Rollins College in nearby Winter Park. We looked forward to his coming for he was a disciple of Woodrow Wilson, had served as Wilson's clerk during his presidency of Princeton College and even when he was president of the United States and a U.S. delegate at the peace conference that created the League of Nations at the Treaty of Versailles on June 28, 1919. Dr. Holt told us many times that although Germany, France, Great Britain, Italy, and Japan ratified the treaty, the United States never did sign it despite the fact that President Wilson had been one of the first to promote the plan. He spoke to us many times on the failure of the United States to live up to its responsibility as a world power. History, of course, has borne out his predictions. This kind of speech opened our young eyes to the outside world of international affairs. I sat in rapt attention and remember now what Dr. Holt said even though I had not reached my teens.

We also looked forward once a year to a special occasion when Dr.

Holt lured many celebrities who had appeared at Rollins on a program called "The Animated Magazine," to our school. Sooner or later we saw most of the big names in government and in church, as well as many authors. I will never forget the days, when dignitaries like Secretary of State Cordell Hull, Rabbi Stephen S. Wise, Willa Cather, and Jane Addams talked to us. The most memorable for me, now that I am thinking of my schooldays, were the two ladies, well-known pioneers in their fields of endeavor. Jane Addams was co-winner of the Nobel Prize for Peace for her work in founding Hull House, a settlement quarters for poor children in the worst of Chicago slums. Willa Cather, author of many books, was awarded the Pulitzer Prize for *Death Comes for the Archbishop*, a novel based on the teachings of the Catholic Church in colonial New Mexico. Dr. Holt called these occasions "inspiring." Our principal called them "enriching."[3]

We also had many just plain relaxing times. For a very special birthday treat, our teachers took us in a swan boat for a ride on Lake Eola. We would glide along over the waters while the real white swans sailed majestically past our boat. The swans were said to be descendants from a pair imported in 1910 from a private preserve of Edward VII.[4] I had learned not to pester them because they hissed and flapped their powerful wings if disturbed, and we all stayed quite clear of the alligators.

I am heartbroken that the school that offered me so much could not have been maintained and kept as a quality small private school in Orlando. It filled me for seven years with a daily shot of excitement for learning as well as an exposure to a camaraderie with some wonderful girls, many from the North, whom I never would otherwise have known. Our teachers bore enormous teaching loads and gave us inspirational lessons in many inventive ways. They were the model teachers of the time, and we had the benefit of their imaginative pedagogy. Their personalities remain with me always. The Cathedral, Orlando's best, was to be my school home until the tenth grade.

Orlando Senior High School: Grades Ten to Twelve

High school was a different story. The Boom had burst and the Great Depression had made its effect felt everywhere. Although Florida had adopted public school education soon after the Civil War and schools had spread throughout the state, the collapse of the economy in 1929 had resulted in a shortage of books, decreased wages for qualified teachers, and less funds available for improving educational practices and programs. In addition, facilities for a city that had grown to 23,000 residents were crowded.

When it dawned on me that we were just stone broke, I became aware of Mother's anxiety. Daddy, who was a compulsive gambler, had lost all of his assets, including co-ownership of property on Orange Avenue. It was then that I remembered that I had four gold dollars he had given me in my piggy bank. I got them out and gave them back to him. The most terrifying part to me, however, was that I had left all my friends at Cathedral, and I felt lonely and out of place as I crept insecurely through the long, bare walls of Orlando Senior High School. Middies and skirts had been my school uniform since the first grade. Suddenly, as I was forced to enter the tenth grade with no clothes to wear, Mother and I panicked. We went to stores such as J.C. Penney and Sears Roebuck and bought four dresses and some oxford shoes. That would be my total wardrobe for the whole school year.

I was only twelve and a half years old, and my new classmates were sixteen. I was immature, to say the least. Mother, who seemed to sense my worries, tried to smooth the way for me by saying, "There will be all kinds of children in your classes. You must go slowly to make new friends. Those who approach you in the beginning may not be the ones you want to have in the long run." She was so right. I made many false starts. "Just try to keep out of permanent alliances," Mother advised. "Hold your head high; be kind to everyone for pretty is as pretty does."

As I entered the tenth grade, I did not know how or why but I received a bid to join the Pi Kappa Alpha, the high school sorority. This seemed to be my chance to "fit in," and my spirits began to rise. I was thrilled to belong to a group of "cute" girls. During a six-week initiation period the initiates were prohibited from wearing any make-up. I had never worn make-up in my life so this was no punishment for me, but it was for my classmates.

Since the no-make-up edict was not a problem for me, the girls, who were seventeen or eighteen but seemed more like thirty, decided they had to do something else to "initiate" me—and that was to wear lots of make-up. I felt like a teenage call girl or a street walker made up like a circus clown. If I wiped the color off, which I often did, they smeared on more

Newspaper clippings from Phil's high school years.

lipstick, rouge, and powder. For the whole six weeks I endured this punishment. I knew that being tapped for Pi Kappa Alpha meant that I was "accepted" or "belonged," so I tried to I overcome the humiliation.

Pi Kappa Alpha was so important and exciting for me that I would never have had the courage my little sister did many years later when she was a sophomore. Cleona lacked many of the insecurities I had had at her age, and she already belonged to the popular crowd, since she had been at the public junior high school with them.

Cleona and her great friend, Pill McLeod, had been tapped by the sorority at the same time and discovered that one of their acquaintances who was a very nice, intelligent girl was not going to be offered a bid. The apparent reason for this was that the girl's mother was considered a loose woman, whirling around New York and not at home taking care of her little girl. The girl, however, was being lovingly reared by her perfectly acceptable grandmother who was not, alas, in the elite crowd of Orlando. Her exclusion from the sorority enraged Cleona and Pill. No doubt these snobbish teenagers had been told by their parents that the girl was "not our kind."

The episode became a cause celebre for weeks, and Cleona and Pill

Photos from Phil's Orlando High School Yearbook, 1934. She and classmate Buster Keene were listed as Best Dancers (left), while she and Bob O'Rourke were identified as Most Popular.

sat on their invitations for a few days agonizing over whether to accept—join the sorority of girls who could behave so disgracefully or be rather "out of it" for the next three years. Mother told me that on the grounds of moral indignation Cleona decided to refuse, although Pill accepted.

When I was nursing Cleona, dying of pancreatic cancer, she told me something that I had not learned until then. As a result of her refusal, the entire membership of the high school fraternity, Omega Xi, came to call on her and tell her how proud they were of her action. This confidence will remain one of my bittersweet memories of my sister's admirable life.

Simultaneous with my initiation, the Pi Kappa Alpha had its annual "Girl Break" dance at the Orlando country club. Even though I was scared to death of what the evening would be like, I mustered up my courage and invited Burwell Howard, a tall, handsome boy in the eleventh grade, one class above me. I had the most enormous crush on him. Mother, always concerned about finances, immediately reacted, "Phil, you have absolutely nothing appropriate to wear, and I have no money to buy you anything."

Searching my memory for what I could do, I suddenly remembered that I had worn a yellow organdy dress at the May Day Festival at Cathedral. As a member of the Floradora Sextet, I had sung several selections from an old Broadway musical comedy, including "Tell Me Pretty Maiden, Are There Any More at Home Like you?" My dress—lovely for the occasion then—was far from "right" for a tea dance. It was the wrong length, wrong style, wrong material, wrong everything! While my hopes of attending the dance were dimming, Mother proceeded to alter the dress as best she could and when she finished she decided it would do. I guess Burwell was not ashamed of me, and we had a marvelous time. Perhaps this was the turning point in my feeling about public high school.

The good news was that the school work was easy. Cathedral School had prepared me so well that there was always time for extracurricular activity. I could achieve an "A" without opening a book. It was not my style to cease studying so I did more work than required to keep up with my class. Before long I had read all the history books in the school library.

My studious habit was my downfall, however. This fact became very clear to me when I learned of the "Slambook," passed from one student to another for comments—anonymous. Not only was I supersensitive about my dress, but I feared seeing what appeared around my name centered on the page in this horrible book. Imagine my horror at remarks such as "stuck-up," "too brainy," or "too young to be flying so high," whatever that meant. Every time this book fell into my hands, I was grief stricken and dissolved into tears in Mother's arms the minute I walked into our front door.

Another problem of being a so-called egghead, was that one of my favorite after-school activities was the Drama Club. I "tried out" for parts in many plays and was awarded the lead role in most of them. Obviously dramatic skill did not endear me to the frustrated ingenues in the class. They never let an opportunity pass to write some typical slur about me in the Slambook.

Election to membership in the National Honor Society did not enhance my popularity either. To make matters worse, very few girls in my sorority were "tapped" for this honor. My self esteem bottomed out. There were no praises for my scholarship. No one was my friend.

My junior year was not quite so emotionally upsetting. After all by then I was almost fourteen years old. By then, I was driving a car—a great pleasure. Because my Daddy had no time and Mother had no patience, she had one of my classmates give me driving lessons. No one had a driver's license in those days, so, once I had learned, I could drive whenever and wherever I wanted to go.

My senior year turned out to be a delight. I had shed my insecurities and started enjoying myself. I somehow adjusted to the fact that my parents could no longer afford to send me to a private school. I also took in my stride the fact that we kept moving from one small house to another whenever we could find one a little cheaper.

Instead of going home from school every afternoon we went to Mildred Long's house, where we danced from three to five. Mildred's mother had cleared her living room of all furniture, except a tall wind-up Victrola, to provide us with a dance floor. It was the age of Cab Callaway, Benny Goodman and their big bands. We did the "stomp" and the "shag"—too early for the "jitterbug." We consumed gallons of lemonade and dozens of freshly baked cookies. When the boys finished football, basketball, or baseball practice, they wandered in for an hour or two of dancing, tired as they might have been from their sports practice, we were all consummate dancers.

Occasionally I received invitations to the football games, spring house party weekends, or other functions at the University of Florida, where boys in classes ahead of me had enrolled. I was fifteen at the time, and Mother had reservations about these invitations, but she knew that I was "square," and did not drink anything alcoholic or smoke.

A favorite thing to do on Sunday nights was to attend AME (African-Methodist-Episcopal) services where my friends and I believed we were welcome. Black friends would advise us when a particularly good preacher or choir was to be in the church. We would be in a group of about ten boys and girls. We tiptoed up the steps to the balcony so as not to draw attention. It was very difficult not to join in the singing, the rhythm and beat were so contagious. We really just reveled in the melodious gospel music and spiritual singing.

All in all, by that time I was totally adjusted to life in a large public high school. By 1934, when I graduated, almost all aspects of school life were extremely pleasurable, or in words of that year "the cat's pajamas!"

Notes:

1. *Florida: A Guide to the Southernmost State.* Compiled and written by the Federal Writers' Project of the Work Projects Administration for the State of Florida. (New York: Oxford University Press, 1946), 99.

2. Eve Bacon. *Orlando: A Centennial History* (Chuluota, Florida: The Mickler House, Publishers, 1975), 189, 196, 207, 217-18, 235.

3. *Florida: A Guide to the Southernmost State*, 363.

4. Ibid., 226.

CHAPTER SEVEN

College and Prom Trotting

On with the dance! let joy be unconfined
No sleep till morn, when Youth and Pleasure meet
To chase the glowing hours with flying feet.
— Childe Harold's Pilgrimage
Lord Byron, 1788–1824

In the fall of 1934 college doors were swinging open to me. I had been accepted by Florida State College for Women (FSCW) in Tallahassee, where I would spend the next four years to be cherished forever in my memory. Even though tuition was free, there was a dire need of money for college fees, books, and transportation, a major item in Daddy's mind, for Tallahassee was at least three hundred miles from Orlando.

Another major item that concerned me was my wardrobe. I had worked all summer at the Yowell-Drew Department Store (no longer in business) on Orange Avenue to plan and produce a fashion show for the school and college crowd. I earned enough money for several outfits, at wholesale prices, to begin my college life. To keep up with the fashion, I had knit three pastel suits just right for Florida winters. Instead of the necessary computer or small refrigerator of today's freshmen, I entered Jennie Murphree Hall with only my clothes and a knitting bag, complete with needles and yarn. I wore with pride a yellow knit suit, sparkling with a tiny metallic thread, when I was invited to a gala weekend at the men's university in Gainesville. In a way I owe a considerable part of my wardrobe and hence my social success during my college days to Grandmother Annie Powell who taught me the basic knitting stitches when I was a child.

I was one of about twenty-seven hundred students on the Tallahassee campus, where, in 1857, the Florida State College was originally established as a coeducational institution. In 1905 the State legislature removed the male students to Gainesville—with the words "the men's seminary will be separated from the women's seminary by the Suwanee River." They designated the eighty-acre hilltop tract in Tallahassee for women only.[1] In a new role as Florida State College for Women it gained membership in the Southern Association of Colleges and Secondary Schools and was the first in the South to be placed on the approved list of the Association of American Universities. By the year I entered FSCW it already had the reputation of having an important influence upon the professional and cultural life of women in Florida.

College Curriculum

Since my accounting major required many core courses, I had few electives. While I knew from the first week at "Tally" that social life was going to be frivolous and fun, the economic facts of life were too oppressive to be escaped. I **had** to make good marks in my accounting classes, so that I would not disgrace Daddy when I worked for his office in the summers. As a consequence I was enveloped in ledgers and journals on the fourth floor of the Commerce Building, (long since replaced with an outstanding business school). Betty Ann McKenzie, a pretty blonde Pi Phi "Village Vamp Club" member, and I trudged daily up four flights of rather steep stairs and settled in front of the adding machines assigned to us. **We had to balance our books.**

I remained huffing and puffing, always out of breath from the climb because of my chronic asthma, but ready to challenge the rows of figures in front of me. I was well aware that Mother and Daddy would be extremely cool if anything but an A appeared on my quarterly college reports. The tax rules I had to master were contained in the IRS (Internal Revenue Service) Code, later to emerge as about thirty volumes of the Code of Federal Regulations.

My other required courses were economics, money and banking, and political science. They were fascinating but required close attention to specifics. For me that meant long, unwavering time in study and accounting labs during the school week.

Nevertheless, there was still time to daydream while I was sitting in front of my adding machine on that fourth floor. While I needed these

Phil, as seen in the Florida State College Yearbook, 1938.

accounting classes, my dream was of a future when I would be dressed in a slick black dress with a white collar, arguing an important legal case with a worthy set of facts before a jury. I had long wanted to be a lawyer, and in my day dreams, I looked and acted like Kay Francis, so lady-like and serious, just as she appeared on the screen in her many movies of the 1930s. I admired her so much that I had my hair styled exactly like hers. Daddy had urged me "to be a lawyer because they earned twice as much as CPAs do."

My college days were not all grind. I was tapped for the Cotillion Club, a group of attractive girls who liked to dance. On the weekends I did have freedom to enjoy a holiday atmosphere. In fact the festivities began even before entrance day with rush parties for two popular sororities, Delta Delta Delta and Pi Beta Phi. My high school idol, Elinor Estes (now Mrs. William Miller) urged me to pledge Pi Beta Phi. I'm ashamed when I think of it now, but back then most sororities and fraternities were actually antisemitic. I was scared to death I would not get in. When the small white envelope containing my acceptance was in my dorm mailbox, my world was just about perfect. Thinking often of the hours I spent during the next three years considering other pledges, their characters, their hair, their clothes, their manner of speaking, whether they were too sugary or too tart, too shy or too bossy—I wondered how I ever made the sorority of my choice. Academic standing was never a requirement nor even very persuasive to the admission committees.

My sorority sisters and I shared many secrets, had many serious deliberations—we called them "bull sessions"—and exchanged many helpful suggestions, but I knew in my heart of hearts that I was not enormously popular with many members of my sorority. In later life my friends told me that they did not confide in me their innermost secrets because they were intimidated by my approach to learning. Yet Pi Phi membership added much joy to my four years at Tallahassee. I realize now that the ill feelings of my sorority sisters rolled right over my head and got lost in my day-to-day activities.

My bosom friend, Ermine Lawrence, was my roommate at the Pi Phi house. I was thrilled when as president she asked me and Arline Lockhart to share the presidential suite with her. Ermine looked like Heidi, a rather short, very blonde girl with two large golden braids framing her face. We made quite a threesome, it seems, with my dark brown hair, green/blue eyes, and my penchant for studies. Arline was round, chestnut-haired, with a disarming smile and witty comments on everything. She was editor-in-chief of *Distaff*, the literary magazine.

In the fall of 1937, Dr. Mary Alice Eaton, professor of economic geography at FSCW, invited Ermine, Arline, and me to join a small "salon" at her flat on Saturday afternoons. She proposed that we could listen to the broadcast of the Metropolitan Opera, have hot chocolate, and discuss the libretto. After a few sessions, she suggested that we read some of the "great books," assembled by Mortimer Adler and Robert Hutchins for a course at the University of Chicago and St. John's College in Annapolis. We three thought Professor Eaton had a good idea, and we started with Plato's *Republic*. We continued with Karl Marx, Lytton Strachey, then Friedrich Engels. This series of socialist propagandists led Professor Eaton to discussions of the bourgeoisie versus the proletariat and the communist cause.

At that time, although only seventeen or eighteen we were searching for an answer to our economic ills. In the United States we were still in the doldrums of the Great Depression. Distribution of oranges, Florida's principal source of income, had so broken down that farmers, some of whom were Daddy's clients, were dumping their fruit in ditches while children nationwide, suffering from malnutrition or lack of Vitamin C in their diet, could have benefitted from the oranges that were going to waste.

Neither Arline nor I fell for Professor Eaton's hypnotic speeches praising Communism but Ermine did. Thereupon Miss Eaton enlisted Ermine to adopt an assumed name, open a post-office box, and carry her mail received from the Communist Party headquarters. All went well for Ermine until she realized that the scholarship committee of the Daughters of the American Revolution (DAR) would cancel her scholarship if her communist connection became known. Not only that, but Ermine confided that she was secretly married to her childhood sweetheart, and ladies of the DAR scholarship committee extended grants to single girls only. These were both serious offenses, if discovered, which would lead to Ermine's dismissal from college. Ermine's clandestine marriage was understandable. She was sleeping with a young man named K. Bradley and nice girls had to be married to do that!

My so-called illegal activity was less serious but to me it was worrisome. A few of us had been invited by the rector of the local Episcopal Church and the chaplain of Florida Agricultural and Mechanical College (A&M) (Negroes only in the student body) to meet on a weekly basis with the A&M sorority girls (we did not use "black" in those days). We met in the basement of the church and "let it all hang out" as young women of college age would say today. This was the only integrated social activity I ever heard of in Tallahassee, and I learned a lot in our exchange of ideas. The FSCW faculty would not have approved of our association with the A&M girls. In fact, my suspicions were confirmed in 1939 when the DAR refused to allow Marian Anderson to sing in Constitution Hall in Washington, D. C.—an action that was not condemned by the FSCW administration. It was not long before we three became concerned that my activity would not only embarrass the FSCW administrative officers, but would especially embarrass Mother who was a DAR member. As a consequence, these were anxious days for both Arline and me. Every time the doorbell rang at the main entrance of the Pi Phi House which we could see from our suite, we both panicked. I was wrong about Mother. As soon as she heard about the DAR's position on Miss Anderson's recital, she resigned. She never, however, resigned from the United Daughters of the Confederacy.

There were no restrictions on girls from FSCW going to Gainesville to visit the men's campus of the University of Florida, a distance of some ninety miles. The men were more frequently able to visit us than we were to visit them, simply because they were allowed to have cars and we were not. We liked this arrangement just fine but girls who were not the prettiest or the most charming had few occasions for male companionship in classes or gala festivities. For me, who knew many men students at Gainesville, it was an impressive lot. Many were and have remained my good friends. The University of Florida, the men's university, was renowned for its law school and its athletic programs—football, basketball, baseball, and track. Now FSCW has become FSU and has all of the above, but it also has a circus, an appropriate activity for an educational institution in a state boasting the winter home of Ringling Brothers, Barnum, and Bailey Circus. Fortunately for me Aunt Lucy (Mother's "baby" sister) and her husband, Uncle Harry Kellim lived in Sarasota, on Bay Shore Boulevard, near the John and Mabel Ringling's estate. Uncle Harry, who was president of a Sarasota bank, was an adviser to the Ringling family, and Aunt Lucy, therefore, had been a friend of Mrs. Ringling.

The welcome mat was always out for me at the Kellim's. Aunt Lucy had no children and had in a way adopted me as her own. She had a special feeling toward me as I had been a flower girl at her wedding.

My introduction to European art began in Sarasota, where the John and Mabel Ringling Museum of Art opened to the public in 1930. The Ringlings had filled their Mediterranean villa, called Ca'd'Zan, and the exhibition hall adjoining it with stone carvings, statuary, French furniture decorated with ormolu, and exquisite Meissen and Delft porcelains. In 1936 Mr. Ringling bequeathed this collection of more than seven hundred works, including fine examples of paintings from Italian, French, Dutch, Spanish, and English schools, as well as five renowned tapestries, and four important works of Peter Paul Rubens to the state of Florida. The museum is now associated with the Florida State University system.

I especially cherished my visits to Sarasota's art world with Aunt Lucy, since she had gained considerable knowledge about the exhibitions from Mrs. Ringling. The visits also had an added attraction for me—the companionship of young men from Sarasota, college students from Gainesville and Princeton.

Social Life and College Proms

Junior year was a socially busy year. In the fall of 1936, the University of Miami at Coral Gables launched its second Orange Bowl football game inviting Catholic University to play the University of Mississippi. Babs Beckwith, Jack Beckwith's sister, a New York Powers model, was the queen. Jack invited me to be his house guest, as he was studying at the Gainesville campus and, as a member of the varsity teams, was always in "training" for football or basketball. (Therefore he couldn't drink assuring me he was a safe driver.) He was my date for the game and we double-dated with Babs and George Smathers, who later became the Democratic senator from Florida (1951-1969). After an exciting game that ended with Catholic winning by one point over Mississippi, we danced all weekend to popular, background music, "You'd be so Nice to Come Home to," and "Moon over Miami." I had no sooner returned to the Tallahassee campus when an invitation came to me for the Fall Frolic Dances at the University of Alabama from LeRoy Dickson of Orlando. That weekend provided an opportunity to meet the members of the Alabama football team, the Crimson Tide, that had played at the Rose Bowl in 1935. It was also a chance to dance all night to the music of one of the great big bands of the time—possibly Sammy Kaye's. On these gala evenings the orchestra always played a dance set, consisting of twelve or more songs, after which the leader would stop and whisper loudly into his microphone, "All right folks, I'll be back soon. Meanwhile, walk around the floor and make arrangements." That, of course, gave us all time to do just that, arrange for "late dates" anywhere from 2 a.m. to 4:30 a.m. We got very little sleep on college party weekends, but one did not go to college parties to sleep. On the return Tuscaloosa-Tallahassee trip our Greyhound bus, unfortunately, skidded and swerved across a small mountain road during a snowstorm. It took the driver some while to get it turned in the right direction. The fact that I had never seen snow in some respects outweighed the inconvenience of our delay and actually added to the excitement of that unforgettable weekend but made me a day late for my FSCW classes.

The highlight of my prom-trotting years was the Fancy Dress Ball at Washington and Lee University in Lexington, Virginia. George Gilliland, a friend from Daytona Beach, had invited me as his guest many weeks before the event. I was unprepared, however, when I received a telegram from George simply saying, "Wire me your measurements."

"What nerve," I thought. I was indignant and considered sending off a sassy retort, when I realized that he needed my measurements to order my costume! Since the theme that year was the "Congress of Vienna," the dress had to be a particular 1815 style and color. It was a lavish affair even though it surely could not equal the entertainment at the actual event when Prince Metternich represented Austria in 1815 at the signing of the peace settlements to end the European wars of liberation. For a young girl from Orlando, it was a stupendous occasion, and I remember the glitter of it all to this day.

George, who was president of his class, invited me again to the Washington and Lee finals so that I could lead the ball with him. We danced in intricate patterns or steps, known as a cotillion, or quadrille, today. When this occasion was over, George persuaded one of his cadet friends at Lexington's Virginia Military Institute, the alma mater of General George C. Marshall, to include me in the year's final celebrations at VMI. After almost two weeks of picnics, river boat rides, dances, and all manner of inventive entertainment, I was ready to leave for Florida, but not without an unexpected last-minute jolt to my composure.

When George called for me the next morning, he said, "You had better pay Mrs. Smith, your landlady." I immediately panicked for I had not known that I was responsible for fourteen days of room rent, orange juice, and coffee. This was the first time that any of my dates had not paid for my weekend living expenses at their college affairs. I had to call Daddy, collect, at his office and tell him of my plight. I would gladly have committed hari-kari instead. Daddy, bless his heart, whose bank balances were always alarmingly low in those days, wired the money to me and saved my reputation.

My problems were not over, however. To save money—always in short supply for a college student—George had arranged for us to ride to Richmond with a friend, Lewis Powell, who had a tiny roadster. On the way out of town we toured the Washington and Lee campus to see the tomb of Robert E. Lee and George Washington, as well as the beautiful chapel and administration buildings. But, in my flustered state after wrestling with the rent problem, I forgot to visit the ladies room before we started our journey.

In Lewis Powell's "Tin Lizzy" I was seated between two tall men, albeit slender. It was a tight squeeze. In the four-hour drive to Richmond, I became extremely uncomfortable and needed to use a rest room in the worst way, for two cups of coffee and a large glass of orange juice had been a considerable amount of liquid. I really thought I was going to die of an exploded bladder. Throwing my usual Victorian modesty aside, I finally mustered the courage to whisper in George's ear that it was imperative that we stop immediately at a filling station. In 1937 gas stations were few and far between especially on the back roads of Virginia. Although George had discreetly relayed my message to Lewis, he whizzed right passed the next gas station, believing it was too dingy. Little did he know I would have settled for a large tree stump. I wanted to shriek, "Just let me out of this car before I disgrace myself." When I finally conveyed the message that just a bush, a small bush, would do the trick, we reached the train station. It took me several weeks to tell my parents of this agonizing finale to my exciting two weeks in Lexington, Virginia.

My end-of-college celebrations were finished. No sooner was my graduation over in 1938 than I left for Annapolis. A first-class Naval Academy student, Tom Walker, had invited me for June Week at Annapolis to witness the Navy's traditional graduation ceremonies. I saw it all—the Ring Dance when a midshipman walks through a fifteen-foot high ring and puts an engagement ring on his lady's finger; the parade of all four classes, and the graduates tossing their white caps into the air as a signal to their becoming full fledged ensigns.

Academy graduation was followed by the week of the intercollegiate crew regatta at Poughkeepsie. Watching this race was thrilling in the extreme. It was exciting to see eight strong twenty-two to twenty-four-year olds stroking their oars in beautiful rhythmic unison. Their desperation to win, not only for themselves but for their academy, was obvious. Tom and his crew had been in training for the event for four years, but they knew that California or Washington crews were favorites.

The race began in the pouring rain. As the shells in the lead came close to the finish line, the Navy crew sped ahead at the last moment and emerged victorious. What excitement we felt when the favorites of all the sports journalists were the losers.

As we stepped off the observation train to go back to the gym for the dance following the race, I walked with the other dates, "drags," of the Navy crew and several of their mothers who were chaperoning them. Our dates were showering and changing for the dance. Even college graduates had chaperons in those days.

We piled into cars after the tea dance and were taken to one of the date's houses in Port Washington, Long Island. The next morning I had my first English muffins, having lived in the South where homemade biscuits were always served. Our victorious oarsmen took us sailing on sunny, lovely Long Island Sound.

Later that evening and for the next few days we went into New York for sightseeing, returning to Long Island in the evenings. We saw "I Married an Angel" and "I'd Rather be Right," on Broadway and toured the Fifth Avenue department stores. Lord and Taylor was especially memorable, with its garden decor featuring a handsome Italianate fountain bubbling with Dorothy Gray Gardenia perfume. Bonwits, Bests, Altman's and Bergdorf were all decorated in a glorious fashion. For a Florida girl, these were dream stores indeed!

The lovely, carefree day was ending, and with it came the true end of my college life. But before deciding just what to do next, a wonderful opportunity awaited me—a European tour, during the fateful summer of 1938.

Note:

1. *Florida: A Guide to the Southernmost State*. Compiled and Written by the Federal Writers' Project of the Work Projects Administration for the State of Florida. (New York: Oxford University Press, 1946), 102, 281.

CHAPTER EIGHT

Open Road

Strong and content I travel the open road.
— *Walt Whitman, 1819–1892*

During my last semester in college an extraordinary invitation arrived for me. It was from the Open Road, asking me to participate in a
1938 summer tour of eleven European countries, where I would study the
economic, social, and political institutions. This dream trip to Europe
was a graduation present from my parents. In order for them to afford it,
I promised to forego Yale Law School and work my way through the
George Washington University Law School instead. I was passionate to
see Europe while the four years of college "book learning" were fresh in
my mind. The summer of 1938 was a time between Hitler's March
Anschluss of Austria and his September invasion of Czechoslovakia's
Sudeten region. The clouds of World War II were looming darkly over us
all.

My sorority sister from Coral Gables, Florida, Betty Wynn, was going with me. Neither of us could possibly have imagined how much that
trip, at that momentous time in world events, would mean to us.

The trip was advertised to the incoming and outgoing student body
officers of many colleges. The brochure contained an especially tempting
lure—five weeks in the Soviet Union. I remembered what Lincoln Steffens
had written in his famous autobiography after a fact-finding trip to the
Soviet Union in 1919, "I have seen the future and—it works."[1] It didn't,
but we only found that out in the 1960s.

An organization called the Open Road, which we later realized was a
communist front, sponsored our trip. In what I can only believe was a

test, I received at the Pi Phi House, very shortly after enrolling in the group tour, a letter from a college student in Talladega, Alabama. The gist of that letter was that she was happy another "colored" girl was going on the trip to the Soviet Union where there was no discrimination against Negroes. I still cannot figure out who she was or why it was I and not Betty who received that letter. Little did she know what we discovered. The USSR **did** discriminate against Blacks who came there from all over the world.[2] My correspondent was not on the trip and the Open Road people in New York with whom we had our orientation meeting prior to embarking on the *SS Aquitania* insisted that they had never heard of her. Or had they?

The communist underground at that time was very heavily embedded in the student body "left" in universities all over our country. It had reached Florida State College for Women through a Ph.D. from Chapel Hill, Mary Alice Eaton, our professor of economic geography.

Our Traveling Companions

Except for Betty and me, our Open Road group consisted entirely of Ivy League students, recent graduates of Mt. Holyoke, Vassar, Barnard, Dartmouth, Columbia, and Williams. Betty and I, thus, felt very inferior intellectually. A gathering before the sailing didn't make us feel any more at ease about our own ability to "fit in" with our new travel companions. We were determined, however, to make them our friends. That women showed their intellectual prowess was a shock to us for in those days, as southern women, we went to great pains to camouflage that particular ability. If one had a superior intellect, one hid it!

My Diary

Shortly before I embarked on this trip, Martin Anderson, editor and publisher of the *Orlando Morning Sentinel*, a poker playing friend of Daddy's, gave him $300 and a note, "J.B., Give this to Phil and tell her I want 300 plus words a day in a column about her trip. This will buy her a couple of Paris hats." So when Daddy flew to New York to see me off, he brought the check and my portable typewriter.

I also kept a diary which is, 60 years later, still in fairly good condition, with my columns pasted on the pages—newsprint of that era seems remarkably durable. The only weeks on which there was no reporting, just my own handwritten notes, are the first four weeks in the Soviet Union.

This omission deserves explanation. Our sightseeing and interviews of political figures from the far left to the far right could not have been planned better. We toured housing projects, homes for retired, aged, and infirm; city planning projects all over the environs of London; as well as in the three Scandinavian countries and Finland. With all of that on-the-spot learning, we still had the opportunity to enjoy wonderful theater, hear music, see monuments and castles—being young and vigorous, we had eighteen-hour days, at least. to take full advantage of that trip. Yet for a long while Betty and I did not catch on to the fact that the Open Road was a communist-affiliated organization,—not until we reached the Soviet Union. We did know that our conferences, briefings, and many of the professors we met were very leftist, but then that was the tenor of academic life at that time.

On Our Way

As we set sail, we crowded tightly at the railing and looked through the crowds for our families. We located them and waved madly, shedding lots of tears. While the very wealthy made yearly crossings on the large famous liners of the time, the middle class, particularly Southerners, rarely had such a treat. Even though we were going to the seat of Western civilization, we felt that we were leaving our own civilization, our world, our ties, and perhaps we would never see them again.

Transatlantic air travel was really unknown then. One could hardly fly across the continent without changing planes! Tears disappeared and were soon replaced by a certain amount of anguish over our new home for the next seven days. We met our stewards, found our stateroom and our bathroom several doors away. We had lunch to the excruciating music of a talentless American jazz band and spent the rest of the afternoon unpacking and perusing our new surroundings, meeting a few passengers who were, on the whole, very pleasant people. We had a roommate (three to a stateroom) who was most attractive and was going to Greece and Rome to work on her masters thesis in the classics.

The gongs which announced both lunch and dinner would have roused a snail out of its shell, but the food was delicious and welcome. Our hot, salty bath and the rocking motion of the ship made sleep welcome and quickly achieved.

We were seasick for the first twenty-four hours until we realized that a full tummy is the best defense for this most traumatic of all travel complaints. How travelers suffered before the day of Dramamine!

Our group had lectures daily on public housing policies and social experiments in Western Europe—one day a fascinating, well documented lecture by an executive secretary of the Chinese branch of the YMCA who was just back from the front of the Japanese-Chinese War. The rape of Nanking in 1937 and the conquest of Manchuria five years earlier were very fresh news items to us. We had read about them and seen Movietone News short subjects on them since the early 1930s. Lectures were held down in the third class sections of the ship since that was where most of our group stayed. We met a stowaway who had hidden himself under a stairway for twenty-four hours until he became very hungry and gave himself up. The ship's management put him to work and told him to expect to be shipped back on the return trip.

Also traveling on the ship was the movie star/opera singer Grace Moore and a Frenchman who had been fighting for the Loyalist cause in the Spanish Civil War. He had been a longshoreman for a German shipping company when he enlisted. He had seen the enormous tonnage of arms, munitions, and other supplies being shipped from Hitler's Germany to the Franco forces in violation of the embargo on scrap iron and other materials which could be converted into armaments. He reported that the Franco forces were, therefore, very well armed, whereas the Loyalist army, a ragtag bunch, had about one gun for every three men. If a trio of soldiers went over the hills together and one was killed, someone would grab his gun. He reported horrible slaughter of women, children, nuns, and priests by both sides. In 1938 mass hunger and agony prevailed everywhere in Spain. Our visa would not permit us to visit there.

One of the couples at our dining room table of ten was an Indian tea plantation owner and his very handsome wife. She arrived at dinner with a sapphire blue evening gown appliquéd with silver beads and filigree and the mandatory sapphire in her nose. She confessed that her gown was so heavy she could barely wear it. It had taken the dressmaker three months to make, her husband had given it to her, and she couldn't bear to hurt his feelings. Another table companion was from the Friends Service Committee en route to do hospital work at the Spanish front. She also had been very seasick and had retreated to her stateroom in dire straits, feeling that indeed she was at death's door. Her roommate, also seasick, whom she had not met before, said, "I'm Finnish!" Her reply, "So am I," and fell into bed! Fortunately she recovered quickly.

Shipboard life was a wonderful treat full of good talk, movies, horse races, other games, and too much food. The last evening ended with a gala ball, the singing of "Auld Lang Syne," and doing the Big Apple, the current U.S. dance craze, which we all did so badly that my Florida partners would have disowned me. It was all part of the scene.

England

Our first stop was Southampton, England. Betty Wynn and I had discovered that our colleagues on the tour were far more versed in the labyrinths of economic dialectic than we were. We were armed only with our conventional political science and economics courses at FSCW. On reaching London, we therefore charged off to the book shops on Charing Cross Road to buy Marx, Strachey, Engels, Lenin, and their fellow essayists so that we could hold our own during the argumentative evenings en route to the Soviet Union.

In all fairness, Open Road did make an effort to see that we had interviews in all countries with political figures of both the left and right—politicians like Lord Edward Halifax and Clement Attlee as well as Palme Dutt, a communist theoretician in London. We were invited to hear debates in the House of Commons and had time to explore with a fine clerical guide the miracles of Westminster Abbey and the stones of its chapels built in the eleventh century.

While in London we returned several times to the Parliament buildings and the Abbey. We had tea on the terrace with Sir Arnold Wilson and Sir Eric Seering, two conservative party members and our conversation, for the most part, consisted of our questions, but it was constantly drowned out by the sounds of airplane practice flights overhead.

The British were not prepared for the war which many knew was inevitable, but they were gearing up as fast as possible. Every wastebasket had a large sign instructing people to the nearest air raid shelter and a warning to obtain gas masks, which were being given out free. Searchlights blazed all night. This was June 1938, and the fact that it took only fifty-five minutes to fly from Berlin to London was the cause of more and more anxiety in British minds.

There was so much to see and do in England. Sir Harold Nicolson, famous diplomat/author of his day, often guest at "Knole," and husband of Vita Sackville-West, gave us two hours of his time! We had a memorable tour of the British Museum, but only had time to hit the high spots. We viewed the Rosetta Stone, whose hieroglyphic writing reveals a part of ancient Egyptian civilization, and we saw the Elgin Marbles—parts of the frieze of the Parthenon's sculptures—which the seventh earl of Elgin shipped home from the Acropolis in 1802.

When we entered an exhibit dedicated to William Shakespeare, our guide, who was a professor, told us the story of Professor George Kittredge, the famous Shakespearean scholar, who came to the British Museum in search of a specific bit of information. The chief custodian, not knowing the answer, replied, "There is only one person in the world who can answer that question, and that's a Professor Kittredge of Harvard University in Boston." The professor clicked his heels and departed. When Kittredge laughingly narrated this incident to a fellow faculty member, the man, in turn, asked him why he did not have a Ph.D. Kittredge—not a modest man—replied simply, "But old fellow, who would examine me?"

Scandinavia

Our next stop was Scandinavia. We were tossed unmercifully during our overnight journey on a small steamer from Harwich across the English Channel to Esbjerg on the southwestern Danish Coast, but we were young, tough, and by then equipped with stomachs of iron. The food there was much better than it had been in England. We marveled at strawberries the size of tangerines, butter molded in the form of castles, the raw fish, and smoked salmon, all of which proceeded to add pounds to our midsections.

We loved how the soft pink daylight lasted until after ten in the evening and the nights were only about five hours long. In those days, the lovely starlight Danish evenings at the Tivoli were made even more lovely by the extravagant sparkling lights of kerosene lamps! As dusk approached, one saw dozens of street workers mounting tall ladders to the Gothic style domes to light the lamps with their wick-torches. What with delicious Smorgasbords and Carlsberg beer (sampled first on our tour of the brewery of that name) our waistlines were ever in danger. We mainly marveled, as we did in the other Scandinavian countries, as well as Finland, at the lack of unemployment and the excellent public health facilities and public housing. These were orderly societies, the cities spotlessly clean. No one seemed to have the threat of war on his mind.

Now accustomed to our extremely liberal companions, Betty and I were exposed to both political extremes and found such extremes offensive. We saw the great experiments in social medicine, housing, child and elderly care in the Scandinavian countries. These were impressive and convinced us that free societies can take care of their people, give them employment, and still maintain civil rights and free institutions—the Scandinavian countries had democratic governments, and we saw little poverty.

Norway was a revelation. We enjoyed its cosmopolitan atmosphere, warm hospitality, and were introduced to many impressive, high-level people, who gave us a crash course on the nation's politics and economy. We attended an all-day conference on social institutions with Danish and Norwegian graduate students. Very handsome, healthy, pink-cheeked girls and boys, all over six feet tall and looking like Olympic athletes, attended our sessions. One Norwegian, Johan Capelin, attached himself to me. He had just graduated from law school, was from Hamar, somewhat to the North of Oslo, and was going to clerk for a judge of the Norwegian Supreme Court, just as honor students in our law schools did. He spoke no English and I no Norwegian, but we managed to communicate in French, and engaged in some coquetry while dancing and frequenting sidewalk cafes during our three-day stay. When we parted, we promised to write as indeed we did, until our correspondence was interrupted by the German occupation of his country and the resulting pro-Nazi puppet dictatorship under Vidkun Quisling.

At one point, I recall receiving a postcard from Johan with a small hammer and sickle drawn in the corner. Yet in short order, he lost sympathy with the communist cause when Joseph Stalin and Joachim von Ribbentrop signed their non-aggression pact in August 1939. This agreement gave Hitler the freedom to move against Poland, an act which not only signaled the start of World War II, but resulted in the German occupation of Denmark and Norway. After the war, Johan became a highly respected member of the Norwegian Foreign Service and was ambassador to, among other countries, Brazil.

We were welcomed at the town hall by the mayor and shown around by his daughter, who said laughingly that they called her father "King Peter," as he had been mayor since 1918. She feted us with the usual generous Smorgasbord and liquors, and then took us on to Kronberg Castle with its lovely gardens and exquisite rooms, the summer home of the royal family and a fitting one for a much admired and respected family, still enjoying the loyal support of most Norweigans.

Our next stop was Stockholm, where we saw breathtaking views of the harbor with its dozens of little islands and thousands of sailing craft of all sizes. During the day we learned about the Swedish cooperative movement and their Luna factory, (first international cooperative having all Scandinavian countries as well as Scotland as members). Factories in Sweden were spotless and well designed, with the inevitable executive dining room and fabulous food. RyKrisp, Macaroni, and 400 Coop grocery stores had their headquarters in the country. The public housing was, at that time, the best in the world, commodious, well-designed, simply furnished, and affordable at very low rents.

I reviewed these day-to-day events in my mind, as I sat in my room, while the others were shopping or sightseeing, meeting the deadlines of my daily column for *The Orlando Morning Sentinel*. Because my writing would provide me with funds for at least a Paris hat, I couldn't miss a deadline.

Soviet Union

It was, however, not until our train stopped in the Soviet Union, arriving "from the Finland Station" into the terminal of the Leningrad station, that we finally knew who our traveling companions were. Everyone except Bob Spivak, our leader, and Betty and me knelt down on those black gravely tracks and "kissed the soil" as they put it, of the Soviet Union. Wow! Our companions were card-carrying members of the Young Communist League. I have lost track of all of our group and really don't know how many of them had a change of heart when the Stalin-Ribbentrop pact was signed. Many sympathizers of the Russian government and apologists for the USSR communist line did leave the party or its U.S. affiliates at that time.

On our first night in Leningrad, we stayed at the aged but still elegant Astoria Hotel. We were briefed after dinner by the bureau chief of *The New York Times*, Walter Duranty, an apologist for the Soviet Union if there ever was one. He had authored several books on Russia including *I Write As I Please*, and had won a Pulitzer Prize for a series in the *Times* on the Soviet Union in 1932.

During the question and answer period, I asked Mr. Duranty what procedures I would have to follow to send my daily column to *The Or-*

lando Morning Sentinel. I knew all mail in Russia was censored. Duranty asked, "My dear, is it cabled or air mailed?"

"Of course," I replied, "it is air mailed. It is simply a school girl's commentary on a most remarkable trip to eleven countries this summer."

"Then don't worry, just airmail it all, and it will get there safely." How wrong he was! He was so under the cloak of Stalin that his judgment was faulty on even that small problem not to mention so much of what was going on in Russia that summer.

This was the time of the purges, trials without any scintilla of notice of one's accusers, or opportunity for counsel for the defense to make a case. Stalin killed many millions in his agricultural "reforms" as he starved those who would not obey the quotas and rules of the communes. He also killed countless millions during his political purges. Our traveling companions would not face up to those facts at all. It was absolutely fascinating to hear their attitudes at that time. The United States and the Soviet Union were to be allies in World War II—fighting Hitler, Mussolini, and Tojo together—but we did not have to turn a deaf ear to the news of Stalin's murders.

We were in Moscow during an enormous seven hour parade in Red Square featuring dancing peasant girls, tanks, and proud goose-stepping soldiers. We planned to watch the parade from the nearby roof of the American Embassy but we had been warned to cross Red Square by 8 a.m. After that hour, we were told, the square would be closed. Bob Spivak had suggested that we wear a bathing suit underneath our street clothes, as the Russians never started anything on time. We'd be on the roof for about twelve hours, he said, and we could enjoy the August sun.

All spring, prior to the trip, I had earned a little money modeling rubber bathing suits, a short-lived fad, unfortunately, as it made one's figure look divine. I earned little but got to keep the three or four suits I modeled. Mother refused to let me take one with me as she thought Europeans would not think them modest enough. Rather she insisted on my taking an aquamarine faille swimsuit which looked a lot like a decorous tennis dress today.

I mention the swimsuit because of what happened to me later on the day of the parade. After about three hours in the sun, typing away on my portable typewriter, I felt dizzy and knew I was getting too much sun. I spoke to Spivak, and he said, "Just go downstairs and find an empty office. It's a national holiday. I'll send someone down to find you when the parade starts, if it ever does, or when we open our box lunches, whichever comes first."

So I picked up my typewriter and walked down to the floor below, still wearing my modest swimsuit. I rang the bell on one of the first doors I passed, and, to my amazement, a large Russian maid opened it. I could see that she was working in a very beautifully appointed apartment where people were actually living. I apologized profusely and told her I had made a mistake, and continued walking down the hall to find an empty room.

Almost immediately I heard an American-sounding voice, looked back, and saw a tall handsome man who said, "Young lady, can I be of assistance?" I explained that I was part of a student group on the roof waiting to see the parade, and I was seeking a quiet place to type my column until the parade began. He said, "Come right in, there is plenty of room here for you to work." I entered and found, at 11 a.m., a group of men having breakfast on this business holiday, and they asked me to join them. Bliss—American coffee, a week old *New York Times*, English muffins! We chatted and I was having a marvelous time, but I was aware that they were hiding smiles and obviously amused by something. It finally came out. One of them said, "Miss Asher, would you like to know what our maid announced to the breakfast table when she came back from answering your doorbell?"

She said, "there's a naked woman outside who wants to come in!" Imagine their disappointment when I entered in my tennis dress-like bathing suit!

The men, I soon learned, were representatives of General Motors who had been in Russia for months waiting to make a deal for automobile production in the USSR.

Soon after the parade, they invited Betty and me to see a dancing performance in a nearby stadium. When they arrived at our hotel, the hotel receptionist refused to let them call us to announce that they were waiting in the lobby. Experienced in the customs of the city, they came to our floor and bribed the floor lady with American cigarettes so that she would let them come to our room. Those floor ladies were KGB officers who continued for years to cause trouble for travelers in the USSR and have just disappeared in the 1990s.

Walter Duranty stayed with us a great deal of every day. That seemed strange to us as we were, for the most part, only college seniors with no vote and surely no clout at home. He continued to assure me that the Russian censors were not as bad as we portrayed them at home. He told me that when the censors wanted something deleted they usually talked it over with the author so that the whole piece would not sound idiotic when it reached its U.S. editor.

(That sounds strange to me as I see it in my diary of that day because not one line I wrote to *The Orlando Morning Sentinel* ever reached my editor from the USSR.) As I learned later, mail from the American embassy in the USSR was usually sent by pouch. If it was not included in the pouch, it was sent first class, by courier to Greece, then to Paris, and then finally to the United States. Second class mail went through the postal service as a courtesy to the Russians to show that we trusted them (wishful thinking). The Russians always opened mail from the United States, and blacked out some sentences. The English say the Russians opened a sealed embassy document to their embassy in Geneva—as the seal was broken—and it had contained nothing more subversive than a book, *The Forgeries of Stalin*. The Soviet authorities had taken the book apart, copied it, put it back together, and instead of trying to reconstruct the English seal they had put an Austrian government seal on it instead! The British were furious as many pages were missing.

Duranty also kept saying that Russian army authorities did not think Hitler's army was as strong as the Germans would like the West to believe. He cited the German invasion of Austria which had already occurred in March 1938. Apparently many German tanks which had invaded Austria had broken down frequently, and tank soldiers had to jump into the trains to arrive on time in Vienna. Duranty insisted that if the tanks did not hold up on those smooth sophisticated European roads what would they do on rougher terrain? Alas, that did not keep them from overrunning most of Europe and establishing a Nazi regime in Vichy, France, which was as repressive and antisemitic as the Third Reich.

Duranty kept insisting that most of the recent executions that followed Stalin's purge trials were against local party administrators. These, he insisted, were guilty of graft and of disobeying party discipline, essential to their building a socialist state. This all sounds ludicrous to us now that the Soviet Union has collapsed, especially coming from one of *The New York Times's* bureau chiefs.

We often asked questions about Leon Trotsky's exile, citing the constructive role he had played for such a long time in support of the Bolshevik revolt against the Czarist regime. Duranty finally admitted Stalin's lack of confidence in his old ally. Stalin had, according to Duranty's evidence, wired Trotsky, who was ill at the time of Lenin's death in 1924, that he should not try to attend and lied about the date of the funeral. Trotsky assumed that he could not get to the funeral in time although in fact it was held a day later than he had been told which would have given him ample time to attend. In Trotsky's absence Stalin brought in about 5,000 of his followers to win the election as Lenin's successor.

In hindsight, even Duranty admitted that if Trotsky had come to the funeral he probably would have been elected, as he was much the best speaker and the crowd respected and liked. him. (In 1926 Stalin established himself as a virtual dictator, in 1927 he expelled Trotsky from the Central Committee of the Communist Party, and in 1929 from the Soviet Union.)

Duranty was equally wrong in our discussions on Spain. Most liberals in the United States were on the Loyalists side. Franco had not only sided with the Nazis, accepted their planes and tanks to overcome the Loyalists, but had courted Mussolini as well. Il Duce had sent "perhaps a total of 75,000" troops[2] to fight side-by-side with Franco's Spanish troops. These Italian troops were not very effective as the best troops from Italy had been sent on the Libyan campaign. In the summer of 1938, the Loyalists still held Barcelona, a large munitions manufacturing area. All of this may seem irrelevant today, but the Spanish Civil War was on all our minds and the source of much debate in our country. The Abraham Lincoln Brigade, composed of Americans fighting with the Loyalists had many famous people among its members, and its survivors still hold reunions.

During our stay in Moscow we saw many churches, stripped of their ornate gold decoration, and being used for worship only by foreign workers and visitors. The British Foreign Service officers we met said that the NKVD (forerunner of the KGB) watched the churches very closely and, if per chance an old Russian woman visited a sanctuary, she was told never to go in again. Most Russian-national U.S. embassy employees, who felt more secure, hid their crosses behind the refrigerator, moving them out only when they prayed.

People in the USSR in 1938 were dying like flies from malnutrition, filth, and disease caused from all manner of third-world lack of modern hygiene. Several hundred thousand of those deaths seemed to mean little to Stalin, who eliminated millions by death squads and famine.

Housing was so scarce that crowds of people walked all evening in the streets and parks because they had no place to spend the night. Many teenage girls had to sleep in the same room with three or four men. Abortion was legal, thank heavens for their sakes. The Congress of People's Deputies met only once after Stalin became their head of State. Stalin handled all decision-making through the Supreme Soviet, comprised then of his disciples. Most, we were told by the embassy, lived in former merchant and aristocratic family palaces, dressing well (five-ten years behind our styles but the best available).

Anna Louise Strong, the American journalist who wrote favorably about Communism, was in Moscow at the time. In view of the political complexion of our group, our hosts naturally exposed us to her. I found her wonderful, however, as she had the courage to be in both China and Russia during their upheavals, had known how desperate the lives of their peoples had been. She was working for a betterment of their lives, as well as for a little freedom of thought for them. She had just arrived from Siberia and reported that the poverty in the provinces was appalling. There were thousands of forgotten villages all along the Vladivostok-to-Moscow railroad, where the villagers ran up to meet trains stopping to take on water or coal, trying to sell the smallest, most withered cucumber. Yet, she kept repeating, Stalin has given the youth of Russia self-respect and hope that they would never again be a slave to a landlord's whip.

U.S. embassy officials eased our pain those last two days in Moscow taking us around in their cars, giving us Coca-Cola and chocolate bars, getting us into areas where our guides were not taking us, and principally relating their experiences in living there. Their frustrations in trying to do business with the Soviet regime happened so frequently that they could only assume it all was standard operating procedure. We packed and checked out with the ubiquitous NKVD women on the hotel floor who watched us all like hawks.

Trude Mansfield's Story

The story that has made a lasting impression on me was one told me by my friend Trude Mansfield. It took place in Moscow about the same time as I was there. During the later 1930s many foreign couples went to the USSR to work as scientists or engineers which were badly needed. Trude, a Czech citizen, had married a British/Indian engineer in London when they were fellow students at a London university. They had answered the Soviet call for engineers and moved to Moscow from London. The pay was very high, about three times that of her husband's English salary and surely much more than he could have earned had he returned to his native Bombay. After reporting to his Russian job, he left for months at a time on assignments. Meanwhile, as he was away so much, Trude enrolled in medical school at Moscow University. She knew nothing of her husband's whereabouts except from the clothing he packed; i.e., for hot or cold climates. He could only say, "I am going to Factory #4 or #2." One day, when he had not returned after three months (no communication was permitted), she presented herself at the appropriate commissar's office, in the proper line, and asked for information regarding his location. The clerk disappeared for quite a spell and then she came back with the words, "Eliminated as an enemy of the State."

Trude had gone to London to attain a doctoral degree in biology as her Czech parents had discouraged her from a medical education. It was during those studies that she met her engineer husband. Because she had a pre-med education she was readily admitted to medical school on her arrival in Moscow, and speaking a Slavic tongue she had quickly mastered the Russian language.

Trude had been doing some translating for the British embassy and Sir Stafford Cripps, who was the ambassador from May 1940 until January 1942. After the Russians had murdered her husband, the ambassador and his staff helped her find a person to share her apartment for the rest of her pregnancy (she was five months pregnant). As a medical student, she was well aware of the difficulty of finding a bed at a lying-in maternity center. When her pains began, she rushed to the one where she had reserved a bed months before. (She later told me all of this story as we were minding a ticket table at Sotheby's Auction House for a Legal Aid benefit exhibition.)

After only thirty minutes in the delivery room, a matron came in and said, "This patient must go, her husband was killed as an enemy of the state." She was handed her clothing and overcoat (it was winter and snowing at the time) and pushed out on the road. Only after staggering for about an hour from house to house did she find a friendly couple who took her in, delivered her baby, and kept her for a week.

I met the "baby" son, born under these extraordinary circumstances many years later after he had graduated from Harvard Law School. Trude left the Soviet Union with her son on a Moscow-to-Vladivostok train (armed with all the canned baby food the U.S. and British embassies could spare for her 7-day train ride). She raised him in the United States, and her subsequent husband, the distinguished Federal Circuit Judge, Walter Mansfield, adopted him.

Trude, with Walter's blessing, repeated this whole story at a winter house party in Westhampton during the 1970s to our guests the Oscar Reubhausens, the John B. Oakes, and to my husband who received it with horror. Only Trude and I, of that assemblage, had been in Russia during the time of the episode and could readily imagine it happening. Both Trude and Walter Mansfield had been OSS agents working for General "Wild Bill" Donovan during World War II and had been dropped by parachute into Yugoslavia.

To Poland and Czechoslovakia

When our Open Road group left Moscow, we took the overnight train to Warsaw travelling again third class. After breakfast in the dining car, we returned to find an attractive Western-looking man in our compartment. After we introduced ourselves, he announced in a somewhat haughty voice that he didn't like Russia. He appeared urbane, suave, and well dressed. It didn't take us long to realize that he was a Polish policeman spying on us. At the border, the Russians customs police took away many of our travel souvenirs, our photographs of the people we had interviewed in Great Britain and Scandinavia, as well as my beloved portable typewriter. We were infuriated but helpless and we knew we would never see our possessions again.

How thrilling to arrive in Poland, a free state. We stayed at the Warsaw Hotel, a modest lodging but it seemed deluxe to us after Russia. A wonderful hot bath in a clean bathtub with a stopper to hold the bath water (unavailable in Russia) lifted our spirits. But we did not feel entirely liberated since we soon discovered that the suave gentleman in our compartment on the train followed us that day and throughout our Polish stay, demanding to see our passports once we got them back from the reception desk of the hotel.

While we knew that compared to Russians, Poles lived in an atmosphere of freedom of thought and movement, we also could see that the country was in a state of military readiness. Uniforms were everywhere, as Poles feared of a Russian invasion as well as a German one, which sadly occurred a little less than a year after our visit. In spite of the military atmosphere, Warsaw was a city of charm and quaintness. Horse-drawn carriages still performed taxi service, and the city was filled with lovely baroque buildings, old Gothic churches and many cobblestone streets lined with hundreds of little shops selling attractive clothes, and delicatessens with tempting sausages hanging about. We explored the city as well as the countryside where we saw harvested wheat tied in bundles in picturesque farming areas resembling Brueghel landscapes. We could not miss the political and economic turmoil, however, nor the poverty of the farmers and miners—too many people and too little food. In the rich mining towns of Silesia, we saw many weary, ragged workers trudging home from work at sunset.

The same air of freedom greeted us on our arrival in Prague on July 29, 1938. Here we were joined by another student tour group made up, as was ours, largely of Ivy League college students. They had just come from Germany and were raving about the prosperity and spirit of Germans. Our hosts, a married couple, Professor and Mrs. Ambrose, were professors at Prague University. Mrs. Ambrose, in a few welcoming words, explained her feeling toward Germany by stating that "Hitler had done much for his country materially, but spiritually he is preaching a code in direct opposition to all of the ethics and morals that intelligent people hold dear." She went on to predict that his belligerent behavior would eventually create a war which would be suicidal to the German people. This was before Neville Chamberlain's September 1938 appeasement trip, which made it possible for Hitler to break every commitment he had made to the Czechs and the rest of Europe.

As for the Czech people, Professor and Mrs. Ambrose spoke of their will to worship, write, and say what they thought, and to resist the Germans who would take away their rights. They assured us that every male Czech had calmly donned a uniform on May 21 and had resolutely taken his stand against a German invasion.

Lord Walter Runciman, the Ambroses explained, was there trying to negotiate a settlement of the Sudetenland crisis. Hitler, who wanted to annex it to the Reich, insisted that it was German in ethnic composition and that the Sudeten Czechs wanted to be a part of the Third Reich.

Everywhere we went, we could see that the Czechs were so proud of their economic and social institutions, all of which were only ten to twenty years old. Despite the newness of their little nation, they were already famous all over Europe for the great strides they had made in educating handicapped people, managing efficient old age retirement homes, running country schools for underprivileged children, and establishing many other enlightened social institutions.

The highlight of our visit to Prague was our visit to the country's president, Eduard Benes, and the foreign minister, Jan Masaryk. As I look back, I wonder how these two valiant patriots, aware of Hitler's threats and with their country's backs against the wall, could spare time to see our group of American college students. We had photographs taken with them, and that crucial moment in history was not lost on us. Benes looked oddly serene as he explained to us the present plight of his people. He felt that any minute German Luftwaffe planes would be bombing this beautiful city. He said they were living with clenched fists and a "bottle of brandy!" Many concessions had already been made to the Sudeten minority. All minority people only want to live their own lives in peace, he explained, and his government resented the arbitrary tactics of Lord Runciman.

In Prague we found beauty everywhere we went: the terrace of the parliament, where we had tea with three of its members, the baroque churches, Wenceslas Square, whose apostles in the famous town clock paraded on the hour with faces of the virtues and the vices, the stately Charles River Bridge, the ancient Jewish synagogue and cemetery. The old tombstones had no family names, only occupations described simply as "butcher," "baker," or "tailor."

This small country was making a success of free enterprise. Its Skoda works, the Bata shoe factory, the Pilsener brewery, fine furniture and fabulous Bohemian glass factories, all evidence of what can be done with a free, trained, well-educated populace. We reveled at so much—the cafe's Gypsy music, the mesmerizing waltzes, and those pastries!

I had quickly decided that none of the men on our trip were particularly appealing, either in looks or manners. At dinner the first night in Prague, however, I was happy to be seated next to a handsome young counselor in the Czech Foreign Affairs Office. He was soon to go to England to try to plead his country's case. His last name was Stiasny, a very common Czech name.

The rest of my Czech evenings were spent with Ruth, from our group,

Stiasny, and a fellow member of his office. Together we visited all manner of cafes—elegant ones with Louis XV decor, and little dives frequented by millionaires and streetwalkers. Ruth and I were invited to both of the men's homes and met with their families who were gentle, aristocratic people. Their homes were filled with Meissen figurines and priceless art. We had manydiscussions over the next two evenings about how their social customs differed from ours, but concluded that basically we shared the same values.

I had assumed, as a Southern girl, that nice girls didn't drink or violate their virginity before marriage. *Au contraire, les Europeans*! Our Czech escorts assured us that if they were attracted to a young lady they would live together until one or the other decided to part. The women would, indeed, be accepted at the best social milieux, that of their family or the diplomatic set, and when it was over they would shake hands and remain friends. If the girl became pregnant, as we immediately assumed might happen in our country, they said, "oh, but the man has total responsibility. He always pays for the abortion." These were the years when abortion was illegal in the United States. It all sounded pretty heartless to a small town girl from Florida.

At an appropriate age, a man would choose a wife from a correct social class, who was well educated and shared his interests and goals in life. If she had other affairs—discreet ones—during their marriage that was all right, as her husband most assuredly would be having his own. Ruth was as wide-eyed as was I. We could only stammer weakly that in our circles at home, this was not the accepted conduct.

From these gay and marvelous evenings we returned to our hotel about 5:00 a.m., having seen our dates fling the equivalent of $20 bills to the various orchestras to play our favorite dance tunes. We kept saying that they couldn't afford to be so extravagant if they were paid anything like our State Department employees. They simply retorted that Hitler would be there soon and their money would be worthless.

Seeing the sun rise over that exquisite Charles Bridge lined by centuries-old statuary—it was all too beautiful to believe true, so indelible in my memory—that I never wanted to return to Prague during the Cold War. Not until 1995 did I return, and after a great trip down the Elbe, I spent three nights in Prague, a city now quite like Paris in the 1920s, a mecca for foreign writers, composers, and all creative people.

Switzerland

After crossing through Zurich and Germany we arrived at what was to be our final destination in this political-economic-social study of the countries visited. Our Open Road group was invited to a conference sponsored by the International Student Service, including groups of young people from all over the world, at a place high in the Swiss Alps above Montreux called Les Avants. Our beautiful chateau was splendid. Betty Wynn, my Florida tour mate, and I finally were billeted together and had two balconies from which to drink in the beauties of the Swiss scene.

The first plenary session was impressive in that so many nationalities were represented. Bill Fletcher from Yale summed up the American students' points of interest, and Dick Credick rose to add that while our frontiers were de jure closed, our mental frontiers were de facto open and tremendously receptive. Two girls from France, two boys from Oxford, two from America, and one girl from India, and I spoke at this session. Most young people everywhere were concerned about the distribution of goods and services and their own chances, once graduated from university, of getting a job. Sounds like today's graduating classes!

On August 1, our first night on the Les Avants mountainside, we had a delicious picnic supper punctuated with marvelous Swiss Neufchatel and wonderful local cheese. The day was a national holiday, since on August 1, 1291, the Swiss fought to the last man for their freedom. They assured us they would do it again, and have kept their neutrality ever since.

To have been a part of this conference was surely, up to that date, and much after, the most enriching experience of my life. I was grateful to the International Student Service for putting it all together and especially for including our Open Road group. To hike, picnic, debate, eat, and play with students from twenty-nine different countries in that time and place was to make the conference alone worth the trip. At least the Open Road did something right!

We celebrated Swiss Independence Day on that mountain with its graduated necklaces of lights from the villages around it with two English students from Leeds who were witty and brilliant. That they seemed to carry steins of beer with them morning to night did, however, diminish their appeal. I did not want to leave the party but felt obliged to return to my room in the hotel and write my daily column. My work constantly

interfered with my late night pleasure, and dancing with everyone—
Swedes, Indians, Italians, and others. This was the Depression, not just in
America, but everywhere. $300 was $300!

The International Student Service was founded after World War I to
aid needy students in procuring higher education, and at that time dealt
principally with student refugees from countries invaded and occupied,
who could not continue their studies. The service was then concentrating
on Austrian students after the German occupation of their country, and
Chinese students whose universities and cities had been destroyed by the
Japanese. The service fostered lectures, debate tours, and conferences
annually such as the one we were attending. There were sessions on "Students and Religion," "Students and Social Problems," "Students and Politics." We, who came from Florida were suntanned, healthy looking, and
well dressed. In contrast the English students were shoddy, badly dressed,
and had uniformly bad teeth, greasy, dirty hair, and were altogether puny
looking. Their superior education, intelligence, and wit made up for all of
these shortcomings in appearance. We climbed Mont Blanc with the two
skinny students from Leeds. We were huffing and puffing halfway up—
and they were leaping up higher and higher like mountain goats.

On the last night of our conference, the students from the delegations
presented a skit. The Dutch students performed superb at cabaret acts. I
think we placed next. We had collegiate attire, the girls in saddle shoes,
bobby socks, sweaters, and pearls (the girl uniform on campus in the
South at least) and boys in white slacks and sweaters with athletic numer-
als. We danced tap and Charleston and the popular ballroom steps of the
stomping era, and just before the end two of the boys came in like Al
Capone and Dutch Schultz, robbed and shot us, and when we revived, we
sang "Hand Me Down My Walking Cane," "Swing Low Sweet Chariot"
and the like. The groups, in general, directed much satire to the German
delegation of twenty which had failed to arrive.

There were some representatives from Austria and the Sudeten region of Czechoslovakia who said "Heil Hitler" constantly. We were told
by the conference staff that for the past few years the Germans had not
sent bona fide students. Afraid that students would be contaminated by
democracy and Western thought the Germans sent young people from
their foreign office who gave antisemitic speeches and then walked out
when there was no applause.

From Montreux our next stop was Geneva—a dessert! The League of

Nations was still in session when we arrived there, and the Russian Foreign Minister Maxim Litvinov was making a speech about collective security, pleading for the Western nations to come to the rescue of Czechoslovakia in resisting Hitler's annexation of the Sudetenland. As we entered the assembly hall to hear him, we noticed the marvelous murals done by José Maria Sert (who also has some murals at Radio City and the Waldorf Astoria in New York). The murals depict the victors and the vanquished both carrying their dead, indicating that no one ever wins a war. It will always be in my memory how Litvinov, if he had succeeded, might have averted World War II, if the Western industrial democracies and the USSR could have banded together. Stalin finally fired Litvinov and the United States never joined the League, a fact that broke Woodrow Wilson's heart.

France

In the beautiful city of Paris, we did as much sightseeing as possible, and visited many important monuments. We had interviews at *L'Humanite*, a communist newspaper, where we were fed the party line. We met the editor of *L'Oeuvre*, another socialist newspaper, as well as Edouard Daladier, the premier of France, who was united with Chamberlain in not going to the aid of Czechoslovakia.

It was here that Betty and I left the Open Road group. We had learned so much from them—especially humility. They had bragged all during the trip about what they knew, what they had done, but we knew they had bluffed a lot when they didn't know something. Betty and I had kept quite a low profile, keenly aware of our inferior college education.

On Our Way Home: First Stop in Germany

After braving the Open Road trip, Betty and I were to have a week on Lake Lucerne at a Youth hostel before joining an art appreciation group tour of Italy. Such hostels in the United States are very clean, and while primitive in accoutrements, pleasant enough. Not this one. We could not eat the food which, as soon as it was put before us, was so attacked by bees that we simply had to abandon the whole project.

We might have stayed if it had been warm enough to bathe in Lake Lucerne. We could have managed, despite the straw mats with no sheets on which we had to sleep, for we had been roughing it in Russia for so many weeks. But what we couldn't tolerate were the large groups of Hitler Jugend in residence at the hostel. All day long, they strutted around the hotel saying "Heil Hitler" every few minutes! We desperately wanted to move out.

Our opportunity came once we met with our art appreciation group with whom we would tour Italy. Our wonderful new leader was a darling. He was about sixty-five, very fatherly, and a great art lecturer. He did not enjoy the youth hostel at Lake Lucerne any more than we did. He arranged for us to get back a small percentage of what we had deposited for that week. Gone was the Paris hat I had hoped to buy with some of the money earned writing the column.

Since the tour of Italy was a full week away, Betty and I left Lucerne by a boat that took us to Brunnen, then a train to Zurich, and a further train to Munich, where we finally arrived at night.

How dated it all seems. We were wearing our Pi Phi sorority pins, just in case we might run into an American who would recognize them, and, by gosh, it worked. A professor from the University of Michigan was in Germany for a year, and he recognized our pins He befriended us and told us of a safe, inexpensive place to stay, and also told us where to find some good, cheap restaurants. He was an enormous help to us, as we spoke no German. We registered at a hotel near the railroad station and fell into a deep sleep from exhaustion only to be awakened at about 3:00 a.m. by the terrible sound of sirens. We raced to the window, where we saw the most horrifying sight. People were being pushed out of their homes, beaten, and dragged onto trucks and carts. This was our first sight of Nazi terrorism against the Jews, and it was a sight we would never forget. Berlin's *Kristallnacht* was only a few weeks in the future, occurring in early November 1938.

We were terribly shaken but after some discussion, we decided not to leave the country yet. We, of course, had no idea of the enormity and savagery of the Nazi terror that was to come.

We had very little money to see us through the week but had resolved to hear the opera—a Wagner festival was in progress—every night. We went to the American Express office where an aged lady offered to sell us two tickets for the rest of the week, as she was forced to leave Munich earlier than she had planned. Was she a Jew escaping the Nazi vise? We never knew.

The tickets cost $3.00 each and were orchestra seats. We felt that we had splurged. That ticket purchase left only about $1.00 a day on which to eat. We had paid our modest hotel charges in advance which included, thank heavens, breakfast; *"Brot mit Butter, mit Marmelade, mit Kaffee."* We managed to sleep and eat breakfast late, have supper about 4:00 p.m. and a little coffee at opera intermission. We had planned to look up a girl doing her college Junior year in Munich named Linnea Lundberg. Having had no success thus far, lo and behold, we bumped into her at the opera. She took us in hand thereafter and showed us Munich, the twelfth century Bavarian city in the foothills of the Alps.

Her first instruction was to salute back and say "Heil Hitler" each time someone saluted us, so as not to be conspicuous. My notes simply rave about the good looking men, all in uniform, which made up the entire male population. I couldn't know then how deceiving those looks could be. Recently a New York friend, who was born in Germany, told me about her life in Europe in the 1930s. She and her family had left Berlin in 1933 to live in Paris, since, as Jews, they feared for their future. But as she approached her seventeenth birthday, she wanted to celebrate in Berlin, and her family arranged to grant her this wish.

All of the male guests at her elegant dinner-dance were in Nazi uniform and several in SS uniforms; she, a seventeen-year-old Jewish girl being whirled about by Gestapo officers, thought nothing of it at the time! Even very young teenage boys were in Hitler Jugend outfits. We had to keep telling ourselves that these men were being made to do dreadful things. (We had not at that point known about the actual dimension of the concentration camp and gas chamber horrors. Recent scholarship indicates that many German citizens became aware of the atrocities before it meant death to protest.)

These uniformed soldiers also sang all the time, and much later a New York stockbroker told me of his years in the Hitler Jugend. He described how they had sung military songs for each hour of the day— while brushing their teeth, going to meals, making their beds, doing all of their chores, and that it was mesmerizing for them. He said, as a teenage boy, he would have reported his parents and grandparents to their leader had he suspected they might not have been loyal to Hitler.

Those in Munich during our visit, who were not in military uniform were in Bavarian dress—the suede or other leather—Lederhosen with suspenders and knee socks. Our other companion that week was a Swiss/French student who spoke no English so it was good for my French. He was in a panic one night as he heard from his fellow students that all military leaves had been canceled. He had phoned his father in Geneva who told him to stick it out until the end of the summer term.

Linnea Lundberg was, by the time we got to her, quite pro-Nazi, while Georges Lanvin, our Swiss friend, would caution us to remember the strict spy system and to observe the fear written on most German faces. He said that it was difficult to keep in mind what the Nazis were up to when you heard their gorgeous music and reveled in the masterpieces in the Alte Pinakothek and the Residenz Museum.

I had asked the U.S. Information Service, or whatever our government liaison office was called, if I could get an appointment with a head of the Women's Activities in the Nazi Government, as I was writing a column. He arranged an appointment with a Frau Scholtz-Klink. She was forthcoming with her comments and answered a lot of my questions. Toward the end of the interview, I grew more bold and asked about the women and children that we had heard were being shipped out and put to death if they were disabled, handicapped, or retarded. She stood up and said that the interview was at an end; but, as I was leaving she said, "Dear Miss Asher, please go home and tell the Americans that the Germans do not eat babies for breakfast!" That had been a chilling interlude to an otherwise delightful sightseeing morning.

Most cafes had their own small chamber music concerts so we had a little coffee in each one, and did finally get a seat at the large beer hall, where Hitler staged his abortive 1923 *Putsch*. We ate lots of butter on everything, but Linnea and Georges reported that butter in other parts of Germany was rationed. Clearly, Bavaria was the last place where Hitler commanded all private cars. He was eager to cater to its populace who represented the only remaining native opposition.

To Join the Art Tour Group in Italy

It was time to journey back to Lucerne. On the train, we shared a compartment with a pair of Swiss/French college students who had been staying with a Munich family for a year. The family's small son grieved for his father who was in a concentration camp, where he could see him only once a month. This man, a pastor of a protestant church, was later killed. I have thought so often of that train ride and the protestant minister killed in the concentration camp. As we know now, it was not just Jews who were eliminated and tortured.

I often think of the famous statement of Protestant pastor Martin Niemöller: "In Germany the Nazis came for the Communists, and I didn't speak up because I was not a Communist. Then they came for the Jews and I didn't speak up because I was not a Jew. Then they came for the trade unionists and I didn't speak up because I was not a trade unionist. Then they came for the Catholics and I was a Protestant so I didn't speak up. Then they came for me. By that time there was no one to speak up for anyone."[3]

We had a few pleasant days in Lucerne in spite of the terrible conditions at the lake hostel. We had a gorgeous boat ride on Lake Lucerne, enjoyed good food in Swiss coffee shops (all we could afford), and true to custom, our hotel near the Old Cathedral was marvelous. We even got to see the famous Passion Play. It was a sincere and unostentatious production much the same, we understood, as the citizens of Lucerne had produced it four hundred years ago. How lucky we were to have seen Munich and Lucerne, instead of staying in that Hitler Jugend and bee infested hostel!

The rest of that summer was spent learning about and seeing art in Italy with a much nicer group of students and a charming leader. We were the nineteenth group whom he had taught art history and appreciation in the summers. He proudly sported decorations of the Légion d'honneur and other medals from foreign nations. We could only believe that he deserved them all.

Italy was clearly in the grips of a police state mechanism, but nothing so oppressive, it seemed to us at the time, as Hitler's Germany. True, they took some of us to the Prefecture of Police in Rome. They thought we looked subversive—as we giggled while Mussolini was giving one of his long tirades from that famous balcony at the Piazza Venezia. One call to our embassy released us. We learned later of their daily antisemitic actions and the many innocent people who were jailed and never heard from again.

During that fateful summer of 1938 when I was so very young, ignorant, and innocent, I did not dream that I was at the scene of such momentous happenings, seeing history in the making. Europe would never be the same again.

Americans thought, in that year, that we could stay out of war, and that we could just provide the materiel for the Europeans and Russians to defeat Hitler. Within a year, Hitler had broken every commitment to Chamberlain and Edouard Daladier and had overrun most of Europe. Today, as the only superpower surrounded by smaller and less responsible powers possessing nuclear capability, we need to exercise caution. We now must think in long-term visions, using our power to reduce poverty, to provide health care, to conquer illiteracy, and work for population, nuclear, and pollution control. In addition, we need a proper Western power structure, bolstered up by a United Nations with enough resources to execute peace-keeping and peacemaking.

As a twenty-year-old about to move to Washington and work my way through The George Washington University School of Law, I was not as terrified of the future as I should have been. Now, in 2000, after a lifetime of participation in the world of international affairs, I am more frightened than ever before.

Notes:

1. Paul Johnson. *Modern Times: The World from the Twenties to the Eighties*. (New York: Harper & Row, 1983), 88.

2. Hugh Thomas. *The Spanish Civil War*. (New York: Harper & Row, 1986), 978.

3. Lewis D. Eigen and Jonathan P. Siegel. *The Macmillan Dictionary of Political Quotations*. (New York: Macmillan Publishing Company, 1993), 130.

CHAPTER NINE

My Introduction to the Law

The rule of joy and the law of duty seem to me all one.
— Justice Oliver Wendell Holmes Jr., 1841-1935

From the day Evelyn (Suzi) Fisher and I set up housekeeping in Washington, D. C., we felt as if we were the first liberated women. Eve could not have been more excited about the apple. Neither Suzi nor I had ever lived away from our parents except for our dorm days at Florida State College for Women. This was high noon. Over the years many young people have traditionally migrated afar to study, work, marry, and settle in parts of the United States quite new and foreign to them. But in my day the numbers were few, especially for young women.

The milieu into which I was thrown in September 1938 as a first-year student at The George Washington University School of Law had an unsettling effect on me. I had emotional baggage gathered from my "consciousness-raising" Open Road trip. I was torn between the various ideologies which whirled around in my head.

In 1933 Franklin D. Roosevelt had begun his first term as President of the United States by assuring the nation, still troubled by a grave economic crisis, that "the only thing we have to fear is fear itself." As he approached the campaign for his second term, he had already attained one of his primary objectives in the passage of the Social Security Act, giving relief to all in need, old and young alike. Until then middle class folks had no savings after the depression years and no "security" of any kind for their old age.

In April 1936, when Mother and I sat under a tent in Deland, Florida, listening to FDR's appeal for support, I was so impressed with his words that I noted them as best I could, and my school girl script is still legible.

"You ought to thank God tonight if, regardless of your years, you are young enough to see visions, to dream a vision of a greater and finer America that is to be; if you are young enough in spirit to believe that poverty can be greatly lessened, that the disgrace of involuntary employment can be wiped out, that hatreds can be done away with; that peace at home and abroad can be maintained; and that one day a generation may possess this land, blessed beyond anything we know with those things spiritual and material that make man's life abundant. If that is the fashion of your dreaming, then I say, hold fast to that dream. America needs it."

I still have the yellow foolscap-lined pad with these words written on my unsteady lap. On my arrival at the YWCA for my first night in Washington I burned with the desire of becoming a lawyer and making a "difference" in my country. I was only one of the idealists who invaded the nation's capital during the New Deal. Many of our parents' friends thought "that man" in the White House was ruining their country. The previous summer Mother, Cleona, and I were treated to lunch by a classmate of my father's, Stuart Commeaux. He turned to me during our delicious lunch and said, "So, what do you think of Mr. Roosevelt?" Being only fifteen I replied, "Oh, Uncle Stuart, I think he is wonderful." To which he replied, "Young lady, you are not half as pretty as I thought you were." But it was with my head full of FDR's dreams for America that I joined Suzi to look for an apartment in the fall of 1938. To add to my enthusiasm, shortly after my arrival in Washington, I attended a lunch at the YWCA and found myself afterward sharing the elevator with Mrs. Roosevelt. This seemed like a wonderful omen, as her very presence was inspiring to me.

Before my arrival, Suzi had scoured Washington hunting for lodging for us. She already had a job, and she knew what our budget for rent would allow. Her parents were as concerned as mine about the propriety and safety of our future location. Suzi found us suitable quarters at 2700 Q Street, N.W., in "Kew Gardens," located just west of the Q Street bridge. Two majestic bronze bison flanked either side of the bridge and made the short approach to our gardens dramatic.

The apartment was attractive. **One**, I repeat **one**, pleasant but unfurnished room with a kitchenette and bath. Since we did not own a stick of furniture and had no money to purchase any, we decided to rent what furniture we needed. We looked at want ads and found one source at 7th and F streets. About halfway up two flights of rickety stairs, Suzi began tugging at my skirt and whispered hoarsely, "white slave traffic!" Concluding that Suzi had been reading too many dime store novels, I laughed and continued upward. Since no white slave traders were present, we proceeded to rent the bare necessities, which included roll-out twin beds, convertible during the day to a sofa. I immediately signed up for afternoon law classes, from 5:00 to 7:00 p.m., Monday through Friday, and started job hunting.

My deal with Daddy was that, if he would send me on the European trip, I would find a job and work my way through law school, and find one I must!

Job Hunting

For two and one-half months I walked the length of Pennsylvania and Constitution avenues from Capitol Hill to Twentieth Street. Although I had a B.S. degree and CPA credentials, I discovered no one would hire me unless I could type. Further, all of the accounting and auditing positions available in government involved travel. Not only that, but housing restrictions required an accountant to share his or her overnight lodgings with another accountant. To require that two of the opposite sex room together during auditing trips violated even today's proprieties. Very few women CPA's applied, but those who did were denied employment as the agency could not pay for single occupancy.

Since finding suitable work in my special expertise seemed to be out of the question, it was obvious that I had to look for another kind of employment. At Daddy's suggestion, I asked Claude Pepper, who was serving his first term in the Senate, to help me. I called the senator's office several times a week and occasionally visited his staff to impress upon him how desperate I was. Finally, one afternoon his secretary telephoned me with the message, "Get over to the National Archives building right away. The Department of Justice has established an office there to publish something called the *Federal Register* and will be hiring a junior typist. Most of the slots are already filled but they want you to take a typing test right away."

Every now and then in my job search, I splurged on a taxi in order to be on time for an appointment. On this occasion, I was in a hurry after an interview at the Agriculture Department, and did not want to be late for my National Archives appointment. As I was climbing into a taxi I heard the driver laughing to himself. While I fished around in my papers for the name of the officer I was to interview, he kept on laughing. I had been so depressed over my inability to procure employment that I begged him, "Please share the joke with me, I need a laugh."

"Well, lady, you won't believe this," he chuckled, "but a few years ago I had a fare to the Agriculture Department. He was Will Rogers." Rogers was a famous man in those days and wrote a nationally syndicated political column. He also appeared regularly on numerous radio shows. He did "stand up" comic routines on Broadway while he twirled his lasso and performed quite remarkable rope tricks.

The taxi driver continued, "Mr. Rogers said he liked it in Washington a lot, but he thought if they would double the salary of the dollar-a-year men they could get better men!"[1] As Rogers paid his fare, complete with a nice tip, he winked at the driver and said, "Well, I've got an appointment with the Secretary of Agriculture. I guess he'll try to give me a package of seeds."

Perhaps it took less to make me laugh in those days, but the driver's story sent me off with a good giggle, and I approached my interview with an upbeat feeling, although I dreaded the thought of taking a typing test.

To prepare for the test, I found an inexpensive business school, four flights up in a disreputable location on F Street and enrolled in a crash course for two ten-hour days pounding away at an ancient Remington typewriter. "Passing" was to type fifty words a minute with no more than five mistakes. How my FSCW classmates would have teased me! We had vowed, with our college degrees in hand, never to accept a secretarial job under any circumstances. Now I was begging for one.

When I appeared at the National Archives for the testing process, the administrative and clerical staff to whom I reported were sitting around gabbing, doing crossword puzzles, or engaged in some other frivolous undertaking. I thought, "Oh, if I could just land this job, I would work so hard that I would put them all to shame."

I proceeded, however, to flunk the typing test twice, and only finally passed it at 4:00 p.m. on the afternoon before the hiring and the Civil Service blanketing process was to take place. Talk about the eleventh hour! At any rate, hooray! I had landed a job. But what a job! (In retrospect, that sentence should read: What? A Job?) It carried the lowest possible work classification, that of a CAF-1 in the Clerical Administrative and Fiscal category. Further, it paid only $100 a month. But, I was so relieved and happy that I might not have traded places with FDR himself—Eleanor, perhaps, but not FDR. At the base of the marble steps approaching the National Archives building are engraved the immortal words, "What is Past is Prologue." Even though I had read the quotation when I climbed the beautiful stairway that afternoon, the past was not one of my concerns. I was dreaming of the future. I was enchanted just to be living in our nation's capital. Whenever I had a few hours, I walked and walked to explore the museums, public buildings, squares, and parks. I often stood awestricken in front of the Lincoln Memorial. This city was, indeed, my oyster.

Quite by chance, my work gave me my first introduction to the Supreme Court's review of legislation. The publication of the *Federal Register* had been mandated as a result of a court decision which involved that of a single farmer's violation of a Department of Agriculture regulation. The farmer's defense stated that he did not know of the existence of any such regulation and, therefore, could not be held accountable for violating a rule which had not been posted in a public place or sent to him via the mails. It was the opinion of the court that unless the law, rule, or regulation was published and available for those responsible for its compliance, no one could be held liable for its violation. The Congress recognized this communications gap and directed that there be a codification of all federal rules and regulations, that it be made accessible to all who must obey them. This was the real reason that the Congress established the Office of the Federal Register, under Act 44, U.S.C. Chapter 15.[2] The daily publication, called *Federal Register*, provides official notice of the existence and contents of all regulations and legal notices issued by the federal departments. As a junior typist in that bureau I was never asked to type a word—we edited and footnoted galley proofs instead!

My Law School Calendar

At night law school my study of civil procedure was illuminated by one professor, James A. Pike, who had been a Sterling Fellow at Yale Law School. Jim Pike had worked on the New Federal Rules of Civil Procedure with Dean Charles E. Clark at Yale who had been ordered to draft them. Jim was a spectacular teacher and made a dry subject like trial and pretrial procedure come leaping out of the case books. His father had died when he was two years old, he told me, and it was during his early childhood that he began searching for the meaning of life. He had graduated from the University of Southern California and had received a grant to attend Yale Law School, where he distinguished himself. In Washington he worked at the Securities and Exchange Commission (SEC), while teaching his procedure course at the evening sessions at George Washington's law school. I was lucky to be in his class. Jim gave me an "A" in his course, not, I hope, because I went out with him several times. On our dates he prepared supper and played his spinet organ for me. Twice we attended an Episcopal church in the southeast section of the District of Columbia, an unrestored and slum-like area. The high church services were punctuated by richly aromatic incense. Jim was deeply religious, and I wondered how he would focus his enormous physical energy on a combination of law and religion.

On the weekends I spent any remaining part of my tiny salary flying up to Cambridge to see Philip Graham, then a student at the Harvard Law School. Phil had gone to the University of Florida in Gainseville, and I had dated him and his roommates during my college years. Going steady was rare in those days. During my weekends in Cambridge, I stayed at the home of the Felix Frankfurters, who acted as gurus to gifted Harvard law students.

Phil embarrassed me in a rude way on the first of those many visits when he introduced me to Marian Frankfurter at a *Harvard Law Review* party in the stately Copley Plaza Hotel. She graciously said "Oh Phil, Phil has been anxiously awaiting you. We are so glad you are here!"

Phil Graham proceeded to add, "Oh Phil is a nice girl. She has a nice body!"

I was stunned and turned purple with embarrassment. I had only "kissed" that wretched boy in a most proper way! I was sure his remarks must have convinced Mrs. Frankfurter that I was sleeping with him and that he knew something about my body. I was furious! When I reported this humiliating exchange to my roommate, Suzi, her reply was "Why didn't you say, well, it's a great deal better than yours, Phil." It was, indeed. Phil was no Adonis, but Suzi was cleverer than I, and hindsight is always infallible.

The morning after the party Phil and Edwin Pritchard took me to their Harvard Law class on real property, taught by the famous Edward H. Warren, called "Bull" by everyone. His nickname, I soon learned, indicated his personality—overbearing. Professor Warren eyed the three of us as we arrived late and sat in the last row of a large teaching amphitheater. He yelled "Mr. Pritchard."

"Yessir," roared two-hundred-pound, rosy-cheeked Pritch in his Kentucky drawl as he sprang to his feet.

"G to A and the heirs of his body . . . such and such factual problem . . . . What's the answer?"

Pritch hemmed and hawed and came up with the wrong answer. Everyone was well aware that neither he nor Phil had attended Warren's class for weeks. Warren knew this and found them arrogant. Quite true, incidentally.

Warren thundered, "Wrong, wrong, wrong. If you'd attended my lectures, you'd know the law on the subject."

Pritch replied, in an even thicker southern drawl, "Suh, it's not ignorance that makes me give the wrong answer. It's the terror of the monster before me."

That broke up the class and the incident was duly reported in *Time Magazine.*

Pritch and I became good friends. I often saw him when I visited Phil. Those were exciting times, and even instructive for me. Phil was editor-in-chief of the *Harvard Law Review,* the law school's most prestigious post, one that reflected his academic excellence. Once Pritch said to me when he picked me up at the Boston airport, "I'm having a terrible time with your pal Phil, Phil." (Both of us having the same first name posed somewhat of a problem.) "Every other sentence he says "y'know. It's driving us all crazy."

We struck a deal during the cab ride. Every time Phil said, "y'know," we would answer in unison "Yes, Phil, we know!" In two days, we broke him of that irritating habit of speech, so often used today. I recommend our method.

The only other excursion away from my duties at the Office of the Federal Register was a weekend at Ponte Vedra Beach, Jacksonville. My first cousin, Locke Brown, Uncle Fletcher's son, who was then twenty-four-years old, telephoned me out of the blue to say he was going to Florida to visit his parents and invited me to go along because my parents would be visiting there also. His proposition was that he would drive me if I would keep him awake. I agreed without hesitation and about 1 a.m., while we were on our way, he offered to explain Albert Einstein's theory of relativity to me. Although that was the last subject I would have expected to hear, he showered me with difficult, mind-exploding, abstract thoughts for more than two hours.

On that long, long ride he confessed, "you know, Phil, when I was a student at Gainseville I used to see you at the University of Florida surrounded by tuxedos and being the queen of the military ball, and queen of this ball and that ball, and I was just too shy to cut in on you."

I retorted, "Locke Brown, how could you possibly say that? You are my first cousin. You know I would have loved to have seen you!"

"No," he said, "I don't think you would have, and I would have been too shy to have enjoyed it."

Isn't that sad? My cousin standing in a huge gymnasium wondering whether to dance with me and I had not even known he was there!

My trip with Locke to Florida was my last chance to see him, but even in that brief weekend he impressed me with his charm and thoughtfulness. Soon after that he became a lieutenant in the Marine Corps, married a Marine colonel's daughter while on duty in the Philippines, and was the first pilot shot down on a mission over Guadalcanal. His son was born after his death. I regret that I did not get to know Locke better, but I am pleased that his wife and son were always a part of Uncle Fletcher's and Aunt Maude's family.

I treasured my weekend respite from working in the daytime and studying at night. But while my regime was grueling, I made many friends in Washington who were government bureaucrats and clerks to justices of the U.S. Supreme Court Through them, I participated in many extracurricular activities that gave enlightening peeks into high court procedures and decisions.

The Supreme Court and New Deal

During my last two years at Tallahassee, I studied constitutional law and followed the acts of the U.S. Supreme Court.President Roosevelt had received Congressional support from both conservative Republicans and southern Democrats for his New Deal proposals during his first term. In his second term these Congressmen began opposing his programs. This change of Congressional support coincided with the fact that the Supreme Court, in a number of important decisions, had rendered him powerless to deal with pressing economic and social problems. His reaction was to "pack" the court with judges who would support his efforts to promote the general welfare of the nation.

The court, as FDR once said, was composed of nine old men. Willis Van Devanter (78), an old Taft appointee, was almost senile. Charles Evans Hughes (75), had been governor of New York state from 1906-1910 prior to his appointment to the court by Taft. James C. McReynolds (75) was kicked upstairs from the post of U.S. Attorney General when Wilson no longer wanted him in that office. George Sutherland (75), who had been prominent in Utah state politics, was a Harding appointee. Pierce Butler (71) was also a Harding appointee and a railroad lawyer, who had fought for the railroads who were against the Federal Employers' Liability Act. Owen J. Roberts (62) was a successful lawyer unanimously confirmed during the Hoover administration. His contributions were in the area of civil liberties and business regulation. My memory tells me he was against both. There were three liberals in place: Louis D. Brandeis (81), Harlan F. Stone (65), and Benjamin Cardozo (67).

The legendary Justice Oliver W. Holmes Jr. was no longer on the court when I arrived in Washington. His presence was looming large over the court, nevertheless, and I relish the tales of this great man told to me by Phil Graham's friend, Professor, later Justice Felix Frankfurter.

For more than twenty years the distinguished Justice Holmes and the Harvard law professor exchanged letters. Their contents ranged from personal chitchat to the philosophy of law, supplemented by notes on cases and persons involved in them.

In 1917, Holmes sent Frankfurter a note concerning one of the professor's students who had just been selected as his clerk. "The lad here calls himself a pacifist as well as a socialist and exhibits a thin and stubborn rationality. I find myself very fond of him and even liking his society above the average of secretaries."[3]

On April 21, 1921, long before Felix Frankfurter joined the court himself, he recommended Benjamin Cardozo to Holmes, as a "sensitive man who deals sanely and bravely with realities." Within two days the justice acknowledged his agreement with these evaluations. "You feel the edge of his blade cutting and not merely sliding down the lines of least resistance. He certainly is a razor and not a kitchen knife." When Holmes retired eleven years later, he considered Cardozo a most worthy successor.[4]

Brandeis was a Wilson appointee whose confirmation was opposed by Wall Street as well as by the U.S. Congress. Coolidge did not "vet" Stone as to his political philosophy since he was the eminent dean of Columbia University Law School. Cardozo was similarly unvetted by Hoover as he had served as chief of the New York Court of Appeals.

Rumor had it that the conservative justices rode in the same automobile to and from the court for oral arguments. The Saturday conferences, when all nine justices attended, were at that time held in their homes. We knew the court was very polarized principally on the New Deal regulatory cases.[5] Joseph Rauh Jr., who had graduated first in his class from Harvard Law School in 1935, was Cardozo's clerk at that time. He told me the liberals met at Brandeis's home at 6:00 p.m. on Fridays to plan their strategy. He reported never having seen Justice Cardozo more unhappy than after one of the Friday sessions when the justice revealed that Brandeis and Stone were not going to dissent with him, despite their feelings, and that another wrong decision was going to be made.

The Supreme Court was, to a law student in Washington, the apex on the Richter scale. My friends were thrilled to be chosen as a clerk to a Supreme Court justice. When Phil Graham, with whom I was then informally engaged, came to Washington to clerk for Justice Stanley Reed, a recent Roosevelt appointee, he invited me to lunch each Monday to hear the proceedings. He was wonderful to ask me so often for he knew how exciting it was for me to hear the decisions and just to *be* there.

Court Packing

In January 1937, I listened on the Tallahassee radio to President Roosevelt giving his inaugural address for his second term. It was then, I finally realized, that he gave a faint warning of his plans to pack the Supreme Court. Justice Brandeis, although he remained an admirer of Roosevelt, opposed the plan vigorously. Not deterred, however, the president appointed a "kitchen cabinet," whose membership included Thomas Corcoran (called "Tommy the Cork" by the president himself) and Benjamin Cohen, to get his programs in place. The key measures in question were included in the National Industrial Recovery Act (NIRA), termed by the president as "the most important and far-reaching legislation to be enacted by the Congress."[6] Tommy and Ben had dreamed up such schemes as passing a law that would forbid less than two-thirds of the court from invalidating federal or state laws, and permitting the majority of Congress to overrule a court decision.

Roosevelt got nowhere with his plan to pack the court, since there was strong congressional opposition. But social reform was given an enormous boost when Justice Roberts promised to uphold the minimum wage laws of Washington State. He cited an unfair labor practice when a laundress had been made to work ten to twelve hours a day "to finish her washing and ironing." Eight hours were a maximum daily work load, according to the state law.

The biggest change came in April 1937, three months after the president's inaugural address, when Chief Justice Hughes defended the position taken in an oral argument concerning the constitutionality of the National Labor Relations Act (the Wagner Act). The Wagner Act granted employees the right to organize and bargain collectively with employers.[7] In effect, he overturned the original 6-3 vote against the act, when the court had denied its constitutionality, to a 5-4 vote to uphold it.[8]

Joe Rauh, Cardozo's clerk at the time, said the justice was elated and smiled saying "a switch in time saves nine," meaning the **nine** Supreme Court justices. In another leading decision, the court sustained the administration's amendments to the Social Security Act that had passed both the House and the Senate. This was referred to in all "legalese" conversations I heard as a victory for social reform. Justice Van Devanter, a staunch New Deal critic, opposed the victory and promptly resigned.

Hughes was a very able administrator. He had ascended to the bench as chief justice in 1930 in the midst of the most serious and steadily worsening economic crisis in American history.

Rumor had it that Chief Justice Hughes would state facts at the opening of the regular Saturday conference on cases under consideration. He would first state his own view. Then the justices would vote from the most junior up, in order of seniority. This was done so that the juniors would not be intimidated by the seniors. To be perceived as non-political, the 1938 court did not vote in elections, either national or state.

In 1941, when both the minimum wage and social security were at last a reality, Chief Justice Hughes resigned at age seventy-nine. He had led the court with great fidelity through a decade rent with bitter difference. Despite Roosevelt's impatience with the court in delaying his New Deal program, Hughes did quicken the pace of judicial reversals. Frankfurter, in his usual flair for words, added, "To see him preside was like witnessing Toscanini lead an orchestra."[9]

Stubbornly, FDR continued to try to pass his court packing plan by turning to the Congress, inviting all 407 Democratic Congressmen and Senators to a White House picnic where he laid on his considerable charm, but to no avail. The outrage felt by the great majority of the American people lingered for months and support for the plan steadily ebbed away. In 1938, Justice Cardozo died. He had been firm in his position that adherence to precedent should be relaxed in the face of changing conditions. He will remain a legend throughout the legal world. Cardozo memorial lectures are still delivered annually to bar association groups all over the United States.

Flag Saluting Case—Individual Liberties

When Frankfurter succeeded Cardozo on the court, he wrote the president, "Dear Frank: In the mysterious ways of Fate, the Duchess County American and the Viennese American have for decades pursued the same directions of devotion to our beloved country, and now on your blessed birthday I am given the gift of opportunity of service to the nation which in any circumstances would be owing, but which I would rather have had put at your hands than at those of any other President barring Lincoln."[10]

It was obvious that Frankfurter adored Roosevelt. In turn Frankfurter's Harvard law students, whose teacher he had been since 1914, recognized his brilliant, probing mind. Great excitement prevailed in Cambridge when his appointment to the court was announced, the third Jew (Brandeis, Cardozo, and now Frankfurter) to have been chosen for this prestigious body. In praise of Roosevelt's choice, Phil Graham wired me to say "How splendid to have a president willing to spit in Adolph's eye!" FDR himself later referred to the circle of students who worshipped their professor as "Felix's Hot Dogs." Joe Rauh, who had been one of Frankfurters students at Harvard Law School, was his first clerk in the court.

Harlan Stone's record during his long service on the court was well known and his reputation had been established in 1940 when he registered a lone dissent in the compulsory flag saluting case involving the public schools of Pennsylvania.[11]

Frankfurter, in a sudden change from a civil libertarian, surprised one and all by not supporting Stone in his dissent. Pritch, who had replaced Joe Rauh as his clerk during the arguments on this case, tried very hard to dissuade Justice Frankfurter. Phil, who was to be his clerk the following year, joined Pritch, but did not succeed. Most everyone believed it was Frankfurter's way of expressing, as an immigrant Jew, his love of country and its flag. Even Mrs. Roosevelt supported the press in saying that there was something very wrong with forcing little children to salute the flag when both they and their families felt that it was an act denying the supremacy of their God.

The court which had looked up to Frankfurter as the famous liberal Harvard Law professor did not ever after that, it seemed to many of us, so revere him. His period of leadership at the court gradually came to an end.

In January 1940, when Justice Frank Murphy finally accepted an appointment to the Supreme Court to fill the vacancy resulting from the death of Justice Pierce Butler, he wrote President Roosevelt that he would prefer to serve his country directly in the war effort, and added, "I know too well that there are many men of greater stature than myself available."

Tommy Corcoran, realizing Murphy's sense of inferiority, called Ed Huddleson at the U.S. Solicitor General's office to persuade him to return to the court (he had already served a year as Reed's clerk) as Murphy's law clerk. Ed, who accepted reluctantly, had invited me up to the court to view Murphy's first session. When he joined me in the audience, he told me the justice had touched his arm on his way to the robing room and asked, "Should I take Black's Law Dictionary with me to the bench?"

Ed said he shook his head in the negative, but he admitted he thought in his own mind, "If you don't know the law by now, Black's dictionary won't help."

Ed served Murphy as a scholarly amanuensis. During his nine and one-half years on the court, Murphy gained self-confidence and emerged as an independent figure in cases involving separation of church and state.[12]

After the 1940 decision on the flag saluting case in Pennsylvania public schools, Hugo L. Black, who had never graduated from any law school and who had little legal or judicial experience, began to emerge as one of the finest scholars on the court and the leader of the liberal majority.

Three years later Stone turned this 1940 decision around when a question of saluting the flag relating to West Virginia public schools came before the Court. This time Black, William O. Douglas, and Frank Murphy, plus two new justices, Robert H. Jackson and Wiley B. Rutledge, joined

Stone and his view won the day. What was formerly an eight to one in favor changed to a vote of six to three against.[13]

In 1941 when Roosevelt named Stone chief justice of the Supreme Court, he chose the son of a New England farmer and a solid, peace-loving man. The president's wartime government by its very nature created a new set of priorities and aroused new feelings and causes among the American people. It was then that the civil rights movement could make gains and civil liberties could be sharpened. In these circumstances Chief Justice Stone met antagonists on all sides. When the delicate problem of whether pacifists must take an oath to bear arms as a condition to naturalization arose, on the other hand, Stone wavered in defense of individual freedoms.

As Joe Rauh pointed out to me when we discussed this case, "one beauty of our government is its resilience. When one engine sputters, another reaches out to meet the nation's needs."

Roosevelt's Appointments to the Supreme Court

During my years of closely watching the process in the Supreme Court and my discussions with several clerks of the justices, I remain constantly astonished at the way President Roosevelt conducted his affairs of state and especially with the court. His first appointment made in 1937—the first of a total of nine during his four terms in office—was Justice Black, a fifty-one-year-old liberal senator from Alabama. Unfortunately, Black was in no position to assist the president in the court packing plan because he was, himself, involved in a problem defending his connection with the Ku Klux Klan.

Stanley Reed, Roosevelt's next appointment in 1938, had been solicitor general. His clerk, Phil Graham, filled me in on Reed's major opinions in support of the president. The general opinion among my friends was that Roosevelt had, in effect, pulled the Supreme Court back together with his choice of Reed. He reasserted that his plan to pack the court was a continuation of his New Deal program, planned at least two years before he announced it. Most of my friends tended to believe that, but they also knew that Roosevelt's support seemed to have slipped between the time he thought of the plan and the time he tried to execute it.

Roosevelt's appointments thereafter proved he was true to his cause and the cross currents of the nation as he saw them. In 1939, Felix Frankfurter and William Douglas were next, about whom I had learned a good deal from my personal contacts with them. In 1940 Roosevelt convinced Frank Murphy, an Irish Catholic from Michigan, to leave his post as attorney general and join the Supreme Court. He had been governor of the state in 1937 and had settled a forty-four day sit-down labor strike by 135,000 General Motors workers. Soon thereafter, in 1941, the president named Harlan Stone to become chief justice. He had already served on the court with great distinction for sixteen years. Also in 1941, the president named James F. Byrnes and Robert H. Jackson to seats on the court. Byrnes, a southerner from South Carolina who had supported the president when popular support for the New Deal was lagging, was one of the ring leaders at the 1940 Chicago convention to secure the president's nomination for a third term. Jackson had worked with Tommy Corcoran and Ben Cohen in drafting New Deal programs. He had served as solicitor general and attorney general and often briefed the president in his bedroom during breakfast and later lunched with him.[14] When Roosevelt asked him to be an associate justice, he replied, "Mr. President, that's a long way from the farm in Spring Creek." He said he went through the battle with FDR to fight the "crowd who were opposed to reform in an economic and social field."[15]

Wiley Rutledge, who took his oath of office in February 1943, was Roosevelt's last appointment. He had been a member of the Court of Appeals in the District of Columbia. Roosevelt said he appointed him because of his "geography"—Iowa. FDR died before Rutledge had written his most important civil liberties dissent.

I find it interesting that many of the constitutional rights for which FDR fought in 1938 are being threatened today. If I have spent an inordinate length of time dwelling on the U.S. Supreme Court, it is because of my fascination with that hallowed institution. Friends who were clerks of the justices widened my vision of the nine men who sat behind an immense mahogany bar in their magnificent red-draped chamber, and that respect has only increased with the current presence of two wise women, both of whom I am proud to know.

S Street and the Aftermath

In addition to being a weekly guest of Phil's at Supreme Court Decision Mondays, I saw a great deal of the other clerks at the court in the evenings or on weekends. Most were my contemporaries, friends, and headed for brilliant careers.

There was Allison Dunham, a graduate of Columbia Law School, clerk for Justice Stone; Edwin McElwain and Adrian "Butch" Fisher, both clerks for Chief Justice Hughes, to name a few. All discreetly reported comments of their bosses concerning the "goings on."

It was not unusual for Felix Frankfurter, Hugo Black, and Wiley Rutledge to join us at Phil's house where Phil, Pritch, and Ed Huddleson lived on S Street. On several Saturdays Phil and I had lunch with Justice William Douglas who was only forty-one years of age and seemed lonely among the august group of older justices. Phil and I were invited to his chambers to listen to a football game on the radio, share a chicken sandwich, or simply to chat.

Other frequent guests at S Street were in a variety of fields. John L. Lewis, the maverick labor leader dropped in at S Street occasionally. In his absence Pritch gave a perfectly hilarious imitation of him, right down to his bushy eyebrows. Jerome Frank, not yet thirty years old, argued with anyone and everyone and sometimes had a good story about his colleagues at the Securities and Exchange Commission. Tom Harris, number one in his class at Columbia Law School, Justice Stone's law clerk in 1935–1936, and his wife Lucy were two of the very few of our crowd who were married. They became Sam's and my close friends as well as our neighbors on 30th Street.

Two young scholars, also S Streeters, had just returned from England after completing their Rhodes scholarships, often made the discussions livelier. They were budding young journalists—Hedley Donovan, later editorial director of Time, Inc., and John Oakes, later editorial page editor of *The New York Times*. In those years they both worked for Eugene Meyer, owner of *The Washington Post*. Hedley often brought along his divine Dorothy Hannon, whom he married with enormously happy results. Lucy, Dorothy, and I often sat on the floor together and whispered. Those evenings were exciting and stimulating, quite heady for a little southern gal.

Pritch, my long-time friend, knew many journalists. He invited me to dinner at the Salle de Bois, a snappy restaurant at DuPont Circle, and he took pleasure in pointing out to me, sometimes in an ostentatious way—much to my embarrassment—Walter Lippmann and Arthur Krock. His asides about these famous Washington political commentators usually ended with, "You see, Ash (he often shortened my maiden name), I'm just a bumpkin about celebrities!"

Ed Huddleson, whom I had known since he was editor-in-chief of the *Harvard Law Review,* often asked me to go horseback riding with him on weekdays or Saturday mornings. We did equestrian spins and even galloped around Hains Point before breakfast, then stabling our horses just in time to report for work. What an invigorating way to begin the day! How great it was to be young, healthy, and burn the candle at both ends. A visual reminder of those days are snapshots of Ed and me in riding habits. He started each morning date with a gift, a piece of milk glass or other bibelot, before we saddled up. I still display these treasures proudly in my home.

Once when I told Ed I had friends on the National Labor Relations Board, he became red in the face and exclaimed, "Why that's unconstitutional!"

"What," I asked, "to have friends at the Board?"

"Gosh no, it's the NLRB that's unconstitutional." This is just one indication as to the troubles collective bargaining faced at that time. Ed had been law clerk to Justice Hand in 1938-1939, an attorney in the Office of the Solicitor General in 1939-1940, and law clerk to Justices Reed and Murphy in 1940. From 1949 to 1996 he was a senior partner in Cooley, Godward, Castro, Huddleson, and Tatum in San Francisco, serving on the boards of the Rand Corporation and many other institutions. Ed died in 1996.

Before leaving to memory the many friends I enjoyed during my studies in law school and their connections with S Street and "Hockley," the other bachelor pad, I must note an unhappy end of life to two very special people. They both committed suicide.

Phil Graham was my friend, companion, and fiancé in my first year at law school, but we separated at the end of that year. He had given me much pleasure along the way. Nonetheless he had hurt my feelings so often that I had not worn his ring publicly, only on a chain under my blouse, and I began to wonder what would happen when the rules of courtship no longer applied. Perhaps he may have thought I would be amused when he, in an offhand way, had written me to say "he could not love me any more after seeing how much I ate at Childs." That was the end for me. I concluded then and there that I was too sensitive to bear his irreverent and sardonic humor. Phil missed me not a whit and proceeded to marry beautiful Katherine Meyer, daughter of Eugene Meyer, owner and publisher of *The Washington Post.*

Unfortunately, when in his late sixties, Phil became mentally disturbed and committed suicide—a tragic end to one who contributed much to the law, government, and to publishing at *The Washington Post*, *Newsweek*, and other enterprises. His brilliant widow grabbed the torch and performed her tasks in a wise and courageous way.

Another tragic ending came to my law school professor, James Pike. He had married a beautiful brunette, Polish-American girl named Esther, one of the three women in my class at law school. Soon thereafter, at the beginning of World War II, he enlisted in the Navy. His first child was born while he was overseas. In his absence Esther continued to edit and publish law review articles and case law notes dealing with the Federal Rules of Civil Procedure in a loose leaf publication called the Pike-Fisher Service. Military pay was not a living wage, even with an officer's stipend, so the proceeds from this service supplemented the Pike family coffers.

In the late 1940s, Jim devoted himself to the church and was ordained as an Episcopal minister. He became dean of the Cathedral of St. John the Divine in Manhattan and then Bishop of Southern California. This was the beginning of the end of his career in the church. He quarreled with Cardinal Spellman over church doctrine and, after divorcing Esther and marrying his assistant, he went off to Israel to search for Dead Sea Scrolls in the caves at Khirbet Qumrân, where archaeologists had begun scientific excavations in 1949. He wandered off into the desert in the Judaean Valley and was not seen again. While we do not know for certain that he committed suicide, his mental state was so impaired that those of us who knew him well are concerned that he deliberately ended his life. What we do know for certain is that this brilliant legal scholar, who spoke and wrote five languages and had published twenty books on Episcopal church teachings, died all too soon.

My first two years of law school were profoundly enriched by such friends and acquaintances. I had no doubt that I had chosen the right career. The law has continued to be ever more fascinating.

Notes

1. FDR persuaded many talented and dedicated people to serve his New Deal without salary, hence they were paid a dollar a year.

2. *Federal Register,* LXI, 135.

3. Robert M. Mennel and Christine L. Compston, eds. *Holmes and*

Frankfurter: Their Correspondence, 1912-1934. (Hanover and London: University Press of New England, 1996), 70.

4. *Ibid.*, 109, 110, 234.

5. Leon Friedman and Fred L. Israel, eds. *The Justices of the United States Supreme Court, 1789-1969: Their Lives and Major Opinions* (New York and London: Chelsea House in association with R. R. Bowker, 1969), III, 1903, 1916.

6. Ibid., 1909, 1916.

7. Ibid., 1910, 1911.

8. Ibid., 1912.

9. Ibid., 1913.

10. Ibid., 2405.

11. Ibid., 2230.

12. Friedman, IV, 2499-2501.

13. Friedman, III, 2232.

14. Ibid., 2549.

15. Ibid., 2562

Chapter Ten

Wartime Washington

There is no more lovely, friendly and charming relationship,
communion, or company than a good marriage.

— Martin Luther 1483-1546

Courtship and Marriage

My bachelor days continued. Suzi and I found a new apartment next to the National Arts Clubhouse on the second floor of a Victorian brownstone at 2001 I Street, only two blocks from the George Washington's law school, where I was to begin my third year. We were thrilled to have a bedroom! And then, disaster struck. Suzi lost her job. The employers at the news magazine where she had worked for two years discovered that she and a few other employees had joined The Newspaper Guild, a union founded in 1934.[1] Today it would be illegal to punish an employee for exercising the right to seek collective bargaining and freedom of association, but not in 1939.

Suzi and I shed a lot of tears the night she came home with the note terminating her employment. We made lists of places where she might apply for a job, and she began to pound the pavement the very next day. It was all to no avail, however, and after about six weeks of non-stop job searches, she was forced to move back to Florida to live with her parents.

With Suzi gone, I had to find a roommate to share the expenses. Phil Graham said he knew a lawyer in the Antitrust Division at the Department of Justice who was living in a hotel and was anxious to find an apartment. I told him to have her call me, and she did the next day. We set a time for her to inspect the premises.

Her name was Marianne Bell, daughter of Minnesota Federal Judge Robert C. Bell. Judge Bell had been the local U.S. attorney during the investigation of the famous Tea Pot Dome Scandal in the Harding administration.[2] I had heard that Marianne was a brilliant, attractive brunette, who had graduated from Carleton College in Northfield, Minnesota, and the University of Virginia Law School. I first saw Marianne as she walked into my modest second floor apartment with a quiet step and greeted me in a formal ladylike fashion. She had apparently asked for recommendations from people who knew me and after a few moments, all it took to see the rooms involved, she allowed as how "they would do" and said she would move in within a few days.

She then outlined the guidelines of her lifestyle: 1) she never bought alcoholic beverages. Her beaux could do that if they wished; 2) she never invited a man in after 10:30 p.m.; 3) she always wore white doeskin gloves, cleaning them nightly with acetone; and 4) she routinely gave 10 percent of her salary to the Democratic Party.

Since Marianne had professional status, there were some differences between us in a practical sense. She earned a lawyer's salary and I a miserable stipend of $100 a month. My work began at 8:30 and hers at 9:00. An extra thirty minutes of sleep would have been a heaven-sent dividend to me. If she was running late, she could afford to hop into a taxi. A few years later when we were out every night and working all day we would giggle uncontrollably about how exciting life was. All we needed to make it perfect was just a little more sleep.

When she had taken possession of her half of the apartment she called me at my office to ask if our household had a dozen cocktail glasses. My answer was "yes." She went on to say that her brother Bob, a recent Harvard Law graduate, was in town, and she wanted to give him a party. I could not resist inquiring, "What does this have to do with your iron-clad lifestyle rule about buying alcohol?"

"Well," she admitted, "when it's my handsome brother, I make an exception." That little party was to launch our first week together.

Some time earlier, during a ten-minute intermission between lectures, a law school classmate named Sigmund "Tim" Sichel[3] had invited me to dinner in his apartment in Tacoma Park, Maryland. He went on to say that the dinner was to be two months hence in honor of Samuel Gates, a lawyer with degrees from the University of Paris, the University of Southern California, and Harvard. The advance date made refusal impossible. I

said "yes," thinking that I would have several much more attractive opportunities as the time of Tim's dinner approached, and I could then grace-
fully regret.

It was not that Tim was dull. He was far from the run-of-the- mill law
student. He was a protégé of Mrs. Roosevelt, had been a Sterling Fellow
with Jim Pike at Yale graduate school, and he was in Washington doing a
study for the Federal Reserve Bank on the *Reichsmark*. Like me, he attended late afternoon law school classes. He had been admitted to the bar
in Germany but being a Jew he had fled Europe to save his life and had
not yet become an American citizen. Tim was 4 feet 10 inches tall, his
face was pockmarked and pimpled, and he was about the ugliest little
man I had ever seen. He was an excellent linguist who read Greek and
four other languages as easily as I could read *The New Yorker*: that still
did not encourage me to look forward to his dinner.

Meeting Sam

Sam, Tim explained, was head of a government department, the International General Counsel's office of the Civil Aeronautics Board (CAB),
the quasi judicial, quasi legislative agency regulating commercial civil
aviation. Sam needed someone to write a study on cartels, Tim said, and
he was very eager to get the job. He added that Sam was a devotee of
beautiful women and good food, as well as a fancier of fine wine, having
acquired such tastes in Paris during his studies there. I conjured up a
picture of an old man of about fifty!

I later learned, as the appointed day approached, that Sam was expecting a visit from a beautiful model from Canada whom he wished to
romance. He was as reluctant as I to attend Tim's dinner. At the last minute
Sam's secretary, whom he referred to as a bossy Irish colleen, reminded
him that he was to escort Mary Bendalari, a lawyer in the Antitrust Division of Justice, and she shoved him out the door and on his way to drive
Mary to Tacoma Park. When I reached the tiny basement apartment, Tim
was obviously eagerly awaiting my arrival to make his foursome complete. His face fell, however, when I walked in. He had sent me a gardenia
with instructions to come dressed "à la Baudelaire." I had scant knowledge of Charles Pierre Baudelaire's poems but I assumed he meant rather
"à la Bohème." Wrong. I still don't know how I should have costumed
myself, but Tim's disappointment was evident.

As we settled in, Tim announced he had prepared dinner all by himself. Mary, a very statuesque member of a well-known Italian shoe manufacturing family in Rome, added a witty and amusing note to our casual introductory conversation, while the three of us sipped sherry and munched on cheese straws. Tim had set a card table with the family Meissen china and had a printed menu for each of us itemizing the food and wine of each course. It was obvious, as Tim told us, that he had spent three days conceiving the dinner, three days purchasing the ingredients, and three days doing the preliminary cooking. Between courses he played a Brahms concerto on his record player while he disappeared into his kitchen to make last-minute preparations.

We dined sumptuously for several hours. Tim had outdone himself. Sam whispered to me that he would like my telephone number! I said "It's in the phone book." He later admitted that he almost decided not to pursue me as he thought my answer extremely cheeky. Indeed it was an intriguing way to begin a forty-year romance. I still have Tim's menu, framed and displayed in my kitchens in both Westhampton and New York City, for it was his dinner that soon changed my life.

Sam was a dashing, ambitious, young legal transplant to the later New Deal. Our first date was a "coming out" party in celebration of the removal of his roommate's (Albert "Cot" Forster's) plaster cast. Cot, a blond, all-American javelin thrower from Stanford University and its law school, had hurt his shoulder sledding in Rock Creek Park. Sam's other housemate, Fred Glass, was good looking and congenial. Later, Sam and I drove out to Normandy Farms, a picturesque restaurant with French farmhouse decor where we dined, talked for hours, and "got acquainted."

On our next date Sam invited me to dinner and dancing at the Shoreham, and we included Mother, who was visiting from Florida, and Cot. Mother was impressed to be dining under the balmy summer skies to the music of the then most popular band leader of the day, Barnee Breeskin! I think I am one of the few alive who can remember his last name, yet he was the Lester Lanin of pre-World War II Washington. On our way home we stopped at Sam's house. Mother noticed, displayed over the door of this Tudor-style building, a plaque on which was embossed "The Mayflower." Intrigued by the name, she inquired about its origin, and Fred, a Mississippian wit, filled Mother in on their secret, "Oh Mrs. Asher, that's because so many Puritan girls have come across in it." Mother was not amused. Cot tried to smooth over Fred's quip. The next time I saw Sam was at the cocktail party Marianne gave at our apartment for her brother.

Sam (with Phil), preparing to leave for Alaska on PAA's first flight, 1940.

There is no doubt that this evening I was antisocial, as many people said, for I did not want to mingle with any guests except Sam.

During this period Sam left on a three-month fact-finding trip to prepare for a very important rate-fixing case (for mail subsidy) involving Pan American Airways. Sam and Tom Hardin, a high ranking official of the Federal Aviation Administration, covered all of Pan American's stops in South and Central America.

Just before Sam left for this trip he said, "Phil, I would be delighted to let you use my new Chrysler during my absence if you would like to have it." I leapt at such a chance to have a car in Washington, so "I'd adore that!" was my immediate response. Then he said, "Let me see your driver's license." PANIC! I did not own one, since as I've recounted Florida had not required them. So I said, "Sam, by the time you leave on your trip, I'll take the driving test and have one," which I did. My study for that test was more careful than for most law school exams! I didn't dare flunk or I'd lose the use of that snappy new green car.

With Sam gone, I needed to fill up my life with activities or I would have become quite depressed, I'm sure. My friends rallied around me and happily Kay and Phil Graham invited me to their house right after they were married in Burleith, a small section of town near Georgetown. Kay had said that Senator Pepper (my patron) and George Smathers as well as some other Florida friends of mine would be there. She used her lovely wedding china and flat silver and we dined very well in a VERY small dining room, and when the evening was over Pritch asked if he could take me home. He was still asking me to dinner from time to time, and was always scintillating company. I said, "Pritch, a friend has loaned me his car for a while, so I can take YOU home instead." All the way back to S Street where he still lived and where I dropped him, he told me he was working very hard at the White House and his two best girls were Evangeline Bell (later Mrs. David Bruce) and me. I said "that is nice.

Sam as Counsel to the Civil Aeronautics Board in Washington, D.C, in 1941.

Evangeline and I can share you!" He did nag me mercilessly about whose car I was driving. "Come on, Ash, you can tell me, your good friend." I refused in no uncertain terms. "You, Pritch, are the last person I would confide in. You are a big gossip!" Luckily for me I never got a scratch on Sam's precious possession and could return it intact.

Despite other social outings, I was concentrating my full attention on Sam, for he seemed at once to be everything I wanted in a husband. He had been married briefly and divorced, no children. He wanted very much to be married again and have children. He warned me that his wife would have to put up with his outrageous work habits and the fact that he never wished to be rushed into dinner. I would have agreed to anything, I had fallen so much in love with him. I had been to every nightclub I could ever want and had dates with hundreds of men since the age of thirteen. I was really ready to settle down even though I was only twenty-two-years-old. Soon after Sam returned home, we decided to tie the knot.

Our Wedding

Our original plan was to marry in Orlando in June 1941. We impetuously decided to be married in Washington during April so that Sam could prepare for a complicated case involving Pan Am and I could cram for my third year law school finals. (My law degree required four years as I had been limited to two hours of class work a night.)

Mother, Daddy, and Cleona drove up for our wedding. When I drove them by the adorable corner Georgetown house in which Sam and I were to live, my little sister cried out, "Mother, it's slums." Jack Beckwith, my old Florida friend and Phil Graham's University of Florida roommate, called me for a date on April 25, and Mother answered. Jack was puzzled at hearing her voice. "Mrs. Asher, what are you doing back here? I just took you

Phil and Sam on their wedding day, April 26, 1941.

and Phil tea dancing at the Mayflower two weeks ago?" Mother announced that I was getting married the next morning and invited him to the wedding. The wedding ceremony took place in the attractive, homey atmosphere of Sam's living room at 1220 30th Street. The Episcopalians would not let us be married in church as Sam had been divorced even though his papers proved **him** the injured party. So a Methodist bishop, friend of the father of Sam's Methodist minister, performed the ceremony.

Sam and Phil on their honeymoon in California, 1941.

Afterward, Mother and Daddy gave a lovely breakfast party at Mrs. K's Toll House in Maryland, a pretty restaurant surrounded by azaleas, cherry blossoms, tulips, and daffodils. Fred Glass was Sam's best man. Marianne and Bob McConnaughey, Tom and Lucy Harris, Jack

Beckwith, Cot Forster, and my family threw rice at us as we drove away in Sam's new green Chrysler for a three-day honeymoon at Virginia Beach.

Sam was in the midst of a hearing at the CAB. His adversary, counsel for Pan American, was Henry Friendly. Henry was famous for having made the highest marks at Harvard Law School since Louis Brandeis. Sam knew Henry to be a formidable but congenial opponent so he asked Henry to appeal to the hearing officer for a postponement. When Henry learned that Sam was requesting the postponement because wanted to have a three-day honeymoon and did not feel, as a CAB staff member, that he should ask for this kind of favor, Henry's support was enthusiastic. He made an eloquent plea for a delay, citing a New York conflict on his own calendar.

Years later Judge Friendly would occasionally announce that he had arranged our honeymoon.

Daddy's Death and Aftermath for Our Family

We had just returned from Virginia Beach when I received a devastating midnight phone call from Mother. I knew that Daddy had looked and acted unwell at our wedding. He had made a valiant effort but appeared gray and tired. Mother said at the time that she was very worried about his anemic condition and that the doctors were checking his blood count. I was so anxious about him that I apologized to Sam for his lethargy. He had never seen my handsome Father before. I asked him "how did Daddy seem, what did he say when you asked for his permission to marry me?" Sam cleared his throat and replied seriously, "He said, if I ever broke your heart, he'd break my neck." That was Daddy alright!

Just after we had taken off for our short wedding trip, Daddy had collapsed. Thank heavens that Jack Beckwith, with his medical training, was nearby. In our absence he supported Mother and helped her arrange for Daddy to return to Orlando and see a doctor as soon as possible.

When Mother telephoned me a few days later with the news that Daddy had lymphatic leukemia, I was devastated. Sam and I telephoned our doctor, confidante, and friend, Eugene de Savitsch. He assured us that he had kept an aged Belgian count alive with that condition for years. Because he loved Sam and liked me, he volunteered to fly down and examine Daddy.

What a wonderful act of friendship that was! Imagine what it cost him to close his office and fly down to Florida at his own expense to help us. Yet the news got worse. It was discovered that the laboratory slides had been switched. Daddy was suffering from the more virulent myelogenous not lymphatic leukemia and lived only about three more weeks.

I managed to return to Orlando just twenty-four hours before he took his last breath. Mother was frantic. She had spent all of the family's ready cash for the many blood transfusions required for a leukemia patient. Red Cross blood banks seemed unknown, or at least we didn't seem to use them. Many of Daddy's cronies, former employees, and club compatriots lined up around the block of the hospital to be tested to give him their blood. Only a few had the correct type, so several pints a day had to be bought.

My poor little sister was so vulnerable in her teenage anxiety for her adoring father. She was always his "sugar." My Aunt Zuleim (wife of Daddy's brother Edward) remained at Daddy's bedside while Mother, Cleona, and I were taking a break. We all broke down when she came into our waiting room and uttered in choked, teary words, "We've lost J.B."

After making the usual awful decisions with the funeral directors, we went home. Many of Mother's Brown family came in to be with us for the service. My wonderful Uncle Adrian came in bearing a cooked turkey, salads, and cakes for everyone to have after the church service and burial.

Mother was left alone with mountains of debt. Her home was free and clear, but she had little else. She was worried in the extreme as she had a teenage daughter to support and put through school and college. I had one more year of law school and was still not ready for "real" employment. Those were tearful, anxious days for our little family. The following editorial on my father appeared in the *Orlando Morning Sentinel* on June 17, 1941.

A Real Sportsman Passes On

In the death of J. B. Asher, Orlando sportsmen have lost a real friend. Mr. Asher was a man who played the game square and clean. Though he was not much of an athlete himself, he was very fond of athletics. He contributed generously to movements to advance sports in this section and was always willing and ready to shoulder whatever responsibilities were asked of him.

Generous to a fault, Mr. Asher helped many who were less fortunate than himself. The cherished memory which lingers in so wide a circle of friends should be a source of much consolation to the family in their bereavement.

Mother Re-enters her Profession

Mother never wanted to remarry. She still had a youthful beauty, and she focused her full concentration on re-entering the nursing profession. It was a struggle for a widow of fifty-one. To her credit, however, she was plucky and practical, trying day-by-day to get through her life and pay her bills.[4] First she renewed her registered nurse's certification and studied for her masters degree at Rollins College. With those qualifications, she started to work at the National Public Health Association and in the Tuberculosis Sanitorium, transferring from there to the Public Health Service program for venereal disease. We teased her unmercifully when she was treating persons with VD, saying that her mind was "in the gutter" all day. She defended herself by replying that she had cured half of the population of Orange County of syphilis and gonorrhea.

Once I visited Mother in Orlando to see how she was holding up. I had fixed lunch and was waiting for her to return from the VD clinic. When she arrived, she was fit to be tied. She charged tempestuously through the front door saying the "worst possible thing" had happened to her that morning. Remember, she was a redhead with a short fuse. She told me that one of her colleagues had said, "Mary, before you go home for lunch, you are going to give each one of us a Wassermann test." This test involved intravenously taking a blood sample, a procedure that only medical doctors performed in her nursing days. She begged her co-workers to let her practice in the afternoon on the large, muscular laborers who lined up daily for the test. Their veins were enormous. "Nothing doing," said the staff, "now or never."

So Mother had had to perform ten Wassermann tests before lunch, and she was a wreck! What courage she had!

Despite an occasional outburst, Mother continued to go about practical matters with great perseverance. She remodeled her home into three separate living quarters and redecorated the garage apartment where our servants had once lived. She then had three revenue-producing properties to rent, reserving only the ground floor for Cleona and herself. She managed her finances carefully and paid her bills as best she could.

Amanda and the Ku Klux Klan

It was many months after Daddy's death that I told Mother of an incident that had occurred on the day of his funeral. She had been much too grief stricken at the time for us to bother her with housekeeping problems. I reminded Mother that Sam, for his part, had undertaken to greet Daddy's friends who came to pay sympathy calls, while I had gone to the kitchen to talk with Amanda, Mother's housekeeper for fifteen years, about preparing food for our family. To my surprise and even consternation, Amanda told me she was leaving the house at noon.

"Please, Amanda," I begged, "stay and help us just this once."

"Oh, Miss Phil, I got my church circle meeting, and I don't want to miss it."

I pointed out in no uncertain terms that Daddy had given up several important commitments to accommodate **her,** when she needed **him,** and now we needed **her.**

I remembered several occasions when Daddy had loaned her money, had arranged for her marriage in his office to her long-time, live-in boy friend so that she could qualify for admission to a housing development, and had been her **best friend** for years. My pleading was to no avail.

"Absolutely not," Amanda replied. I threw up my hand in resignation.

I reported my plight to Uncle Adrian, my favorite uncle, who said, "Oh, she'll stay."

After listening to my story, Mother said, "I know what had happened to change Amanda's mind. Adrian just threatened Amanda with a flaming cross or a Klan visit!

Mother's statement revealed that her brothers must have belonged to the Ku Klux Klan. I was reassured of this fact when Uncle Adrian's son told me that after his father's death, his wife and sister-in-law had found some Klan trappings in his father's closet. They had simply thrown them in a wastebasket and never referred to them again.

Uncle Adrian's adopted hometown was Sanford, Florida, the celery capital of the world at that time. The ratio of blacks to whites in 1921-1941 was approximately seven to one. Both Adrian's son and I had been brought up with stories of impending race riots, uprisings, and possible murder of us all by the overwhelming majority of aggrieved blacks.

I relate this story merely to report that the fears of race riots, so rampant today in big cities, were much more rampant in Uncle Adrian's time.

Military Service

Within a month after Sam and I married, Hitler's conquest had swept through Western Europe and the United States moved ever closer to aiding our allies, Great Britain, in particular. On May 28, 1941, President

Roosevelt instructed his Secretary of War to establish the Ferrying Command with services extending beyond the U.S. continental boundaries. The first in charge was then Colonel (later Brigadier General) Robert Olds, whose performance in World War I had earned him a Distinguished Flying Cross. He set up offices with two civilian assistants in the basement of the Munitions Building on Constitution Avenue in Washington. The command pioneered new parts of the world and stretched the skills of men and the capacities of their planes. Its operations began in June 1941 and within five months it had made more than 1,000 aircraft deliveries.

In September 1941, when FDR sent Averell Harriman to Moscow, the Ferrying Command transported him and his mission to England. From there the staff left for Russia by boat, but Flight Captain Major Alva L. Harvey continued on non-stop from Scotland to Moscow with the senior officers. The plane passed North of Scandinavia over the ocean at night to avoid German interception. That was a daring flight in those days.

Major Harvey described this top secret mission in his crudely converted, battered Liberator bomber, a B-24A, saying, "Thirty-two hundred miles in fifteen hours without one radio signal. And twice iced up badly. I'd been flying for twenty years and didn't like that flight one bit."

Quentin Reynolds, who was one of Harvey's passengers, recounts the whole experience in two of his stories, "Only the Stars Are Neutral" and "Potluck at the Kremlin." I have read both and was moved to tears. He landed at airports of unknown capacity and runway length, took off for long hops with no briefing, weather information, or adequate maps. On his way home Flight Captain Harvey headed east via Singapore, Fort Darwin, Wake Island, and Hawaii, finally landing in Washington. Sam often stayed at the ATC office overnight to monitor these dangerous missions in case he could assist if some mishap occurred. Fortunately, we— the wives—were not told about the flight until after the pilot's safe return.[5]

By July 1942 the Ferrying Command merged with the Air Transport Command (ATC), under General Henry "Hap" Arnold, chief of the Army Air Forces. He named General Harold George to replace General Olds. George, although an experienced officer, found his duties too much and called on the president of American Airlines, Cyrus R. Smith (known as C.R.), to be his deputy. With this combination of George and Smith, General Arnold said he did not worry about the service any more. Sam, who had been international counsel for the CAB since 1938, joined C.R. at the

ATC's Washington headquarters about May 1942. He served first as a civilian in the ATC and then as a colonel in the U.S. Army Air Force.

ATC's mission, as stated in brief by General Arnold, devoted exclusively to ferrying, was:

1. Ferry all aircraft within the United States and to destinations outside the United States;

2. Transport by air personnel, material, strategic cargo for all War Department agencies and for any government agency of the U.S. or its allies, subject to directives and priorities;

3. Control, maintain, and operate establishments on air routes outside the United States which are the responsibility of the Commanding General of the Air Force, or assigned to the Air Transport Command;

4. Utilize to the fullest extent possible, within and without the continental United States, the services, personnel, and facilities of the civil air carriers;

5. Assist the movement overseas of combat units in accordance with directives;

6. Administer priorities for air travel and transport of cargo by air on its aircraft and on civil air carriers (except that handled by the Naval Air Transport Service); and

7. Maintain and operate all facilities, planes, airfields.

The ATC had versatile ground crews capable of establishing repair shops wherever required and of providing lodging for air crews between flights. In fact the ATC had to be ambidextrous because no two bases used by the ferrying crews could be manned in exactly the same manner.

In the ever-growing, ever more complicated demands on ATC, Sam, as deputy chief of plans, worked with a number of high calibre civilians, notably James H. Douglas, Jr. and Malcolm A. MacIntyre.[6] Their duties required them to exercise a quality of courage, judgment, and concentration that they never realized before that they possessed.

Sam often reminded me that so many directives had to be made "retroactive," as urgent situations needed action to take place instantly. The planes were in the air before the paperwork was finished authorizing their flight. These functions added up to a world-encircling air operation—an exciting and definite challenge to a handful of career Air Force generals and hundreds of U.S. airline officials, employees, and lawyers who had enlisted to help them.

Sam's responsibilities mounted. The ATC took planes to the West Indies and South America and left them there, where the Allied air forces were supposed to take possession of them. The U.S. crews came home by Pan American.

For the ATC to undertake long ferrying flights on a regular schedule, the command had to establish meteorological stations in the far North, as well as in the tropics, to report weather. These were more complete weather operations than anything the world had ever known. The ATC's scientific crews went in groups of eight or ten men to "dig in" before the freeze in the North and remain completely cut off until the following July!

In the Pacific, Wake Island and Guadacanal were lost to the Japanese almost immediately thereafter. The charge then was to try to supply as much materiel and plane strength as possible to the Allied forces in the Orient. The Philippines could only be reached by a round-about route from Australia or via South America, Africa, and India. The main portion of the Philippines was soon overrun. General Douglas MacArthur escaped from the Philippines and set up the Southwest Pacific Command in Australia. Singapore, the Dutch East Indies as well as Burma had fallen to the Japanese. Supplies were being flown to fronts which shortly collapsed. Airfields were built but had to be abandoned. The Air Transport Command managed to fly Army and Navy personnel half a jump ahead of the Japanese, who controlled more and more of the island area. The pilots told us of stripping their planes of armament in order to carry more supplies, dodging the enemy while clouds, darkness, and bad weather helped them evacuate troops, literally from bases under fire—packing seventy to eighty passengers in planes whose capacity was twenty-four!

The ATC started its China-Burma-India operation after Pearl Harbor and extended its service already begun on the Brazil-Central Africa-Cairo-India route. The command doubled or tripled its operations over the Himalayan "hump" to China, and FDR took the pains to announce to Congress that we were flying more lend-lease equipment to Chungking than had ever been moved over the Burma Road.

In the Pacific theater General MacArthur called upon the ATC for intertheater services, such as transporting transients, providing for their lodging and meals, taking them to and from billets, and handling their luggage. This service was essential in such an enormous military zone where there was no alternative. It was then that the ATC developed routes intended to remain in operation over an extended period of time. The ATC officers and men also became endeared in the hearts of many who had nowhere to turn when they needed a helping hand. These included, for example, a Red Cross girl with a broken arm who was trying to drag her footlocker across the platform at two o'clock in the morning or an enlisted man who had missed his plane through no fault of his own and was afraid he would be given a demerit of "absent without leave." It is no wonder that a *New Yorker* cartoon depicted two men in uniform sitting under a straw shed in the pouring rain on some distant Pacific island saying, as a plane, presumably with an ATC pilot, was about to land, "I hope that's Eleanor Roosevelt bringing me my laundry!"

One incident became famous in the ATC as its participants filtered back home. An Air Force bomber being ferried across Africa's Sahara Desert was forced down at an oasis where a small tribe of Arabs were camping. Crews carried chewing gum, cigarettes, candy, letters of introduction in French as well as in Arabic, and a few gold coins always came in handy as well. These goodies paved their way so successfully in that desert that when a transport plane arrived the next day to pick them up, the sheik came out leading his prettiest daughter as a gift to the pilot. The aviator was equipped with more diplomacy than one would expect. He escaped without insulting the sheik or his daughter.

Sam, his generals, many former airline and corporate officers—all high calibre "civilians in uniform"—literally ran this whole operation from their desks in seedy offices at Gravelly Point, Washington National Airport. They "produced what was militarily, a revolutionary solution" by eliminating tables of organization, groups, and squadrons and setting up "stations" with their own "manning table," a system adapted from civilian airline practice.[7] Sam was totally dedicated to ATC's mission and received a Distinguished Service Medal for his service.

My Role

During these years, 1942 to 1946, I was attempting to manage our home at 30th Street and to achieve good enough marks at law school to make the *Law Review*. In those days, when one was interviewed for a legal job, one was asked at the outset two questions, "Where did you stand in your class?" and "Were you on the *Law Review*?"

More and more I realized that Sam expected that I would become familiar with his work and with the people with whom he was associated. After C.R. Smith arrived in Washington, Sam called one afternoon to say I was to meet him at the Mayflower Hotel where C.R. was staying. Although I was at the office, I felt improperly dressed to visit this well-known captain of the civil aviation industry, Sam's request was a command performance.

I should not have worried. Sam was there when I arrived. C.R. turned out to be utterly informal, with a nice sense of humor. C.R.'s chief new officer for his Washington office, Carlene Roberts, arrived later. She was attractive, friendly, totally involved in the airline conversation, and only somewhat diverted by Gene Autry, who had his guitar, and brought a lighter note to our gathering, especially because C.R. liked Country and Western music. Carlene had caught C.R.'s eye when she single handedly managed American Airlines' headquarters move from Chicago to New York City with great efficiency and few complaints from the hundreds of employees involved.

As it developed during the visit, Carlene wanted very much to meet her Washington competition, Ann Archibald, the public relations and government liaison officer for Pan Am. Ann's reputation was that she could have bills favorable to Pan Am introduced in both houses of Congress, passed through the Senate and House committees, released from the joint conference committee, and signed by the president in forty-eight hours. Understandably Carlene was apprehensive of this kind of competitor. I offered to help Carlene, arranged a black-tie dinner, and invited Ann. Our gathering at 30th Street included Harold Harris, president of Panagra (Pan Am's Latin American subsidiary) Bill Harding, one of the heads of Smith Barney, but at present serving as an ATC officer; Carlene, and Ann—the honored guest. Ann arrived in a "frumpy" Helen Hokinson type outfit, and Carlene wore a gorgeous Madame Grès kind of draped white jersey. All the men were in uniform.

Carlene, under stress, talked a great deal—perhaps too much—and powdered her nose several times. When the party guests departed, Sam and I were convinced that she was not going to succeed. We were wrong! Carlene made an extremely good impression on the Congress, the top Washington bureaucrats, and the leaders of the civil aviation industry. In the end, she became vice president of American Airlines, the first American woman to achieve that position in that industry. Ann was never so promoted by Pan Am.

Lunch Breaks

These were very busy times for us. Sam was head-over-heels involved in his wartime duties. I had finished law school, was working for the Office of Price Administration (OPA), and was expecting our first child. While I was at OPA, I spent most of my lunch hours browsing in the art galleries. Most frequently I carried a simple lunch of cottage cheese from home and ate it in the restroom of the National Gallery of Art (then called the Mellon Gallery) in order to have time to look at the Italian primitives, the Flemish Memlings, and the French impressionists, especially Renoir's "Child with Watering Can," one of my favorites. One night while Sam and I were visiting Eugene de Savitsch, I discovered a gorgeous copy of this painting in Eugene's bathroom. I could not believe my eyes. Next morning, when Sam and I tried to purchase this copy from Eugene, he told us it had already been sold to the first secretary of the British embassy and taken away. I was saddened, but I reasoned that painting was not meant to be ours. During other lunchtime forays into the art world, I visited the Phillips Collection on Dupont Circle, where Duncan Phillips and his mother opened two rooms in their home in 1897. Duncan conceived his museum as a "joy-giving, life-enhancing influence" in the community. Over a fifty-year period, Duncan and his wife, Marjorie, collected more than 2,000 works of art, not only masterpieces but works of artists not fully recognized. One day, when I was about eight months pregnant, Duncan grabbed me and said, "Come, Phil, to the basement I have just hung a charming show of a Swiss mathematician named Paul Klee! You will love his things on paper." They were "winningly playful" and so cheap—only $35.00. Again I had no money except for Gilda's layette. In 1999, Yale University Press published a marvelous book of this distinguished collection entitled *The Eye of Duncan Phillips* by Erika D. Passantino and David W. Scott.

Off-Duty Hours

The circle of Sam's associates included talented people who had come to Washington from all over the world for the war effort. One was a jet-propelled friend from Brazil, Gilda Sampaio, whose husband, Paulo, was chairman of the Civil Aeronautics Board of Brazil. Bill Burden, Undersecretary of Commerce, and Sam had been in charge of Paulo's "year in the U.S.A." to study how we regulated air transportation. Paulo and Gilda had made an enormous hit in Washington. In fact, the Sampaios were infinitely more popular than the then Brazilian ambassador.

A memorable social event I attended, as a consequence of our friendship with the Sampaios, was a grand luncheon, hosted by Mary Truxton Beale. Her great pal was Mrs. Alice Roosevelt Longworth, who was in attendance, and the two grande dames presided at either end of the long table for sixteen. Alice, an *enfant terrible*, was known throughout Washington for her impish antics and irreverent wit. The *crème brulée* arrived. Mrs. Longworth took up her dessert spoon to crack the crust of this elegant dessert in a classic manner and shouted, "Mary, it worked!"

I was seated next to (later Sir) Isaiah Berlin, a leading scholar, when this culinary feat aroused enthusiastic compliments from all the guests. He turned to me and whispered, "Phil, I want to remember this moment." He was in his early thirties and was already famous in the rarefied atmosphere of English intellectual elite. He told me that he was working for the Foreign Office in Washington. As we exchanged a few light comments, he ventured to talk about his translation of one of Turgenev's novels, surprising me with the statement that Turgenev, like many of his nineteenth contemporaries, had "no vision of Utopian dreams." After my experience in the Soviet Union in the summer of 1938, his evaluation of one of the greatest Russian writers chased me back to the library in search of a better understanding of what Isaiah meant.[8]

Whenever we had a free evening, we would have cozy, small dinners at our home just to chat with our friends. On one evening in January 1943 we invited Sam's colleagues at ATC, including the Leylands—Bob and Helen—C.R. Smith, the Douglases, and John Russell of the British Embassy. The day before the dinner, I began to have labor pains and telephoned my neighbor Helen to ask her to call all my other guests and tell them not to come as I would be in the hospital. I was disappointed because I had fresh, thick and juicy-looking salmon steaks marinating in my refrigerator. I had dessert already made in a mold. She said, "Hang on, Phil, I'll come right over and get your food. I'll have the dinner party at my house and we'll toast the new arrival, if that has occurred." She did just that, and thereafter, we became fast friends.

Gilda did arrive on January 15, 1943. She was a beauty and I named her after Gilda Sampaio, who had brought so much charm and joy to our lives. Furthermore the "G" "G" alliteration appealed to me. We were soon sobered by the fact that Gilda Gates suffered from colic. As new parents, we were at our wit's end with sleepless nights caring for a baby who could not digest her food with comfort. Sam and I took turns with night duty. Sam was superb at giving bottles and changing diapers and even, during this period, giving enemas to relieve that tiny, eight-pound, little girl of gas pains. Awakened from sleep one night, I heard Sam's valiant efforts to "burp" her and quiet her tears. I rushed to the nursery and found he had put her on her stomach on a pillow on his lap and was rocking and patting her (I thought rather too vigorously) while singing "I've Been Working On the Railroad" and "The Eyes of Texas Are Upon You," the only two songs he knew.

"Darling," I said, "you have to be on duty at the Air Force at 8:00 a.m. tomorrow and I can sleep a little later. Please let me take over so that you can get some rest." He handed over his little bundle willingly, but with fire in his eyes he insisted, "Thanks, honey, but first thing in the morning I am going to call that goddam pediatrician and tell him if I did not know any more about law than he knows about babies, we'd be starving to death."

Sadly, he fired Dr. Benjamin Stein who had done the best he could and hired another Johns Hopkins's physician, a Dr. John Washington, who proceeded to prescribe exactly the same treatment as his predecessor!

Peggy and Bill Burden were very supportive and encouraged us on with our colicky baby. Bill sent me an extravagant orchid spray in celebration of her birth with a card asking, "What's your secret? We've been trying for twelve years to have a girl and all we've had are four boys—all blond, round-faced, who look exactly alike."

A Working Mother

One evening in April, the phone rang in the basement kitchen of our 30th Street home where I was washing and Sam was drying our dinner dishes. Sam answered, and I heard him say, "Why yes, Mr. Branch . . . why yes, indeed, Mr. Branch . . . yes she is, Mr. Branch. Well that would be wonderful, why yes, Mr. Branch, I think she'd love to." He hung up and grinned.

I inquired, "What was all that about?"

He replied, "Boy, do you have a good job!"

I cried out, "Who said I wanted a job? I haven't slept in three months with our new baby."

Ignoring my objections, Sam announced, "You're going to be the confidential assistant to my old boss, Mr. Harlee Branch, the chairman of the Civil Aeronautics Board. He asked whether or not you were a CPA as he wants to dissent on all of the "rate" cases. He needs someone who can reallocate all the data on the operating statements submitted by the airlines."

There was a shortage of men, otherwise I would not have been offered such a

wonderful job. When I cooled down and stopped objecting, I went to see Mr. Branch and accepted the job. I quickly found the office atmosphere pleasant, the job fascinating and instructive. Mr. Branch was an extremely intelligent man who enforced moral and intellectual standards for the quasi-judicial and quasi-legislative board, to which he had been appointed in 1938 and became chairman in 1940. He had made his way as a journalist, beginning as typesetter, composition foreman, and finally served thirty years as correspondent, reporter, and editor of the *Atlanta Constitution.* He entered politics, beginning as second assistant postmaster general under James A. Farley, FDR's postmaster general and former campaign manager. He also had raised money for FDR. He adored his wife "Buntsie." Each day, as soon as he arrived at his office, he would telephone her and inquire about her plans. If it were an especially chilly day, he would caution her to "bundle up."

At the CAB, one had to learn from scratch, as there was no public utility law course at George Washington's law school at that time. It was my duty to master the knotty government rate fixing procedures and decide whether to use the "prudent investment theory" as opposed to the "cost of reproduction" theory. These were simply accounting practices now in force in government agencies (which regulate and frequently subsidize business) to "fix" the rate at which a subsidy would be determined. In the CAB's deliberations this was the rate Uncle Sam would pay the airlines under government contract to carry the U.S. mail by air. What good fortune I had to work in that important development of our airlines and for such a wise and patient boss! I stayed on this job until a week before Sharon, our second daughter, was born on March 24, 1945.

At that time we were living at 213 Prince Street in Old Town Alexandria (called "Poor Man's Georgetown"). We had created a nursery in a corner of a large bathroom adjoining the third floor master bedroom, where we had arranged a crib, dressing table, and chest of drawers for the nursery area. had a lamp beside a rocking chair so I could read and rock my baby.

While I loved our new home, I had not anticipated how difficult it would be to manage a five-floor house after we had babies to care for. **If** I could have considered the pleasure of living in this eighteenth century home with its honey-colored floors, its ornate moldings, its aromatic smell, and robin's egg blue boiserie in the formal dining room; and, **if** I could have staffed it with several pairs of household help, but that was not possible on my salary even added with Sam's full-colonel pay.

Sam and I were so enamored of this old house that we took the time and effort to work for the enactment of city ordinances to protect such architectural treasures.[9] From the moment we had walked into the street-level door we felt welcoming vibrations that permeated the whole house, one of about one hundred of such homes in Old Town, and we wanted to preserve it for others to appreciate.

On the date of Roosevelt's death, April 12, 1945, I had just come home from the hospital after Sharon's birth and had been sleeping when Mamie, our nursemaid, came into the bedroom bringing me a cup of tea. Her eyes were streaming with tears. Through sobs she told me that FDR had died. She managed to say, "Mrs. Gates, he was the only one in government who ever cared about the colored people. He **was** the only one who saw to it that the dirt road in front of my house got paved."

It is almost impossible to describe the anguish which was shared by a multitude of Americans when FDR died on April 12, 1945. Not just Mamie. All the way from Warm Springs, Georgia, to Washington, D.C., the railroad tracks were lined with weeping people waiting for the train carrying his coffin. These were not the tycoons of industries, who indeed were not sobbing. These were the everyday workman, stenographer, and textile worker who knew they had lost a great leader and a great friend. Grown men in supermarkets and assembly lines openly wept. We had all known, somehow, that he was a very ill man. We saw his face so gray and heard

President Roosevelt dedicating National Airport in Washington, D.C. Sam and Phil are seated in the third row from the front.

his apologies for sitting down while he delivered his report on the Yalta conference. We simply did not want to believe that FDR would not see the war to its logical conclusion.

Even Sam, a rock ribbed Republican, could not stop a tear running down his cheek when he left for the European Theater of Operation to plan how to fly our troops from Europe to Japan to finish the war. It was a period of national grief. Assembly lines apparently shut down for 15 minutes while grown men sobbed. They knew who had been their friend, who had fought their union battles against thugs hired to break their steel strikes. FDR was a man to the manor born, an aristocrat who had insight to "feel their pain." As a very young wife and mother, I will never forget that day.

On V-E Day, May 8, 1945, Sam was in London and Paris and wrote two letters to his babies, Gilda and Sharon, telling them about the celebrations going wild in these cities. He said London secretaries were so excited that they stripped off their clothes and splashed in the fountain on Trafalgar Square. In Paris, he reported, the girls were hugging and kissing every American serviceman on the Champs Élysées. On one occasion, during the celebrations on May 8, he was ensconced in Herman Goering's suite at the Ritz Hotel in Paris, commandeered by the U.S. Air Force for billeting its officers. From the balcony of the Ritz, he could enjoy the excitement below on the Place Vendome, as the U.S. soldiers marched through the city.

All this was going on in Sam's life, while Sharon and I were locked in each other's embrace, rocking away. I imagined Sam living it up in the center of all the celebrations in Europe at the war's end. I spent many hours with the wee baby, singing lullabies or reading Bob Hope's account of entertaining the troops overseas entitled *I Never Left Home*, and administering sweetened water so that the baby would be sleeping through the night when her Daddy came home.

Harry Truman became president after Roosevelt's death and made the decision to drop the atomic bomb in August of that year, an event that marked the end of the war. By the time of Japan's unconditional surrender, Sam was home and we celebrated V-J Day, August 15, 1945, with our Alexandria friends.

Soon after the Japanese surrender, Sam and I moved back to Georgetown. This time we bought a house at 3410 P Street, N.W., and restored it to our complete satisfaction. This is where Sam and I proposed to live for the rest of our lives.

Kathe, our third baby, was born on October 18, 1947, while Sam was attending a general meeting of the International Air Transport Association (IATA) in Petropolis, Brazil. I, who had often accompanied him and Henry Friendly to these meetings, was obviously in no condition to go this time. Cleona, my twenty year old sister, drove me to the hospital during the afternoon. On the way I attempted to ignore the labor pains by admiring the cherry blossoms in full bloom around the Jefferson Memorial. When Kathe peeked her little head into the world, after fourteen hours of labor, she weighed only a little more than four pounds. As soon as possible I called Sam in Rio, who never once said he was disappointed not to have a son. He professed his undying love and did not even comment on her "preemie" weight.

When I was ready to go home, the doctor gave me instructions on the care and feeding of our tiny baby. Something, he said, had clogged the placenta during the eighth month, and her nourishment had been impaired. He instructed me to sleep in the room with the newborn and feed her on demand, every two or three hours. To adjust her to a more comfortable schedule seemed like an endless ordeal. Needless to say, she captured our love and responded to our close watch over her. Even as a tiny infant, she began to show signs of a dazzling personality.

Meanwhile, Sam had been complaining of dizziness. He had been to the Leahy Clinic at Massachusetts General Hospital in Boston and, after extensive tests was told, "Nothing wrong with you, Mr. Gates, that a month lolling about a beach will not cure." He had been under enormous stress during the five years of the war and hadn't had a day off for all of that time. Sam told his Boston doctor that was clearly impossible as he and his wife had just had a baby who had to be fed every two or three hours. He refused to go without me and I couldn't leave Kathe. Our problem was solved when Mother unselfishly came up from Florida to care for our baby and the two little girls, allowing me to go to Varadero Beach, Cuba, with Sam. Mother was a highly qualified registered nurse, and I could go away and not worry too much.

The doctor's prescription was exactly right. Cuba was a tonic for Sam, and soon he was feeling his old self. I had our little family settled again, and was eager to try my hand at practicing law. It was then that my old friend Joe Rauh, who had clerked for Justices Cardozo and Frankfurter, offered me an opportunity. He had served under General MacArthur in the Pacific, had left the army as a lieutenant colonel, and had entered private law practice. He was an advocate of the Americans for Democratic Action (ADA), a liberal organization that devoted itself to opposing Communism, and he asked me to research the statutory history and legislative intent of the Taft-Hartley Act, passed over President Truman's veto in June 1947. Joe was interested in the act as it applied to labor union funds being used for political purposes. He supported labor's political activity, but was firm in his resolve to keep ADA free of Communist infiltration and influence. So far as I know, he succeeded.

When I was working for him I saw him scrupulously avoid all overtures made by various subversive groups. He advised many other organizations, including the National Association for the Advancement of Colored People and the exclusively black Brotherhood of Sleeping Car Porters to do the same. The Brothers were led by Philip Randolph whom Joe always addressed as Mr. Randolph. Joe was often quoted as stating, "Mr. Randolph is the most dignified gentleman I have ever met, period!"

Joe never failed to stand up against Joseph McCarthy's attacks on civil rights, and he cleared Lillian Hellman and Arthur Miller of

McCarthy's wild charges against them in the Federal Appellate Court. Joe once commented to me, "I am proud of our laws and what our generation has done to bring equality in law. The next generation has to bring equality in fact."

Our coterie of friends gave us much pleasure during our Washington years. Marianne Bell, my roommate on I Street, married shortly after we did, to the distinguished and handsome Bob McConnaughey. He was an attorney in the Solicitor General's office and frequently argued cases before the Supreme Court resplendent in his morning coat and striped trousers—the uniform for government attorneys appearing before the court.

Bob Bell, Marianne's handsome brother, married Mary Katherine Morris, one of the two other women in my law school class. Mary K. was a Stanford graduate and former president of Woman's Student Government at Stanford. She, like me, was trying to break into the legal world against mountains of odds. Mother flew up from Florida with fresh orange blossoms packed in wet Spanish Moss for the wedding veil headpiece Mary K. was to wear for the ceremony at St. John's Church on Lafayette Square. All three of us chose the same silver pattern; Marlborough of Reed and Barton. In the future, if we needed to borrow from one another, the silver would match! It was a nice idea but we never took advantage of it.

Immediately after the marriage, Marianne gave Mary K. and me some advice: "Don't get pregnant the first year, girls, its just not very good form." What did she do? She bore her first born exactly ten months from her wedding date! She explained that she and Bob were afraid, because he had been crippled after a ski accident, that they might not be able to have children at all. Those fears proved groundless. They raised four splendid, handsome sons who have achieved a great deal. I saw her and her second husband (Bob died 20 plus years ago) often until her death. She remained very beautiful and was my comforting and caring friend for over fifty years. After Bob's death, Marianne accepted a seat on the Board of Immigration and Naturalization Appeals at the Justice Department. It was only then that she could devote the necessary time for a board position. She had, for over twenty years, used all her vacation and sick leave to care for her husband and four boys when they were ill.

Goodbye to Washington and Old Friends

For Sam, post-war plans meant that he resigned from the Air Force reserve, despite the insistence of General Laurie Norstad that he remain

From left, Gilda, Kathe, Phil, and Sharon Gates.

in the service. He then formed his own law firm composed of two of his colleagues at ATC—Jim Douglas and Malcolm MacIntyre—and Bob Proctor, a Boston lawyer friend. Initially Douglas, Proctor, MacIntyre and Gates had one large client—American Airlines. Sam also had a commitment, made during the war, to represent the Scandinavian Airlines System as soon as he was out of uniform. Organizational plans for the creation of SAS had been designed in our living room in 1943.

Imagine my disappointment, at this moment in my life, when Sam announced that he would have to move his burgeoning law practice to New York. I had just installed made-to-order draperies in the living room, and, our baby, Kathe, was fifteen months old and becoming a very comfortable and congenial member of our little family, leaving me more time volunteer for legal aid practice.

But move we did. Sam and I were headed for a frightening foreign land in which we knew only about five couples. We had never lived anywhere in the Northeast. Sam's two years in graduate school at Harvard pursuing his Ph.D. did not really count. We knew the Adolf Berles, the

William Burdens (our next door neighbors in Washington during the war), the William Hardings, also Georgetown neighbors, the George Brownells, and the Mord Bogies, he of the Schroeder Rockefeller Bank. That was all!

What Sam and his partner, Malcolm MacIntyre, planned to do was join their business, including the lucrative American Airlines account, with a large established New York firm. Their choices were Sullivan and Cromwell, where Mac had been an associate, and Debevoise, Plimpton, and MacLean. Because of Sam's and Mac's age, experience, and enormous law business, they had to be senior partners in whatever firm hired them. Most firms insisted (at least then) that partners go through eight years of training in legal representation and ethical standards in order to attain partnership. Sam was hesitant about joining Sullivan and Cromwell. He said they had twenty-four partners, and he'd never get to know that many! (Ironically, within three decades Sam's firm, then called Debevoise, Plimpton, Lyons, and Gates, had more than eighty partners!) As for Sullivan and Cromwell, three of the partners—Allen and John Foster Dulles and Arthur Dean—very much wanted Sam and Mac to join them but there was resistance from two other partners. The Debevoise, Plimpton, and MacLean offer, therefore, won out to Sam's delight and Mac's disappointment.

I was devastated to leave our comfortable life in Washington. How could New York City, so huge and so impersonal ever compare? How can our lives ever be so full again? I was in for a wonderful surprise.

Notes

1. Heywood Broun, a well-known newsman in New York City, participated in the creation of the guild and was its first president. Journalism awards are still made in his name.

2. Teapot Dome is a region near Casper, Wyoming, which was set aside as an naval oil reserve in 1915. A scandal erupted in 1922 during the Harding administration when Secretary of the Interior Albert Fall leased this oil reserve to Harry F. Sinclair and another, Elk Hills, to Edward L. Doheny. Secrecy surrounding the leases and the sudden wealth of Fall caused a Senate investigation into the matter. It was discovered that Sinclair had befriended Fall and that Doheny had "loaned" Fall $100,000 without security or interest. Both Fall and the Secretary of the Navy Edwin Denby

resigned and in 1927 the Supreme Court ordered that the reserves be returned to the government.

3. Unfortunately Tim Sichel became severely depressed in the 1960s and committed suicide.

4. When my own husband died unexpectedly, I decided to write a book that would guide wives when they experienced the same loss as I had. It is entitled, *Suddenly Alone: A Woman's Guide to Widowhood.* New York: Harper & Row, 1990. (paper edition 1991, Harper Perennial.)

5. Quentin Reynolds. *By Quentin Reynolds.* New York: McGraw Hill Co., Inc. 1963. For an historical account of this whole period, see Oliver La Farge. *The Eagle and the Egg.* Boston: Houghton Mifflin Company, 1949.

6. Douglas, MacIntyre, and Gates all ended the war as full colonels. See LaFarge's history of the Air Transport Command, 256.

7. Ibid.

8. Isaiah Berlin, 88, died in Oxford on November 6, 1997. He has been remembered by his associates, students, and friends in the following articles: "Isaiah Berlin, Philosopher and Historian of Ideas" by Marilyn Berger in *The New York Times*, November 7, 1997, p. 1; "On Isaiah Berlin (1909-1997)" a series of essays by Michael Ignatieff, Stuart Hampshire, Alfred Brendel, and Aileen Kelly in *The New York Review*, December 18, 1997, 10-12; "Postcript" by David Remnick in the *New Yorker*, November 17, 1997, 73: 35 (1997): 39; and *Foreign Affairs*, March/April 1998, 77: 2.

9. In our effort to protect Alexandria's historic homes, we cooperated with Henry and Trudye Fowler. Henry was Secretary of the Treasury in the Kennedy-Johnson administration.

Chapter Eleven

New York: Our New Home

Forward, forward let us range,
let the great world spin for ever
down the ringing grooves of change.
— Alfred, *Lord Tennyson 1809-1892*

As we pulled three little children off the train at Penn Station with masses of luggage, we saw a patch in New York's quilt—the diverse elements of humanity which was to be our town. Men and women of all races, colors, and creeds were rushing, elbowing strangers, pummeling others with their bags unmindful of anything but "getting there." I panicked. Would we ever feel at home in this huge high-powered city of concrete and glass after living in a more homogeneous, quaint, civilized Georgetown, in Washington, D.C.? These people's hearts seemed to be as hard as the materials their buildings were made of. Sam tried to comfort me by saying, "Remember, I am not joining any 'White Shoe' Wall Street law firm. I am joining an absolutely wonderful group of brilliant partners."

Two taxis were necessary to transport us to our furnished, rented apartment—we were on our way with our Gang of Five. It was the fall of 1948.

During our first year, we rented a large ten-room flat at 860 Park, directly across the street from a big, noisy hospital—Lenox Hill. We felt unsettled with someone else's furniture and NOISE. Quiet little P Street had its trolley cars; but they were silent compared to the screeching taxi brakes and the ear-splitting sirens of the ambulances coming and going from the emergency room across the way.

After a year of enduring the cacophony of sounds, we moved to an eleven-room rent-controlled apartment at Park Avenue and 83rd Street, where we stayed until after our then first grader was married. Initially there was no television, as we were determined to have our little girls develop good reading habits. We were glued to the radio—and cheated occasionally by watching the McCarthy hearings on neighbors' television sets—the O.J. Simpson trial of that time.

The Hiss-Chambers Case

As we were making final preparations to leave Washington, the House Committee on Un-American Activities (HUAC) opened hearings on communist infiltration of the U.S. government. The first witness was Elizabeth Bentley, a former Communist undercover agent, whose disclosures initiated the Hiss-Chambers case. Alger Hiss and his wife Priscilla, as well as his brother and sister-in-law, Donald and Katherine Hiss, had been our Georgetown neighbors when Sam and I were first married, and again in 1945 at the end of the war. Donald Hiss was a partner in Washington's most prestigious law firm—Covington, Rublee, Burling, Acheson, and Shorb. Alger served in the State Department until 1947 when he moved to New York as president of the Carnegie Endowment for International Peace.

On a hot summer evening in 1948 we were on our way to dinner in the air-conditioned dining room of the Metropolitan Club in Washington when we bumped into Alger in the club's elevator. Sam greeted Alger with the words, "Alger, old man, I do not know any of the details of the HUAC hearings. I only know you are being accused of all manner of things by this guy Whittaker Chambers. I do hope it all comes out all right for you."[1]

Hiss replied, "Well, Sammy, you've heard of this," and he began to draw a square design around his head several times. "Well, that is my situation, and I am going up to the steam room and try to forget the whole thing."

"What was that all about," I asked Sam. He just said, "Oh honey, Alger means he's being framed—he was drawing a frame around his head and maybe he is right."

The next time I saw the Hisses was in the New York Federal Court House during the Hiss-Chambers trial. Since I was not working then, I was eager to see how Ed MacLean, one of Sam's partners in the Debevoise law firm, would conduct Hiss's defense. In the noon break, Priscilla and

Alger invited me for lunch. I regretted and later thought, "What in the world would I have said to them?" Small talk would have been disingenuous and embarrassing. Any conversation would have involved the merits of their defense and plunge me into a discussion which I should not enter.

Sam and I had read the transcripts of the pretrial depositions every night. Even though Sam was not a part of the defense, Ed shared the documents with him. Our reaction was, "How can a jury believe Whittaker Chambers, an acknowledged perjurer, pimp, homosexual, among other damning characteristics, against Alger, clerk of Justice Oliver Wendell Holmes, valuable advisor to President Roosevelt at Yalta, holder of many top level diplomatic jobs in U.S. foreign affairs? Secretary of State Dean Acheson, Alger's last boss, endeared himself to many of us during the trial by stating, "I do not intend to turn my back on Alger Hiss."[2] In January 1950 Alger was convicted of perjury and went to jail, after two trials and one hung jury.[3]

Alger was disbarred and when released from prison sold stationery door-to-door. I remember Sam saying that he had been in the law firm's office seeking help to restore his driver's license. I saw him at matinee performances of the New York Philharmonic in Helen and Ben Buttenweiser's seats. Helen was a prominent civil rights lawyer and Ben a successful Wall Street financier. The Buttenweisers invited the Hisses to stay in their home during one of the trials, and they also gave financial support to Alger for his legal bills. Lloyd Stryker represented Alger in the last trial and lost it. Having witnessed Stryker in action, I always felt that he did not give that case his best efforts.

On November 15, 1996, Alger Hiss died at age 92. One letter printed the next day to the editor of *The New York Times* said he "did a tremendous disservice to this nation. Death does not change that."

A second—this a paid note—attested, "He would not, could not, did not ever lie, yet he became the most lied-about figure in history. Ruined in fortune and reputation in THE American nightmare he lived, endured, and fought gallantly for truth, and, in these last weeks for life itself. He was defeated only by death." (Signed by Kennett Love, someone obviously with him during his last year.)

A third on the same day states, "Many labeled him a spy and dismissed his defenders as foolish believers. If thinking him innocent is an act of belief, so, too, is the vote for guilt."

A front-page obituary in *The New York Times* on November 16 described the question of his guilt or innocence as "one of the great riddles of the Cold War . . . . At Mr. Hiss's death, nearly 50 years after he was first publicly accused, followers of the case remained bitterly split over whether he was guilty, innocent, or something in between."

Evidence against Hiss consisted of typed government documents found in a pumpkin, and Chambers's personal knowledge of the two Hisses, a fact which could easily have been made available to him because the FBI had tapped Hiss's telephone for years. Some of the believers in his innocence do not trust the work of Richard Nixon and J. Edgar Hoover in connection with his prosecution. The former could have manipulated evidence for political advantage, and the latter's secret files on the case were hidden in the basement of his house and destroyed when he died.

I did not attend the memorial service at St. George's Episcopal Church downtown, but hundreds did, remembering Alger as a man of generosity and wisdom as well as lover of poetry, books, and friendship. John Lowenthal, a retired law professor who had known Hiss for 67 years was reported as saying, "For an important part of Alger's life, there is no satisfactory closure, since what he had hoped for in his lifetime was vindication from his own government."

Mr. Lowenthal added that Alger had introduced him to poetry and to Shakespeare's sonnets as well as much of English literature. When his eyesight failed, he asked to be read a book on Alexander the Great and rejected *The Arabian Nights* in favor of *The Decline and Fall of the Roman Empire*.

Many of us, his contemporaries and neighbors knew him as a rising foreign policy star, a founder of the United Nations, president of the Carnegie Endowment. Several dozen books, including one called *Perjury* by historian Allen Weinstein, a documentary film about the case, a TV miniseries, a play, and a novel based on the affair have all been released. He outlived most of those involved, but a few of us still have memories of being on the fringes of those days. Recently it has come to light that Adolph Berle had been given papers indicating that both Alger and his brother, as well as Jack Service, handed over secret government papers to the USSR. It goes on and on!

The McCarthy Witch Hunts

The Hiss-Chambers case, in effect, was the forerunner of McCarthy's witch hunts. It was a linchpin in what was termed a "communist conspiracy" that had invaded and taken over the government in the Roosevelt and Truman administrations.[4]

The Senate hearings of the "McCarthy Subcommittee"[5]—as everybody called it—spread over our nation like a nuclear mushroom cloud. In mid-1953 the junior senator from Wisconsin, Joseph R. McCarthy, received authorization to conduct congressional hearings on communism and subversive activities in his capacity as chairman of the Permanent Subcommittee on Investigation of the Senate's Committee on Government Operations. Before the summer was over he launched his campaign with a bang in what was called the Army-McCarthy hearings. On a less formal basis he had already started his witch hunt in the State Department, soon after the Hiss conviction. In the early 1950s he had attended the HUAC hearings and began assembling his lists of persons in the State Department whom he tagged as communist tools.[6]

One of the first military victims of the McCarthy Subcommittee was Secretary of the Army Robert T. Stevens, whom the senator accused of subversive activity and disloyalty. In weeks of heated discussions, Joseph Nye Welch, a brilliant attorney with long experience at Boston's superior trial bar, represented Stevens. At one point in the procedures, Welch said, "Senator, you have almost succeeded in doing what the British army under General Cornwallis failed to do—bring down the United States Army. You are trying, but you will not succeed."

The British had just survived an agonizing affair involving espionage. Two highly placed foreign service officers, Guy Burgess and Donald Maclean, found guilty of selling defense secrets to the Russians, had fled to Moscow in 1951. After the British learned of the extent of the communist infiltration of their country, their paranoia spilled quite naturally to our shores. The Cold War dominated U.S. foreign policy and was at its coldest during the 1950s, or so it seemed to those of us who were living it.

J. Edgar Hoover, whom Sam and I often saw dining with his "friend" at Harvey's Restaurant in Washington, was in his glory. Many observers commented that the more McCarthy shouted about the communist conspiracy, the more money Congress gave Hoover's Federal Bureau of Investigation (FBI). He kept reminding us that a third of the world's population was communist. Hoover had files on everybody who was anybody, and a lot of nobodies like me. Too many of us were scared to death of him. Most Americans had done nothing illegal, immoral, or unpatriotic, but his distortions could make it seem so, and we could lose our jobs. His policies caused many careers to end in ruins.

I became more alarmed each day. McCarthy boasted that he had a list of hundreds of subversives in and out of government. He would wave around his head papers purporting to be the "list." No one ever saw the list. It was a sham, another technique to frighten those who had **at any time** been sympathetic to any form of socialism. Many people had been attracted to socialist causes. Most university students were well aware that 90 percent of the wealth of our country was in the hands of one percent of the population, and that kind of statistic offends the young as well as most fair-minded citizens. The rest of us knew that our system of distribution of goods and services had still not been rectified by the New Deal. So at the time, socialism had its adherents.

McCarthy made an extensive tour of the United States delivering anti-communist oratory, at one time citing eighty-one "card carrying Communists" who were employed by the State Department. He went so far as to superimpose a photograph of Senator Millard E. Tydings of Maryland on a photograph with Earl Browder, head of the U.S. Communist Party, to prove Tydings was "conniving" with Browder. His duplicity was uncovered and his tactic failed. Within days the Senate appointed Tydings chairman of a special subcommittee of the Foreign Affairs Committee and empowered him to investigate McCarthy's allegations.

McCarthy's abusive behavior during the Tydings hearings stirred harsh responses throughout the world. Sam and I spent hours agonizing with our friends, Herbert and Doris Wechsler, over McCarthy's treatment of James, known as Jimmy, Wechsler. Herbert, Jimmy's brother, was the famous Constitutional Law Professor at Columbia Law School. Jimmy had been leader of the Open Road tour the year before I took it, and was editorial page editor of the *New York Post* under its publisher, Dorothy Schiff. He was one of five well-known anti-communist friends and political commentators—including Wilson Wyatt, Arthur Schlesinger, Jr., Bernard DeVoto, and Archibald MacLeish—whom Joe described as being "soft on the Reds." McCarthy paid to broadcast this accusation from his podium in Chicago over fifty-five television stations and five hundred fifty radio stations, in order to guarantee that it reached the widest of audiences during Adlai Stevenson's campaign for the presidency. McCarthy, of course, was convinced that Stevenson would be "soft on communism." After that broadcast, Jimmy was summoned twice by McCarthy and "subjected to blistering excoriations."[7]

We knew that when Jimmy tried to obtain a copy of his testimony in the McCarthy records, he was told that he could have it only if he furnished the committee with the names of former Young Communist Leaguers (YCL). Jimmy did not deny having been, in his impressionable youth, a YCL member. Under oath before the McCarthy Subcommittee, he swore that the date of his resignation from that body was 1937. He also said that he withdrew from *PM*, a Chicago-based publication, where he had played a major role in fighting communists, because of its imminent domination by party supporters.[8]

At one point in the Tydings hearings McCarthy leapt to his feet, demanding the names of any former YCL members who worked for the *Post*. Jimmy, believing it was a citizen's responsibility to testify before a Senate committee, named Murray Kempton, Bob Bendiner, Jack Casey, and even Joe Lash, saying that all of them would be happy to tell the committee why they had left the Communist Party. In his book *Age of Suspicion*, Jimmy justified his testimony by saying, "I had resolved much earlier that silence was suicidal in dealing with McCarthy . . . . To put it simply, I did not believe my answers would tend to incriminate or degrade me, but I was quite certain that silence would."[9]

Toward the end of the interrogation McCarthy asked Jimmy if he felt intimidated. He replied, "Of course I have been abused. The suggestion that my break with communism was not authentic is the greatest affront you could recite anywhere. I have fought the battle a long time, Senator, and I have taken plenty of beatings from communists in the course of that fight." Once the session was over, Jimmy vowed he would make a transcript of the McCarthy Subcommittee public and call it to the attention of the American Society of Newspaper Editors.[10]

Finally, Wechsler wired McCarthy that he would submit his complete list "because I do not propose to let you distort or obscure the clearcut issue of Freedom of the Press involved in this proceeding . . . . He added, "I will ask your Committee at that time to decide whether the inclusion of such a list in the record is proper or desirable."[11]

Night after night, Sam and I attended New York City dinner parties that hummed with discussion of one of the most dreadful things McCarthy did. He attacked General George Marshall, who had served as Roosevelt's Army Chief of Staff and Truman's Secretary of Defense and Secretary of

State. On June 14, 1953, McCarthy packed the Senate galleries with any-one who would come to hear his denunciation of Marshall. In a stum-bling, emotionless, three-hour presentation, McCarthy droned on until the Senate chamber was almost empty. At this point, he announced he would insert the remainder of his text in the *Congressional Record.* Im-mediately thereafter William Benton, Senator from Connecticut, an-nounced that Joe should resign.

Sam, who had served under Marshall during the war, did not admire him for refusing to comment on McCarthy's three-hour performance. It was impossible for Sam to imagine that McCarthy would have the effron-tery to condemn at such length this revered, distinguished soldier and diplomat as "a man steeped in falsehood who has recourse to lie when-ever it suits his convenience."[12]

President Dwight Eisenhower felt that he could not oppose the junior Senator's outrages against Marshall. His cautious silence diminished his standing in the eyes of many of his supporters. Yet, all but the bravest congressmen and bureaucrats were afraid to defy this maniac for three more years. Only when the journalists began to say "Joe must go" did enough pressure rise against him, and he succumbed.[13]

Sam was disgusted with McCarthy as well as with Vice President Richard Nixon, who on several occasions had shown support for the subcommittee's investigations, and later led the White House delegation at McCarthy's requiem mass at St. Matthew's Cathedral on the morning of May 6, 1957.[14]

The China Hands

McCarthy had shattered the careers of many of the State Department's Foreign Service officers. Two of the most highly publicized cases were of John Stewart Service and John Paton Davies. They were both missionar-ies' sons and knew and loved China. They were charged with giving se-cret documents to the communists and arrested. Both were dismissed but in time were cleared of the charges and transferred to posts outside of the Asian field.[15] Davies, who had been a first secretary in Moscow, went to Lima. Service, first assigned to German language training, ended his dip-lomatic career in Liverpool.

Our own friend Benjamin Shute, partner at the Cravath firm who had served John J. "Jack" McCloy when he was High Commissioner in Ger-many after the World War II peace was signed, took on the cause of Service and Davies. He applied for restitution of their pension and other personnel privileges due them for their long service to their country, and he succeeded. Yet by 1957, when the case came before the Supreme Court, their careers were in shambles, and they had to seek other employment to make ends meet.

The next thing I heard about Jack Service was that he had accepted the challenge of his good friend Harrison Salisbury, the Pulitzer Prize winning historian, to accompany him and his wife, Charlotte, on a re-enactment of Mao's 1934 Long March. According to Charlotte Salisbury, Service's wife, Caroline, said "You two old men in your seventies are going to die doing that. More than half of Mao's disciples died, and they were younger and hardier than you two. I am not going on such a suicide mission."

Charlotte Salisbury did go and wrote her own riveting account of the trip. She said she simply decided, "Well, we've lived all over the world and survived a lot of hardships. If Harrison goes, I'm going to go with him, and if he dies there, well, so will I."[16]

Charles E. "Chip" Bohlen was an able and distinguished Foreign Service officer. During his confirmation procedure, he said he realized he was "becoming a central figure in McCarthy's political drama against the Foreign Service."[17] He had served with distinction as minister in the U.S. Embassy in Paris but was just barely cleared when Secretary of State John Foster Dulles named him ambassador to Moscow in 1953. McCarthy and his "hitman" Scott McLeod, who was then Assistant Secretary of State for Security Affairs, had not been consulted before Bohlen's appointment was sent to the Senate Foreign Relations Committee for confirmation. McLeod stalled in his support, citing what he called "derogatory information" in the FBI files. Dulles, however, prevailed and Bohlen was confirmed by a 74 to 13 vote.[18]

The McCarthy Era Touches Many More

It's still difficult to understand why McCarthy put so much time and effort in discrediting small bureaucrats, such as I was at the time. It boggles my mind to think of the difficulty I had getting FBI clearance for my job at the Justice Department just after Gilda's birth. Wendell Berge, chief of the Criminal Division, had offered me a job as an entering salaried lawyer, with a P-1 classification at $2,000 a year. The job entailed a study on the status of Civil Rights Law in the forty-eight states. My problem of

FBI clearance lay in an idiotic mistake the investigator made in failing to put the "tail" on the Q of my address on my application for the job. The investigator, therefore, went to 2700 O Street. The residents there were acquaintances of mine, Larry Knapp, whom I had once dated, and his Belgian countess bride. When the investigator asked Larry if he knew a "Miss Phil Asher," he, in a flip response said "Oh yes, Phil lived here with me for a while, but she left me." All bald-faced lies, but taken quite seriously by the investigator, who assumed that I was an immoral woman, and too untrustworthy to be an employee at Justice. The lower third of our law school class went to work for the FBI, so I did not have a very high regard for his intelligence.

The other reason the FBI challenged my character was my membership in The Bookshop on Lafayette Square. During my first year in Law School, Suzi and I found the shop to be attractive with a great supply of paperback books, on which we received a 30 percent discount with our membership fee. The shop also had a program of fascinating lecturers and offered a pleasant, safe place for two single girls to go and meet others. On one occasion, the lecturer had just returned from observing the Spanish Civil War battlegrounds. As young liberals, we welcomed the opportunity after the lecture to sign a petition to the State Department urging that it lift the arms embargo against the Nationalists. The latter were putting up a valiant fight against Franco's troops, who were amply supplied by Hitler and Mussolini with guns, tanks, and planes. When the FBI saw my name on that petition, they put me down as a security risk, and that almost cost me a job.

During those first years in New York City, I had nightmares that the FBI would raid our apartment and pronounce me a communist. Finally one night I arose from bed at 2 a.m. and threw out every Russia connected book and pamphlet I owned, many bought in the USSR during the 1938 summer. I could not risk, or so I thought at the time, being responsible for owning anything that might put Sam in an embarrassing position with his new law firm, or endanger his future. He laughed at me the next morning, but my fear was real and one echoed by many, many others.

McCarthy's witch hunt extended to Hollywood and Broadway, where actors and writers, who were targets of the McCarthy's committee, were blacklisted. While we knew none of them personally, my friend Tom Ervin, who was general counsel and executive vice president of NBC, was very much involved, and he related to me how deep was his agony when he had to refuse to renew the contracts of producers, writers, authors, and actors involved in NBC programs. Advertisers would cancel their commitments if a network hired a blacklisted talent. Those who refused to cooperate with the authorities starved.

The source for untold accusations was *Red Channels,* a paperback published anonymously under the sponsorship of a House committee chaired by Martin Dies, Congressman from Texas. Its mimeographed listings led to hearings on scores of well-known persons in the entertainment industry, on stage and screen.

Anyone seeking employment who was on the list of this ready- reference manual could "turn himself in," so to speak, by telling on "his fellow workers." Because I was a member of the bookshop, my name appeared in the FBI files, and undoubtedly in *Red Channels.*

I had no idea that the bookshop had any connection with the communists.[19]

The most famous New Yorker whose broadcast license was threatened was John Henry Faulk, a popular TV personality. One of Louis Nizer's finest hours (he never wrote about cases he had **lost**) was his representation of Faulk. He brought a libel suit against a publication named *AWARE* which accused Faulk of subversion. Mr. Nizer's efforts on his behalf spanned a five or six-year period, resulting in a multi-million dollar award and complete vindication of Faulk.

Even those outside the orbit of the activity of the House Unamerican Affairs Committee (HUAC) lived through the chilling effects of the blacklisting of Larry Adler, the virtuoso of the classical harmonica, and Jerome Robbins, the famous choreographer. Pleading the Fifth Amendment did not save Lillian Hellman, still receiving accolades for her plays, *The Little Foxes, Toys in the Attic,* and many more. She refused to inform on her friends.

For many generations, Charlie Chaplin is a movie legend. Audiences proclaimed him as a genius from his first film appearance in 1914, even before I was born. Mother took me to see *City Lights* and *Modern Times,* for which he had composed the music. One of his last films was *The Great Dictator,* ridiculing the tyranny of Adolf Hitler. But being lauded by the press did not save him. The FBI brought a series of smear campaigns, saying he was a communist. In addition, it was said that Hoover's group helped a woman named Barry bring a paternity suit against Chaplin, although blood tests proved he could not have been the father of her child. California courts refused to accept the blood test evidence and found him guilty.

In 1952 the Attorney General, prodded by Hoover, would not allow Chaplin, who had moved out of the United States years before, a visa for entry. The only time he came was in 1972 to accept a special American Academy Award. He did produce *A King in New York* satirizing McCarthy's malicious campaign. As Laurence Olivier has said, "He was the greatest actor of our time." He died in Switzerland in 1977, an international celebrity victimized by Joe McCarthy.

Roy Cohn, McCarthy's chief counsel, and G. David Schine, his co-counsel, continued their harrassment of suspects, making a sweep of American libraries abroad and threatening, in the name of McCarthy, to cut funds to librarians unless they immediately got rid of a host of important American novelists. Incredibly those authors included John Steinbeck and Ernest Hemingway; Sherwood Anderson, Pulitzer Prize winning playwright, and Edmund Wilson and James Beard, noted historians. The thought of banning these authors left the embassies abroad quaking in their boots. Having met David Schine's mother at a Girl Scout benefit, I could not imagine her producing an ogre for a son, and I concluded that Schine had become an unwitting ally of Cohn's and had difficulty extricating himself.

Dr. Albert Einstein, one of our greatest scientists, was among the first to speak out against McCarthyism. He recommended that everyone should refuse to testify, as the witch hunt was an affront to all intellectuals as well as society at large. Einstein called upon those accused of un-American activities to risk jail and unemployment, in fact, personal well-being, in the interest of the cultural and moral interests of the nation.

Peter Lewis reported in the *Daily Mail,* "McCarthy is a con-man who is living the part of the hard-drinking, hard-swearing, poker-playing small town boy who belched and spoke his mind." Indeed, that apt description fitted. He spoke his mind, twisted as it turned out to be.

Arthur Miller, after the 1953 premiere of his success, *The Crucible, which dealt* with the witch hunts during Colonial times in Salem, Massachusetts, made a memorable statement: "I have lived through these terrible accusations. The thing to remember is that it has not gone away forever."

Other Events

Just like today, world shaking events seemed to rain down on us in New York, crowding the radio and newspapers. By the time McCarthy was castigating Robert Oppenheimer, the nuclear scientist, for being a security risk because of his communist affiliations, his antics had become a national obsession. When Edward R. Murrow defended Oppenheimer in a courageous attempt to clear his name, McCarthy seemed to withdraw his accusations. The subject that then captured the press was the Hungarian uprising and its defeat by the Soviet tanks as they roared over the bodies of the Budapest youth in the streets. All of these things happened during our first decade in New York. They happened for all the world to see and talk about every night, but it seemed to us that New Yorkers were more concerned than most of the rest of the country, whose principal interest was the World Series.

President Truman's firing of General Douglas MacArthur became the topic of every dinner party for weeks. It was not an easy decision for the president, for he said he had "the greatest respect for MacArthur, a soldier." Then Truman explained, The Supreme Commander of UN forces (mostly American) in Korea "had openly defied the policy of his Commander-in Chief, the President," whose policy was, contrary to MacArthur's advice and actions, to arrange a prompt settlement of the Korean problem with an armistice. There was "Nothing I could do."[20] Jean MacArthur told her friends at my apartment that she was informed of the president's decision to dismiss "her General" by their houseboy who was serving her lunch. He had just heard it over the radio. Many of us remember where we were when we heard the news, just as we remember where we were when Pearl Harbor was bombed.

MacArthur returned to New York to a ticker tape parade of a national Hero. In April 1951 he appeared before a joint session of Congress, emotionally sermonizing, "Old soldiers never die, they just fade away, and like the old soldier in the ballad I now close my military career and just fade away, an old soldier who tried to do his duty as God gave him the light to see that duty."[21]

Douglas MacArthur will long be remembered as a brave public servant. His crowning memorial is the democracy in Japan. For MacArthur not only helped win the war in the Pacific, he supervised sweeping political and social changes in what had been one of the most closed societies.

Postwar Japan emerged with a democratic form of government that allowed women to vote, labor to organize and bargain collectively, and yes, to discriminate against our imports in a most unprincipled way. Modern Japan, with its strong economy and political stability are MacArthur's legacy. His ticker tape parade was larger than Lindbergh's or Eisenhower's. I watched it with awe from lower Broadway holding Gilda's hand. Here was a man, fired by the president, with thousands of supporters urging him to run for that very same office.

New York, Our New World

From our first day, Sam and I were tourists living in the Big Apple. We were forever bumpkins from Florida and California, in love with all that the city had to offer. In the middle of the 1950s, the construction business in New York took off. Great, startling architectural wonders were popping up and down Park, Fifth, Madison, and Third avenues—the United Nations, Lincoln Center, the IBM building, Seagrams, AT&T, the Guggenheim Museum, to name only a few.

The Broadway theater was bursting with great offerings, like *Show Boat, Guys and Dolls, The Heiress, Damn Yankees, How to Succeed in Business without Really Trying, My Fair Lady,* and *West Side Story.* As for drama, there are Arthur Miller's *The Crucible* and Tennessee Williams' *Streetcar Named Desire,* and *Cat on a Hot Tin Roof.*

In February 1952, King George VI's death brought forth the coronation of Queen Elizabeth II, five years after her storybook wedding in Westminster Abbey. We watched it spellbound on our new television.

Throughout the country, civil rights movement began to take shape. Rosa Parks became a modern heroine who defied state segregation laws by being unwilling, after a hard day's work, to "move to the rear of the bus." She was taken from the bus and carried to a Birmingham jail.

In April 1963, Martin Luther King, Jr., who went to Birmingham to force white leaders to begin the process of desegregation, also landed in jail. When he was denounced by eight of Alabama's most respected white clergymen, he protested and wrote his eloquent "Letter from the Birmingham Jail." It became the "most oft-quoted document of the civil rights movement."[22] Four months later he stood on the steps of the Lincoln Memorial and delivered his "I still have a dream" speech to 200,000 peaceful demonstrators who had participated in a march on the nation's capitol.

This was the time when Pope John XXIII, bringing reforms to the Catholic Church, began his all-too-short presence at the Vatican. *Le Grand* Charles de Gaulle's election as the first president of the Fifth French Republic was exciting. Sam and I were fortunate enough to hear him speak at a French-American dinner at the Waldorf Astoria. His speech that night was a literary masterpiece. When answering the questionaire for the Who's Who of France, *Qui est Qui*, he wrote, "L'Homme des lettres, L'Homme Militaire, L'Homme d'Etat."

There were less rosy events during this period. The Russians had launched their Sputnik into orbit, initiated fierce competition between the superpowers, and caused a public relations setback for the West. Although Stalin improved health care and literacy for the workers, his dictatorship soon became a deep betrayal to his people.

Feeling Settled, A Full Time Wife and Mother

How grateful I am to have moved to New York in the fifties—the marvelous city it was then! As frightened as I was of this staid, forbidding city of concrete, it was the ultimate challenge. In the first place, I was "ready" for the life of a full-time wife and mother. My last legal job had been to try cases for the Civil Division Office of the Washington Legal Aid Society, surely not a way to learn to be a litigator. Usually ejectment papers were handed to me, the hearing set for a half-hour later. I would read the pleadings while trotting all the way to the courthouse with my client huffing and puffing in back of me. I would probably have had a nervous breakdown if I had not been forced, by our move, to resign. With three little girls under six, Sam's desire to have a dinner party several days a week for his many California and foreign friends as well as his prospective or current clients, my demanding life left no time for a professional career.

Soon after our arrival in New York, Helen Leylan, who had been my fast friend ever since she rescued me the day before Gilda was born, called me. On our first New Year's Eve in New York she invited us newcomers, whom she thought might be lonely, to spend the evening with her. We actually had no plans made, so she arranged for us to be included in a black-tie party given by her best friend's mother, a Mrs. Milhauser, who occupied a triplex at the top of the Ritz Carlton Hotel. Her daughter, Liz Morris, had the floor below. Mrs. Milhauser, was a long-time patron of the Metropolitan Opera, so everyone who was anyone in music was there. Among the "greats" were the violinist Fritz Kreisler and the composer Sigmund Romberg. I was such a bumpkin, I knew no one, so I just looked around and ate more caviar than I had ever before seen exquisitely served by Henri Soulé, the famous caterer of the Pavilion Restaurant. To occupy myself, I sat down on the piano bench with the pianist, whom I assumed had been hired to play background music. I was quickly on my own kind of "cloud nine" listening to him. After about forty-five minutes I summoned my courage to introduce myself and asked him his name. He said, "Ferde Grofé." His answer rang a familiar bell for I had listened to his *Grand Canyon Suite* played in our college music series. What a thrill! That evening was our first introduction to New York's feast of talented people.

Sam and I went home with a mild case of euphoria, knowing that we had made the right move. New York **was**, indeed, the place for us.

Notes

1. Whittaker Chambers was a journalist, writing for *Time*. He had published his *J'Accuse Against Hiss* in his book, *Witness*.

2. Allen Weinstein. *Perjury. The Hiss-Chambers Case* (New York: Alfred Knopf, 1978) 506.

3. The first jury became deadlocked over who typed the stolen papers on the Woodstock typewriter in July 1949. In the second trial Hiss was convicted of perjury and sentenced January 1950. Weinstein, 469, 504.

4. *Ibid.*, 507.

5. U.S. 83d Congress. Senate. Committee on Government Operations. Permanent Subcommittee on Investigation. *Congressional Investigations of Communism and Subversive Activities*, chaired by Senator Joseph R. McCarthy. Washington: Government Printing Office, 1956.

6. Thomas C. Reeves. *The Life and Times of Joe McCarthy: A Biography*. (New York: Stein and Day, 1982) 278.

7. *Ibid.*, 444-445, 484.

8. Victor S. Navasky. *Naming Names*. (New York: Viking Press, 1980) 60.

9. James A. Wechsler. *The Age of Suspicion*. (New York: Random House, 1953) 268.

10. *Ibid.*, 286, 288.

11. *Ibid.*, 291.

12. Roy Cohn. *McCarthy*. (New York: The New American Library, 1968) 278.

13. Reeves, 372-5, 653, 666, 668.

14. *Ibid.*, 673.

15. *Ibid.*, 324, 356. Harvey Klehr and Ronald Radosh in *The Amerasia Spy Case* (Chapel Hill and London: The University of North Carolina Press, 1996) conclude that the China Hands connived with the communists to undermine their commanders or superiors.

16. Charlotte Y. Salisbury. *Long March: China Epic.* (New York: Walker and Company, 1986)

17. Charles E. Bohlen. *Witness to History 1929-1969.* (New York: W.W. Norton & Co., Inc., 1973) 323.

18. *Ibid.*, 327, 334.

19. Navasky. 21(n), 192; James Trager. *The People's Chronology: A Year-by-Year Record of Human Events from Prehistory to the Present.* (New York: Henry Holt and Company, 1992), 923. The *Red Channels* dates from the Dies Committee (1938-1944), a forerunner of the HUAC.

20. Harry S Truman. *Memoirs by Harry S Truman: Years of Trial and Hope.* (Garden City, New York: Doubleday and Company, 1956) 442.

21. Clifton Daniel ed. *Chronicle of the 21st Century.* (Mount Kisco, New York, 1987) 698.

22. Adam Fairclough. *Martin Luther King, Jr.* (Athens, Georgia: The University of Georgia Press, 1995) 78-9.

CHAPTER TWELVE

Settling in the "Big Apple"

Those friends thou hast, and their adoption tried,
grapple them to thy soul with hoops of steel.
— Act 1, *Hamlet*, Shakespeare

During our first ten years in New York, Sam and I enjoyed the entire patchwork counterpane of the city from the people who knew it well. There were challenges enough for us both. Even raw-boned Sam found a congenial square in the pattern. Debevoise, Plimpton, Lyons, and Gates was expanding because of increase in their law business, and Sam himself was head over heels in work, not only for American Airlines with C. R. Smith, but he had acquired more clients, including KLM Royal Dutch Airlines.

Sam had finally begun to enjoy his membership in India House, a club his partners had wanted him to join. When he invited me for lunch there, he pointed out some of the club's landmarks and its antique memorabilia of ocean transportation. Before we left he told me that he needed another decade to know as many members as he knew at the California Club in Los Angeles. I could believe him for he still wondered whether it was the right club for him! This day, however, he quoted Harry Hershfield, a famous New York figure as saying, "It's a city where everyone mutinies and no one deserts."

Search for Schools

I plunged in to learn as much as possible about the city's educational institutions so that I would have all the information we needed to select proper schools for Gilda, Sharon, and Kathe.

Day by day, I visited Brearley, Chapin, Spence, Nightingale-Bamford, the Friends School in Greenwich Village, and the Lycée and interviewed the headmistresses, with a glimpse of their first, sixth, and twelfth grades. I learned that Brearley was the one where most students stayed for twelve years. Since we wanted to keep our children at home until college age, I decided that Brearley would be our choice. The only problem was that my application for Gilda, our first child eligible for first grade, was placed midway down Brearley's long waiting list. In the interim I placed Gilda, who was five, in the first grade at Nightingale-Bamford. Sharon, only three, went to nursery school at the Church of Heavenly Rest.

When Gilda's acceptance at Brearley arrived in the mail, it was a red-letter day! I knew that Sam cared a lot about school choices for our children, but he simply did not have time to do the investigations that I had felt necessary. He also had definite ideas about education. While I was comfortable that I had made the correct decision by selecting Brearley, I had not consulted him, and he, therefore, had no say in my choice. I was very anxious when we entered the Brearley assembly room for a new parents' dinner the following fall.

As a former Sunday school and junior college teacher, Sam listened with more than a normal father's interest in this evening. After the perfunctory remarks by the chairman of the board of trustees and the president of the student government, the new Brearley headmistress, Jean Fair Mitchell, rose to speak. Miss Mitchell had been a school head in her native Scotland before joining the history faculty of Smith College in Northampton, Massachusetts.

Knowing Sam's preference for women who had pretty legs, and all such external things, I was concerned about his reaction to this stocky lady with a boyish haircut, wearing a man-tailored suit (accepted uniform in her native land for her profession). She also spoke with a definite Scottish brogue. I whispered, "Darling, you will probably not like this lady as much as that attractive head at Nightingale." After Miss Mitchell sat down, he whispered to me, "Honey, there is no comparison at all. This woman is an educator!"

Quite by default, I became president of the Brearley Parents Association when Gilda was in the third grade. During my tenure, I found myself involved in far more interesting duties than just accounting as their treasurer. That was in 1954 when Blanchette Rockefeller (Mrs. John

D. III), as a member of the Board of the Parents Association, asked, "Do we have any black girls as students here?"

Since the answer was "no," Mrs. Rockefeller continued, "We should recruit some. They do not apply because they think it is hopeless or believe they cannot possibly afford the high tuition. I will underwrite some tuition grants for this purpose if we can be sure that the applicants can do the work, without the school having to set a double standard." Most girls awarded the grants met the requirements. They are still well represented at Brearley and make important contributions to their universities and their communities thereafter.

Our daughters benefited enormously by their experience at Brearley and were enriched by their classmates, whether they were the daughters of Warburgs, Rockefellers, or of subway conductors. Patricia Hochshild Labalme, class of 1944, spoke at her fiftieth reunion. She grew up in Manhattan and at her parents' unique "Eagle's Nest" on Blue Mountain Lake in the Adirondacks, one of America's notable "summer palaces." What she said at her reunion was, "If we pause briefly to renew our connection with each other, to this magic school, to remember the songs, the faces, the smell of the labs, the splashed colors of the art rooms, the excitement of the stage, the ideas, the energy, the sense of purpose, the laughter and the love of what we were profoundly engaged in discovering—it's because each of us knows what it has meant to have been formed here, transformed by its alchemy into who we still are today."[1] It **was** a magic school, and I am proud that our three daughters and four granddaughters were educated there.

I discovered that Beatrice Bishop, our Washington friend, who had become Mrs. Adolf Berle Jr., in 1928, was a Brearley graduate and, among her other kudos, was awarded the Distinguished Alumnae Davis Award. Her daughters also went to Brearley.

New Dimensions to Our Lives

The Berles

The Berles, whom we had known in Washington, never made us feel anything but warmly welcomed. They both added extraordinary dimensions to our lives when we moved to New York.

Beatrice was a mother of three and a distinguished OB/GYN practitioner. Adolf, as a very young scholar, had attended the Versailles Peace

Conference and had come home disillusioned.[2] In 1932, while teaching at Columbia University School of Law, he published *The Modern Corporation and Private Property,* coauthored with Gardner E. Means. As a result of his work on this study, Adolf was invited to join Rexford Tugwell, Samuel Rosenman, and Charles Taussig as a member of President Roosevelt's famous Brain Trust. Although he turned down some of FDR's invitations to serve, he did agree to be general counsel of the Reconstruction Finance Corporation in the early New Deal, believing it should take a moderate, middle-of-the-road posture. "It's possible," he once said, "that all the social inventiveness of the world was not explored between the two poles of Adam Smith and Karl Marx."

Adolf's last government post was U.S. ambassador to Brazil during FDR's fourth term. Yet Adolf never left his New York law firm, Berle and Berle. When in New York he continued to participate in state politics, especially in giving advice and assistance to Mayor Fiorello LaGuardia. He founded and served as chairman of the Liberal Party and continued to teach at Columbia. Adolf's contributions were extraordinary.

It was during the period in 1941-1942 that Sam, then at the Civil Aeronautics Board, became acquainted with Adolf, who was then Assistant Secretary of State for Latin American Affairs. One day Sam attended a meeting in Adolf's office in the stately Executive Office Building to participate in decisions to be made with regard to air transportation in Latin America. Sam had just been diagnosed with the mumps. When Adolf, learned of Sam's condition, he said, "Sam, sit in the corner as far away from us as you can. Most of us have had all of the children we want, but you are the youngest of the group and you had best be cautious. I know the risks. My wife is, you know, a doctor."

Adolf and Sam attended the Historic Chicago International Civil Aviation Conference during the war. The conference was devoted to planning the orderly organization of international airlines. Its objective was to produce an agreement that would enable the carriers to fly as unregulated as possible under multilateral treaties between the nations of the free world. The International Civil Aviation Organization and the International Air Transport Association, based in Montreal and Geneva, resulted.

Alas, multilateral arrangements resulting in maximum freedom of the air did not come to pass. Instead, bilateral contracts between nations became the way airlines obtained landing and operating rights in each other's countries. A start was made, however, in an uncharted sea of international law, not too many years after Charles Lindbergh had flown the Atlantic for the first time!

I have thought so much of the Berles lately. We had many philosophical discussions with Adolf over the years. Just before he died, I reminded him of the awe in which Sam and I had initially viewed him and how grateful we were for his kindness. He said, "I don't fit into our world anymore, Phil. I cannot abide these new so-called Leftists who have neither brains nor patience and creativity to develop any system to substitute for what we have. They scream, yell, and demonstrate to pull down our constitutional government."[3]

Beatrice was my mentor. In her autobiography she enlarges upon the stories she told me. She was born in 1902, the only child of Cortlandt F. and Amy Bend Bishop, a family said to have owned everything in New York that the Rockefellers had not acquired and whose independent means disqualified her father from seeking paid employment. She emerged from a miserable, loveless childhood to obtain advanced degrees from Vassar, Columbia, and the Sorbonne, but her life with her parents would have darkened a Brontë Gothic novel. She had felt rejected—neither parent came to Vassar for her graduation—and she was falsely accused of putting her mother in an insane asylum.

Despite her lack of supportive upbringing and guidance, she had the fortitude to establish herself independently, first in Labrador, then in Puerto Rico, Costa Rica, and Honduras, and finally in Brazil, where she was decorated with the *Cruzeiro do Sul* for her work in Brazilian hospitals.[4]

My friends in Brazil say a statue should have been erected to her in Rio in recognition of her invaluable contributions in the field of medicine. She wrote articles about advanced medical treatment, and she taught Brazilian doctors new techniques.

My own indebtedness to Beatrice is enormous. She invited me to see her clinic in Harlem just after I arrived in New York. She introduced me into an art and literary world that I would never have even glimpsed otherwise. Throughout the years I felt that Beatrice's only flaw was giving too much love and blind adoration to Adolf and her three children, Peter, Alice, and her namesake—Beatrice, as well as to her special friends like us.

Sam and I met wonderful people around the Berles's Manhattan dinner table in their Victorian home on Gramercy Park, where Beatrice was born, and at their home in Great Barrington, Massachusetts. Among them were the religious philosopher Reinhold Niebuhr; Max Ascoli, editor of *The Reporter*, an intellectual magazine; and his brilliant wife, Marion, who founded and led the Citizens Committee for Children, on which committee I still serve; Roger Baldwin and Norman Thomas, old New England socialists of the finest quality; and Lionel and Diana Trilling, authors and fellow faculty with Adolf at Columbia University.

While Lionel Trilling was much fawned over, I was quite taken with Diana Trilling. I was even more impressed many years later when she wrote a riveting book about Jean Harris who was imprisoned for the killing of her former lover, the Scarsdale Diet Doctor, Herman Tarnower. Mrs. Trilling, was also an eminent writer and critic for *The Nation* magazine.

Diana and I were able to relate to each other almost immediately having both lived through the depression, the rise of Communism, and fall of Fascism. She and I believed that our first responsibilities were to our families and homemaking. We both credited our husbands with being more competent than we were in our professions. She had published five books and many other writings, had her Ph.D. from Columbia, and not only taught there but was in the center of a lively circle of writers and thinkers. She said that she learned everything from her association with them, not from her Radcliffe degree, which had equipped her for nothing except going to museums, which is exactly what I was doing during my child rearing years.

Someone had told her that I had written a book about surviving the tragedy and pain of losing one's beloved mate. Diana was in her late eighties but still handsome. She asked me if I had good women friends. I said that I had just a few, and they were all getting too ill for me to see or be with often, but that my three daughters were my best friends. This, I added, put a terrible burden on them. Her last words to me were, "I think they can bear it."

Ben Sonnenberg

Around the corner from the Berles, also right on Gramercy Park, was an imposing mansion owned by Ben Sonnenberg. He was known as the most effective public relations operative in New York, yes, in the United States. He was an "image maker." One of his great PR challenges concerned our friend, Dr. Eugene de Savitsch. Gene was a white Russian refugee, a brilliant surgeon and diagnostician. Handsome and unmarried at the time, he was the darling of Washington hostesses, and was a frequent guest of Cissy Patterson, owner of the *Washington-Times Herald.* On one memorable occasion, Gene told Cissy that he would continue to go to her parties, but he could no longer be her doctor because she did not obey his instructions to cut down on her drinking. Cissy was furious. She described Gene in her paper for weeks in a very unfavorable light. He was afraid these outrages by so prominent a Washington press tycoon would hurt his practice, and he enlisted Sam's assistance to counteract Cissy's stories about him.

Sam immediately explored public relations firms to find someone who could improve his friend's image. As a result, all of Washington's P.R. establishments, such as they were in those days, unanimously voted for Ben Sonnenberg, whose offices were in New York.

The chemistry started to work during their first meeting. The three of them, Gene, Ben, and Sam got along famously. Ben boasted that he could arrange to have any client of his listed within two weeks in directories such as *Who's Who,* if the price were right. He also could procure a cover story in *Time.* While he did not achieve either of these feats for Gene, he did restore Gene's reputation in a remarkably brief period.

I remember well my first visit to Ben Sonnenberg's home at 19 Gramercy Park. His was a grand Victorian house filled with the most splendid artworks, furniture, antique brass accessories, French and Bohemian glass chandeliers, and handmade rugs that I hesitated to tread on. That was the beginning of a very long friendship with Ben.

Years after my first meeting, when I had become president of the Girl Scout Council of Greater New York, Sam suggested that I seek Ben's advice on how to create an up-to-date image of Girl Scouting. When, with some hesitation, I asked Ben for an appointment, he set the date the following week at 4:00 p.m. In preparation for my meeting, the public relations office at the Girl Scouts sent him, at my request, a selection of our current publications. They included a proposal I had "cooked up" to "put us on the New York map," i.e., a luncheon to honor women of achievement, including former Scouts. At 3:30 p.m. of the appointed date, I was appearing in the Family Court in Brooklyn, and I could not even leave the proceedings, which had been longer than I expected, to make a phone call advising him that I would be late. One does **not** ask to be excused in the middle of a hearing before a judge unless one wants to lose the case! By 4:00 p.m., I was free and phoned him, explaining that I would take the subway as the quickest way to reach his home, and I offered my apologies.

Ben greeted me dressed in a high, starched Victorian collar, a smoking jacket, a pipe in his hand, and a remark, "Darling, you have kept me waiting an hour. I am, Phil, a twenty-first century man living a nineteenth century life, and I do not like to be kept waiting!" Since I understood that his ordinary fee for an appointment was likely to cost $20,000 and up, I was chagrined. Hoping that he would still give me advice as a friend, at no cost, I timidly absorbed his reproach.

He did not mince his words when he said, "This is trash that your group has sent me. I have had the hour you kept me waiting to examine it all, and it's worthless. Why don't you merge with the Boy Scouts?"

My heart sank, but I did give him the reasons why a merger had been voted down at our national convention. Only then did he settle down to talk to me about fund-raising. He said, "In the first place, never have a luncheon. It takes as much staff, time, and effort as a dinner. You can't charge as much, and it doesn't have the importance of a dinner, so have a dinner."

"Furthermore," he added, "You need prominent names of women on your list who can sell tables."

"You also need other honorees and a chairman," he continued, "who are leaders in the corporate world who can **really** sell the tables." As a result of Ben's advice our first Girl Scout Corporate Dinner (1976) was a smashing success. Recently we had our twenty-fourth dinner, and we have raised over twelve million dollars for the Girl Scout program through these events.

Ben's brilliant advice started New York Girl Scouting on its public path. He was a big enough man to help a girl from the sticks tackle a job she wanted to do well.

Ben urged Sam and me to move to Gramercy Park. We were tempted when we first arrived as we had little children, and the Friends School was close. Gramercy Park, built in 1831, is just as fascinating to me now as it was when I first saw it. It reminds me of St. James's Park in London. Gramercy Park, however, is private, and only people who live around it have a key to its locked gates. It is the closest thing New York has to the Place des Vosges in Paris, one of that city's elegant haunts. The townhouses which surround Gramercy Park are Gothic, Italianate, and seemingly out of another century. The park benches bear plaques of their donors, and some of the trees have their botanical names nailed to them. Woody Allen and Martin Scorsese have used the park in films as a backdrop. Edith Wharton grew up nearby, and Teddy Roosevelt lived next door on 20th Street To have a key to this place is just about the most exclusive achievement one can imagine.

I walk by Ben's house today, now unoccupied and sold after his death. I think of him there in his Saville Row clothes, smoking, cleaning, or sputtering with his pipes. Surely his was one of the most luxurious private homes in Manhattan. It had at one time belonged to Mrs. Stuyvesant Fish, and she had redone it with the help of her neighbor, Stanford White. Brendan Gill, a friend of Ben's, said that Mrs. Fish liked giving parties as well as Ben did, so the house was known as a gathering place for glittering company. She once gave a dinner party for dogs only! Sam and I were abroad when the auction of Ben's furnishings was held. Had I been in town, I would have chosen a pound brass weight to complement a smaller one my sister, Cleona, had bought for us when she lived in England. I bemoan the fact that it tarnishes, and I do not have time to keep it shining as it deserves to be. Ben said he kept a houseboy busy polishing his brass collection five days a week.

At one time, I asked Ben if he knew Ludwig Bemelmans and he said, "Darling, why do you ask such ridiculous questions? I know EVERYONE, besides he lived in one of the apartments that had been my fifth floor." That was sufficient introduction for me to summon up my courage to go to Hammer Gallery, at Ben's suggestion, to an exhibition of Bemelmans's pictures. We still own every one in the series of little *Madeline* books he wrote and illustrated. I had read them all to my daughters so often that, much before they learned to read themselves, they could recite the texts from memory as I turned each page. I **really** wanted an original drawing of his little Madeline. The prices of those exhibited at the gallery were exorbitant, and Mr. Hammer suggested that I satisfy my ambition by writing personally to Bemelmans and asking if he had anything he would sell me that would not abrogate his obligations to his dealer. I did so, and got back in the mail a little sketch in pink and white of Madeline (now proudly framed) with a note which I keep among my art provenances saying, "Give whatever this is worth to the Society for the Prevention of Cruelty to Animals."

An Exceptional Friend

One of the most dazzling people I ever met was Eleanor Belmont, who was seventy when I first saw her. She was a great friend of Beatrice Berle, and Sam was absolutely smitten with her. Known as Eleanor Robson before her marriage, she had a long career on the stage, performing in classics, including Shakespeare's "Romeo and Juliet," Oliver Goldsmith's "She Stoops to Conquer," and Robert Browning's "In a Balcony" and "Merely Mary Ann." Eleanor's late husband, August Belmont, Jr., had worked with Otto Kahn and William Vanderbilt, to establish the New Theater, a medium-sized opera house in New York City.

Sam luckily sat beside Eleanor during one dinner at the Berles. She regaled him with stories of her glittering career in the theater, and how she left it to marry one of the nation's wealthiest, most intelligent, and most active financiers. Suddenly she had homes in Hempstead and a nursery farm in Babylon, both on Long Island; a bungalow in Kentucky on a stud farm for their race horses; a shooting place in South Carolina; a summer home "By the Sea" in Newport, Rhode Island, as well as a mansion in New York City. Sam had never met anyone like her before, and neither had I. The real talent of this great lady was that she made her friends feel important and special. We adored being with her.

Her tales of dinners at the home of Mrs. William K. Vanderbilt, where famous musicians, including Joseph Hofmann and Arturo Toscanini performed, while Giacomo Puccini and Engelbert Humperdinck hung over the piano requesting their favorites. She was a new bride, she told us, when the private railroad car was in its heyday, and she and her husband named one the "Mineola," and staffed it with a French chef. They used it to go on trips to South Carolina for shooting, to Kentucky to inspect their stallions, to their home in Newport, and to another on the Restigouche River in New Brunswick, Canada, for salmon fishing.

Eleanor was an assistant to Henry P. Davison, who chaired the American Red Cross War Council. At the beginning of World War I, she had accompanied him to Europe (only three women in her transport ship) bearing a personal letter from Theodore Roosevelt to General John J. Pershing, Commander of the American Expeditionary Force, who was to support the council's efforts to raise funds for overseas missions. Mrs. Archibald MacLeish, wife of Pulitzer Prize poet and former Attorney General, was one of her able partners and a national director.

Under Davison's leadership, the Red Cross registered over 20,000,000 men and women. Eleanor spoke feelingly about how she had stumbled into fund raising in those days. I only knew there was no one like her in the difficult field of fund raising. In one of the Red Cross's major efforts she had worked with Davison on a campaign that ended with a dinner in New York. The pièce de résistance was the auction of a letter written by President Woodrow Wilson authorizing the fund drive. The bidding had narrowed down to two—Cleveland H. Dodge (of Phelps Dodge Copper Co.) and William Fox, who headed the Motion Picture Committee. Bids, she said, were going up to $800,000-$900,000, and it was more exciting than watching her horse compete for the triple crown! She was seated next to Mr. Dodge and had kept nudging him to "Go on, Go on" until he called the final bid for $1,000,000. With the goal of $100,000, the campaign cleared $1,114,000. In today's currency rates, the actual amount would be twenty times that figure.

The Junior League, Liberty Bonds, and Civil Defense, to name a few, also attracted her talents. Because of her famous acting ability, she was invited to speak for all sorts of causes from all sorts of podia, such as Carnegie Hall, Rabbi Stephen Wise's Free Synagogue, and the New York Stock Exchange.

I could not believe it, nor could Sam, but she admitted stage fright when she walked on any stage or podium. He assured her that no trial lawyer was any good who did not feel perspiration in the palms of his hands as he got up to make an argument or to examine a witness. She said, "Sam, I wish I had had you to tell me that a long time ago. Augie used to tell me of this old saying, 'a lusty bluff well chucked is better than a wavering thrust'." She admitted that advice had not helped her then, and she still didn't believe it.

One of Eleanor's most interesting experiences was her interview with FDR. On that occasion she reported to the president as chairman of the Women's Division of the Emergency Unemployment Relief Commission. She had made a study on methods of coping with unemployment in Europe and had concluded that the enormity of unemployment in the United States was beyond the capacity of the private philanthropy of her Red Cross, and that federal legislation was needed to grant insurance for the unemployed. Not long after this meeting, FDR succeeded in getting the Social Security Act passed.

And **I** thought the Metropolitan Opera Guild had been Eleanor's life! She was chairman of the board of the guild for many years and established its magazine. What an unforgettable woman![5]

Austine Hearst

Another great lady, a bit less famous but much closer to me in friendship and age, was my friend, Austine Hearst (Mrs. William R. Hearst Jr.). I had known her briefly when she was married to Gigi (Igor Cassini), a society columnist known as Cholly Knickerbocker. Austine, Carlene Roberts, and I were singles in Washington in 1938. Once we had moved to New York, I lost contact with the Hearsts, but I have Carlene and her second husband, Justus ("Jock") Lawrence, to thank for helping Austine and me renew our friendship. Will and Austine often invited Sam and me to San Simeon or Wyntoon, the Hearst estates in California, but I first visited San Simeon in the early 1980s. It has been called the most expensive house ever built, or as George Bernard Shaw once said, "This is the way God probably would have done it if He'd had the money."

There are guides who escort tourists around the properties, but guests of the family stay at the Ranch house, a sprawling, beautifully decorated Victorian house. One story told was that William Randolph Hearst Sr.'s mother, Phoebe, had willed him the land, but she waited some time before she gave it to him because she was afraid that he would get "carried away."

San Simeon is a true castle, replete with towers and turrets, surrounded by a park of palm trees with exotic animals roaming in the distance. It was deeded to the State of California in 1958 (seven years after the senior Will Hearst died at the age of 88) and thousands of tourists visit each day.

Austine was a magnificent hostess. She made certain each guest did just as he wished. Her houseguests were always whisked up to the "Enchanted Hill" for a gourmet picnic accompanied by the best of Will's cellar of California wine.

Austine and Will exercised their horses daily. She, especially, loved her rides until the end of her life. She wrote a daily column on the Conference at San Francisco, at which the United Nations was founded. She used her writing talents to publish a beautiful coffee-table book entitled "The Horses of San Simeon."

The castle stands on about fifty acres and the architect was a woman, Julia Morgan. The first thing she ordered was mountains of topsoil to be brought up to the crest of the Enchanted Hill in order to plant masses of camellias. The extravagant gardens are lined by columns linking walkways or garden beds. The stupefying Neptune pool is just that. Breathtaking, as someone says, just out of all imagination except Hearsts' and Ms. Morgan's. Located on a ledge of land overlooking the Pacific, it boasts a huge pool holding 350,000 gallons of water, surrounded by Greek columns. The other pool, beneath the tennis courts, is entirely rimmed by gold-leaf and ceramic tiles set into the cement so that it seems twice as large as the pool actually is. Electrified alabaster torches surround it. There were once marble ladders for the swimmers to climb in and out! I do hope their sons, Will and Austin, and their wives are carrying on in the tradition of their father and grandfather and, especially, of their memorable mother, Austine. I loved her wit, beauty, and warm friendship.

Our New York Circle

Despite fears as we settled into New York, life in Washington soon became a memory, and my circle of friends in New York began to accumulate. Todd Rockefeller (Nelson's first wife) wrote a glowing recommendation for me to join the Cosmopolitan Club. The "Cos," as Todd called it, was launched in 1909 in an apartment in a former stable on 33rd Street, with its initial rooms lighted with gas. It was founded for governesses of German, French, and English extraction who were surrogate mothers, teachers, and value purveyors to the scions of New York's aristocracy, highly educated and culturally advanced women who needed a place to entertain friends or relatives, especially men, or simply have a meal as they could not be seated in most restaurants unescorted.

When I joined the Cos, it had had lots of face lifts and three homes, but its emphasis continued to be on participation, attainment, or interest in the arts and professions. In 1913 the Social Register accepted a Cosmopolitan membership as a badge of respectability. Violinists, ballet dancers, writers—all famous in their time—were members. Willa Cather, Ellen Glasgow, and Elizabeth Bacon Custer (wife of General George Custer, the "Libby" to whom he wrote such ardent love letters) author of *Boots and Saddles*, an account of life in the Dakotas, were members. Amy Lowell, often fascinated her audience there by taking out her famous cigar. The library was replete with classics. The Cos attracted the most interesting women.

As much as I loved my club, it was the scene of one of my most embarrassing moments. I was asked by the Public Affairs committee to introduce the dinner speaker, David Durk, an Amherst graduate, whose life's ambition had been to be an honest cop. He and a more famous "whistleblower" named Serpico had reported serious corruption in the New York Police Department (NYPD). The thanks he'd received for informing on his dishonest colleague was to be sent to "Siberia," walking the beat in a remote section of Staten Island.

A week or so before the dinner, Ruth Plimpton, wife of the former president of Amherst College, heard that Durk would soon be speaking at the club, and she invited me to have lunch with the two of them. During the lunch, I asked him a number of questions about himself that would aid me in my introduction, and I thought I had received a good sense of what his speech would cover. I worked hard on my introduction. All Cos members do, as it is our tradition to make introductions short but very witty, full of facts, and snappy.

The night arrived and the audience was standing room only because of Durk's current headline status. As I rose to do my introduction, I spotted much of the legal aristocracy of the town as well as a number of luminaries of academe. Especially did I spy Judge Whitman Knapp who had headed the famous Knapp Commission which exposed the terrors of the gangs on the docks of the New York waterfront.

After my remarks, David Durk rose and gave a spellbinding presentation, full of drama, riveting stories, and, to my horror words not half so much heard in film and theater in those days as at present—"motherfucker," "shit." Need I add more? The conservatively dressed ladies mostly over forty-five were all squirming in their little gold bamboo chairs, and the men were smirking at their discomfort. Durk paid no attention to his audience and gave us all the lurid details of his "whistleblowing." I have never been so happy to see an evening end as that night. Embarrassing, yes, but like so many of the experiences of our lives in those vibrant New York days and nights—unforgettable, down to the last detail.

Notes

1. Mildred Dunnock, who appeared in Arthur Miller's *Death of a Salesman*, on Broadway, taught drama at Brearley.

2. That was the beginning of a wonderful, rewarding friendship with both Berles. Adolf's life was marked by iconoclasm, in reality inherited from his mother who had left her comfortable New England life to go

west and minister to the Sioux Indians. A Bostonian, son of a Congregational minister, he and his siblings, two sisters and a brother, had an unusual education. His father felt that in the United States there was appalling waste in its secondary education system. Senior Dr. Berle proceeded to take charge of his four children's early education himself. Adolf told us his father insisted that they learn several languages. Lina, his sister, told us that their father made them memorize endlessly, especially long excerpts from Virgil, Goethe, Homer, and Dante, before they had many reading skills. Adolf graduated from high school at 12, but could not enter Harvard until he was 14, where he got his Bachelors Degree at 18 and his Masters Degree at 19. In 1916, he graduated from Harvard Law School cum laude. Thereafter, he joined Louis Brandeis's firm.

3. Beatrice and Adolf had been the subject of a *New Yorker* profile in the fifties describing their lifestyle and extraordinary talents. The article depicted them luxuriating in twin bathtubs facing one another, from which they "unwound" at the end of their professional days. This exercise was quite therapeutic. It also allowed them to explore what had happened to each another since breakfast. They could, and they did, later devote themselves wholeheartedly to their guests—or to each other.

4. Beatrice Bishop Berle. *A Life in Two Worlds: An Autobiography.* (New York: Walker and Company, 1893) 1-2, 83, 87, 179, and passim.

5. Patrick F. Gilbo. *The American Red Cross: The First Century* (New York: Harper & Row, Publishers, 1981) 4, 55, 56, 71, 83, 139, 141, 142; *Who's Who in America*, 1960.

CHAPTER THIRTEEN

Westhampton

A Man's a Man For All That.
— Robert Burns, 1759–1796

Toward the end of our first winter of 1948-1949 in New York, our good friend Marjorie (Mrs. Mord) Bogie called us one evening and asked about our summer plans. I replied, "What summer plans? We like winter vacations, and besides, I am not going to leave my attractive husband alone in this city all summer and go sit on some mountain top."

"It's not a mountain top I'm calling you about," she said. "You cannot raise three little girls under six in Central Park all summer. Mord and I have rented a house in a small town on Long Island called Westhampton. It's less than two hours away, and on the ocean, and its a new place for us. Why don't you come too?"

She further offered to rent an inexpensive house for us, get us into the Westhampton Country Club, and generally be my friend. On a Sunday in late February, Sam and I rented a car and moseyed out to Westhampton to see what kind of summer house Marjorie had reserved for us and locate the large pool at the Swordfish Beach Club where our girls and their friends could play. Our knowledge of Long Island had come from reading novels like *The Great Gatsby*, and we thought it was just one long expanse of tennis, golf, and polo clubs. After we had driven over two hours, we were still not in Westhampton. True, in Nassau County, we were obviously on the outskirts of country clubs with their tennis courts and golf greens. But in Suffolk County, we passed many hay fields, some dairy farms, a few small villages, and acreage soon to be planted with vegetables for large city markets. What in the world had we gotten ourselves into, we wondered.

After three hours, we finally arrived on Main Street, Westhampton, and located the realtor who took us to see "our" house on Tanners Neck Lane. Little did we know, when we signed the lease and paid $800 for the summer, that our house abutted a duck farm that would have horrible odors all summer. Our negotiations completed, we asked our real estate agent to suggest a place for lunch. He said, "There is only one restaurant; it's called the Patio." As we opened the door of this Main Street bistro, we found it packed, wall to wall, with sportsmen. It was duck hunting season, and some of the hunters told us that they had been shooting from "blinds" along the dunes. They were an extremely friendly lot, and invited us to join them around the fireplace and bar. The men sported large red and black plaid woolen shirts and the women wore big thick sweaters. The scene was irresistible!

From that day, we never doubted the wisdom of our choice. We soon discovered we knew more people in Easthampton and Southampton, but they were simply too far out on the island for Sam to travel after work. If he were held up by a deliberating jury or waiting for a corporate officer to call him from California at 3 p.m. west coast time, he would miss the last train to those easternmost villages. In Westhampton, with the prettiest sandy beach closest to Manhattan, Sam could take a late train to Babylon, Patchogue, or Speonk. I could meet him as late as 10:30 p.m., and he could still be at home before midnight, allowing him to wake up "with the birds," as he called his waking habit.

In 1951, after renting for three years, we plunged in and bought our first house, a run-down but well built structure from Mrs. Mortimer Cobb. After finalizing the papers for the purchase, Mrs. Cobb first insisted that we call her "Aunt Gertrude," and then she made clear how she wished us to comport ourselves once we moved into our new home. "There has never been a cross word said in this house," she said.

Sam responded, "Aunt Gertrude, we will try."

Twenty-five years later, when I was peeling potatoes at the kitchen sink, Sam came in from his garden, put his arm around me and asked, "Phil, do you remember what Mrs. Cobb told us about this house? Well, I think we are doing terribly well!"

Most people won't believe it, but very few cross words were ever uttered between us in almost forty years.

The summers in Westhampton became more comfortable and satisfying when we had our own home; we were now a permanent part of the community. Sam was ecstatic with his garden, and life was truly grand.

We spent the summer doing over that great house. I painted the walls of all of the fifteen or sixteen rooms and the trim around fifty-eight windows, most of which had twenty-four panes each. After one exhausting day, I counted that I had painted the trim of over one thousand two hundred panes. I surrendered to a professional for the ceilings and wallpapering as I had made a valiant stab at both and knew they required skills beyond my patience.

Once we were accepted in the Quantuck Beach Club—we had waited three years to be admitted—our life in Westhampton became more fun. The club was where mothers and children spent their days and played together, and fathers came when time allowed. One of the odd rules at the club said that men were not allowed on the beach or at the club unless their swimming trunks had **tops**. Sam flipped over that one. He wasn't crazy about the beach anyway, as he preferred to sail or work in his garden. I implored him to see if he could find a **top** so he could at least go once in a while with our children. He reported one evening that "just to please you, Phil," he had gone to Abercrombie and Fitch in search of a top and learned that such a garment had not been carried for years.

That ended my hopes of getting Sam to the beach when lo and behold, old Dr. Maynard (Dr. Edward Maynard's father), one of the founders of the club, appeared on the beach **with** his **top** but, horror of horrors, without his **bottom**. That rescinded the top rule right away.

Quantuck seemed to me a symbol of the whole community. It was where we joined families that dated back three, sometimes four, generations. If I looked carefully at the younger members, I could identify that they were Shuttleworths, Drivers, Murpheys, or others, just from their cute, round faces, or from the length and shape of their legs, even their carriages. It was where a mother knew at all times where her children were. As I look back at those days, I realize that the club represented a community whose divorce rate was zero in our age group and two in our children's age group.[1]

Thinking of our growing family, we bought two houses at the rear of our property in Westhampton. This afforded us a rectangular private two-acre park extending from one street to the next, only four houses away from the post office. We could walk or bike anywhere we needed to go. With three houses our daughters and their families would have weekend and summer retreats.

We made many friends, played tennis, and sailed. I went daily to the beach and chaperoned junior sports and junior dances. These were the things full-time mothers did in those days. There were few two-career couples. Sam would try to come out on Wednesdays to break his week. "Doing the laundry" was an excuse for me to go into the city Thursday nights. We did not have laundry equipment in Westhampton but did in New York, so that gave us a weekday evening together. That left only Monday and Tuesday nights when we had to be separated. So I was really not sitting lonely on a mountain top. Marjorie Bogie was right!

Historical Setting of Our Summer Home

A local historian, Robert Keene, reminds us in his too infrequent columns in the *Hampton Chronicle* that the eastern section of Long Island was closely associated with the Massachusetts Bay Colony. In 1635 Charles I of England conveyed the Long Island title to the Earl of Stirling.[2] In 1640 English settlers founded Southampton.[3] They were pouring down from New England in such numbers that they purchased a portion of the South Fork occupied by the Montauk Indians, recorded as the "Quoque Purchase of May 12, 1659."[4] This purchase ran from Wainscott in the east (near Easthampton) to Canoe Place near us, and from Peconic Bay to the Atlantic Ocean. Described in the transfer instrument as eight miles square (not eight square miles), it would be today about sixty-four square miles. This transfer was from Wyandanch, the Sachem of the Montauk Indians, to John Ogden.

A second deed, known as the "Quogue Purchase, 1663," transferred this portion of the South Ford—described as "eight miles square"—from John Ogden to John Scott, "who sold it to the town" of Southampton.

A third deed known as "Topping's Purchase, 1662" transferred another stretch of land from Canoe Place to "Speonk Meadows" on Moriches Bay. This deed, including our village of Westhampton, was between Weany Sunk Squaw, Anabackus, and Jackanapes, all resident at Shinnecock, and Thomas Topping, resident of Southhampton. These Indian names are household words in our neck of the woods.[5]

By the 1670s Westhampton (with the Indian name of Ketchaponac) and Hampton Bays (with the Indian name of Wuno'hke) shared seven whaling companies and had potworks for rendering blubber into whale oil.[6]

All this shows that we had landed in one of the oldest inhabited localities in our country, inhabited by Europeans, that is. How long the

Indians had been there is anyone's guess. The oldest house in Westhampton Beach is said to be the house formerly occupied by Barbara (Mrs. Derrick) Betts, who inherited it from her parents, the William A. Gills. It is of museum quality with furnishings appropriate to its age as the one-story, white shingled house it is. A fire ravaged most of its interior in 1997, alas. How fitting that Barbara is one of the movers and shakers of the recently organized Westhampton Historical Society. In the last few years an 1830s house was given to the society and is now moved into the center of town. Currently being restored through the efforts of many town citizens, it is a tribute to those who care deeply about preserving its presence in our midst.

Interests and Diversions

The local grownups had clubs too. The Rotary Club invited Henry Harfield to speak. Marion (Mrs. Henry) Harfield remembered that our beloved family doctor, Dr. Ransom Jagger, was Henry's sponsor or host. In any event, Sam introduced Henry as an "expert" in bank mergers. A partner in the law firm Shearman and Sterling, Henry was a senior counsel to National City Bank and had handled a lion's share of its merger with City Bank Farmers Trust when it became Citibank. Henry corrected Sam, his introducer, and said, to the best of his and my memory, "My distinguished colleague, Mr. Gates, has it all wrong. If you handle one bank merger you are a specialist, if you handle two you are an expert, and but if you handle three, you're in jail!" That brought down the Rotary Club house.

My long association with Marion Harfield continued after my attempt to make beach plum jelly, our principal local delicacy. I picked baskets of red fruit in an area where Madeline Staniford, a garden club member, had told me the fruit was just ripe. All three of our children and their friends helped me pick so that we had a large cauldron of fruit with five pounds of sugar on the stove. It cooked and cooked, and nothing happened except masses of pesky seeds seemed to be emerging from the frothing liquid. I finally telephoned my garden club mentor and said, "Madeline, I picked where you told me to go, and I'm cooking the beach plum stuff the way you told me to, but something seems to be the matter."

She asked a few salient questions and said, "Phil you haven't picked beach plums; you have picked rose hips." Disgusted and too impulsively I chucked out the entire mess—sugar, fruit, and cauldron. The next week I was relating the bungle I had made of this most recent culinary challenge to Marion Harfield (a gourmet cook as well as a cookbook editor). She handed me an article from *Gourmet* magazine which contained two recipes for rose hip jelly, reported to have great medicinal qualities and large quantities of Vitamin C. I could have had pints of this condiment to use for my family and to give to friends and neighbors as presents—all had been thrown in the garbage in that impulsive moment.

At the following week's Rotary Club luncheon, when Henry Harfield introduced Sam as the speaker, he made no mention of Sam's being one of the leading litigators in the country or an expert on international aviation, horticulture, and American political history. Instead, Henry introduced Sam as the man whose wife did not know the difference between a beach plum and a rose hip!

Judge Medina

From the beginning of our Westhampton life Judge Harold Medina was in "loco parentis" for both Sam and me. The judge asked us to call him Dadoo and his wife, Ethel, Madoo. We first met him and Ethel during a dinner party given by their son, Harold Medina Jr. at the Medina compound on Apaucuck Point during the summer of 1949.

We had left Washington in the middle of congressional hearings on the Hiss-Chambers case. During our second summer fears of a subversive element were voiced almost daily in the media which planted redbaiting into our consciences.

Since Harold Jr., a partner of Cravath, Swaine, and Moore, the legal firm that represented Time, Inc., was counsel for Chambers, our conversation turned to this case. Harold believed Chambers' statements that the Communist Party and its major practitioners were going to destroy American values by introducing drugs, instigating the breakdown of family structure, and managing all sorts of terrible things by a "fifth column" of spies.

In January 1949, Judge Medina had opened his "most trying" case involving eleven members of the Communist Party charged with conspiracy "to teach and advocate the overthrow of the U.S. government." At the outset, the judge denied counsel an extension of more than ten days, instead of the usual ninety-day period to prepare briefs, stating, "These fellows are charged with the overthrow of our government by force and violence."[7]

On all counts during the trial "lasting two days under nine months" the judge conducted the tumultuous proceedings with patience and care.

In this dangerous period of our nation's history, radical supporters for the defendants made several attempts on the judge's life. The FBI attended him constantly, both in Westhampton and New York City. After the verdict was rendered by the jury—guilty—Judge Medina addressed himself to the thirty-nine counts of contempt he had pronounced on the many defense lawyers during the trial. One of them shouted that his conduct had been the "price of liberty."

The judge replied calmly, "It is not the price of liberty; it is the price of misbehavior and disorder."

He later gave a statement, "These defendants were not convicted merely for their political beliefs or for belonging to the Communist Party— the jury had to find there was a specific intent to overthrow the government by force and violence." His opinion was appealed to the Second Circuit Court and affirmed and by a 7-2 decision, and later affirmed by the U.S. Supreme Court. His charges to the jury in that case are classics. Many pages have been written about the proceedings, and the judge's opinion is historic.[8]

Those of us lucky enough to have lived through those interesting times with Judge Medina will never forget his professional conduct of the trial in what seemed to me his personal ordeal.

Lee Davis, a local writer, gave us a brief insight into how Judge Medina relaxed when not presiding over the tumultuous trial. Davis had arranged to interview the judge on the Fifth Amendment, particularly as it was used by witnesses during the McCarthy period. At 8:30 a.m., Lee found the judge in his luxuriously-equipped game room and library, practicing billiards. He reported that the judge was fresh as a daisy, his mustache carefully coifed as though he had been up for hours (probably true), and he smelled strongly of Barbasol. He was dressed in sartorial splendor in a white shirt and white pin-striped trousers, supported by suspenders.[9]

Davis quotes the judge as saying emphatically, "There's one thing we've got to combat, and that's the loss of any one of our freedoms, as it's easy to let our rights be whittled away a bit at a time. Once they are lost, we never get them back . . . . I'd rather see all of the Communists go scot-free than lose one provision of the Bill of Rights."

The judge then posed the question, "Will the Bill of Rights become illegal, with some of the recent Supreme Court decisions?" The judge's special kind of ethics would be useful to some sharp practicing members of our legal profession today. He, time and time again, refused to use his personal acquaintance or friendship with a person on the bench or in a position of decision-making. "The difference between right and wrong is not all written down in the books" was his guiding motto.

I always felt deprived not to have been one of Judge Medina's students at his famous bar exam cram course. Over 22,000 budding New York lawyers did take this course, however. It was held in various lofts, The Town Hall on 43rd Street, and a number of large auditoriums. The judge was, I am certain, a born teacher. He enjoyed reminiscing about teaching his cram course and told me of bumping into his former students, who bewailed the fact that their own children about to take the bar exam did not have him around to teach them the pitfalls of that agonizing exercise. During one of our discussions about this course, I ventured to ask the judge to write a supportive affidavit for my admission to the New York Bar. He graciously agreed.

It was not long after that when Judge Medina mentioned to me that he really liked to play golf and offered to introduce me to some of the finer points of the game. He said it would be a diversion from working in his library. I knew he had a lot more free time in the summers because the courts were in recess, and I jumped at his offer. It was timely for me for I was beginning to realize that I must try to play better if I were to be a decent companion to Sam on the weekends. I say "try" because I'm still a poor golfer, if an enthusiastic one.

My habit was to meet the judge on the ninth hole at the tee, where he would be waiting for me. I would park my car somewhere nearby, hop in his cart, and off we would go.

As I teed off one morning and made one or two poor shots, Judge Medina said, "Phil, you waste more shots than any woman I ever saw. Now you pay attention, girl. I bet you ten cents that I will sink my putt in fewer shots than you will."

That was a challenge. I had money at stake and a famous companion staring at me, criticizing my every move. Believe me, I paid attention during my next shot!

As we clopped along in his cart at a fast pace toward the tenth hole, the judge asked, "Where is your ball, Phil?" We'd usually find it nestled in the arms of a tree trunk or a fallen branch. (We have more woods and thick clumps of pine trees at our club than most courses.) Once we spotted it the judge would stop, look in his golf cart, and get out some pruning shears saying, "Now, Phil, what do you think about the shape of that tree where your ball is? I think it needs a little pruning, don't you? I don't like its contours." He'd snip off a few branches so I could get at my ball and take a shot at it. In the meantime he would giggle, "That wasn't really cheating. It was just improving the landscaping of the golf course!"

The eleventh hole, par three, was exasperating for me. To land near that hole, I had to make a long high drive, clear a lot of swampy brush in order to reach the green, sitting up there quite tiny, elevated, and surrounded, of course, by sand traps.

I hesitated and then apologized for my approach saying, "You know, judge, I can never make this green, and that's why I have to aim to the left trap."

He replied, "Nonsense, balderdash, that's not positive thinking. Aim straight for the green."

One day I actually landed on the green on my drive. He said, "You see, you can do it. Keep your head down and watch your follow through-- you did it."

Then he added, "Let me tell you, Phil, I didn't always hit this green. In fact, for years I never made it, just like you. One day I triumphed and with much pride, I marched up, took out my putter, and **"putted off"** the green into the sand trap! So don't feel so proud of yourself. Even if you hit the green, you might 'putt off.'"

On one of those golf-cart afternoons Judge Medina was more chatty than usual. He confided to me that at Princeton (Class of 1909), he didn't know how to make himself likable. He confessed that he knew he was thought by others to be too aggressive as he tried to join everything Princeton offered, and, worst of all, he was considered a clown and a show-off. He was left out of an eating club at Princeton when he became a sophomore so, single-handedly he organized a new sophomore eating club. He said that certain outcasts, like himself, had surpassed the boys who were campus VIP's in their later achievements. He also said that when, after wooing Ethel and overcoming his mother-in-law's objections, his wonderful wife gave him confidence so that his social uneasiness decreased.

At another time, when I thought we were having a "meeting of the minds," I broached the subject of his being the principal speaker at our annual Girl Scout dinner at the Waldorf. He replied, "I'd really like to do it for you, and I believe in the Scouts, but Philomène, I work very hard on that bench. My speeches sound ad lib, but believe me I spend hours on them to make them sound ex tempore. I just about memorize many pages preparing for those things! Sorry." Indeed, his speeches were great and seemed to be casually delivered, albeit carefully rehearsed. Of course, I let him off the hook.

I was so enriched by the judge's friendship. We shared a passion for literature, and spent enjoyable hours in his library, which was filled with valuable editions of English, Spanish, Greek, Latin, and French books, selected with great care. His library was the centerpiece of his gracious Colonial-styled house, situated regally at the foot of Ethel's English garden. He was a church-goer, I knew, because I often sat behind the Medinas at St. Mark's Church from whose pulpit he preached a yearly sermon to standing-room-only. He would offer a five-cent prize to his small sons, Harold and Standish, if they were able to paraphrase in five minutes the contents of the sermon. It did result in their listening, however, more than parents of my age have been able to achieve.

As I think of this sermon episode, I often wonder if the judge's competitive drive put an insufferable burden on his two young children and, in general, resulted in over-hard treatment of the younger generation. His grandson Standish Forde Medina Jr., a litigating partner in Sam's law firm, said a man once accosted the judge saying, "You probably don't remember me, but I was the guy you threw out of your cram course a long time ago because you said I had gone asleep. Well, I was not asleep; it was the fellow next to me." The judge apologized, but it was not an easy gesture for him.

Harold Jr. once told me something he couldn't have told to his father. He said that he could not have imagined what would have happened if he or his brother, Standish, had not achieved Phi Beta Kappa at Princeton, the judge's alma mater, where he had won highest honors in French in 1909.

I remember some of the judge's public interest efforts, as well. One in which he took enormous pride and had a lot of giggles over was his private war with the **tent caterpillars**! I heard him give his version of the story at a meeting of the Westhampton Garden Club. Years later, his grandson, Standish, included the incident in his eulogy of his grandfather.

At one time Westhampton had an epidemic infestation of tent caterpillars that hatch in the spring from clusters of eggs deposited on branches of trees, hedge bushes, and all manner of ornamental plantings. When the worms appear, they immediately devour the foliage around them. Since neither the village conservationists, nor the townspeople themselves seemed to be doing a thing about this threat to the environment, the judge took it on himself and urged his golfing partners to do likewise. He finally sought the help of the local school children. With permission from the teachers, he spoke at the school auditorium and said that he would reward each child with a penny for each five clusters destroyed.

Remember this was a while ago, when the tooth fairy still left a nickel under the pillow, and a dollar a week was a pretty good allowance. In his auditorium speech the judge instructed the students to bring their gatherings to his library at Apaucuck Point. He would reward them in person and let them see him put these wormlike insects into the fire. This was just the kind of challenge which appealed to the students who had become bored with Westhampton's bleak winter weather of February and March and could scarcely wait to get started on the judge's exciting project. To demonstrate to the children that the caterpillars were harmless, he proceeded to pop a few wiggly insects into his mouth! He was, after all, a born show off! His grandson thought he had indeed even smacked his lips after this stellar performance. After all, fried worms have long been a delicacy in Mexico, the former home of some of the Medinas.

Later that eventful day, he received a phone call from one of the high school mothers, who said with a snicker that her daughter had been sick that day and had missed the judge's performance. She was eager to join her fellow scavengers but did not believe that the caterpillars were harmless. Never tolerating an attack on his credibility, he drove immediately over to the girl's house and swallowed a couple more insects just to convince her. What a success the judge's project was! After the onslaught of the local students, tent caterpillars disappeared from our community for a number of years.

Judge Medina had a long-standing, personal interest in his environment, especially his own "point" at the end of Apaucuck Road on Moriches Bay. He had acquired this property from the Raynor family who had run the Point House (an inn just before the entrance to what is now the Medina property), with proceeds from the bar exam cram course. He told me several times about his boyhood dream to own that property. In 1924, he finally had the means to buy the property and build a house. His home, fronting on the bay, had a spectacular view, but it was very exposed to the water, as he found out to his distress during the 1938 hurricane. The storm utterly demolished his home, and even more tragically his beloved library. All of his books were drenched with water and covered with muddy sand, and many ruined beyond repair or restoration. Cast iron radiators were blown a mile away, and his boat, the *Spendrift*, ran aground on the twelfth green at the country club!

He had to dredge the bay and construct a lawn. He then proceeded to tell me that the first bill for his lawn was for manure—a carload for $800, or more—in today's dollars, many thousands. He said, "I never told Ethel, although she was in charge of the gardening!" The judge later built a miniature golf course with one hole in front of his house, requiring more topsoil and manure! Like everything else in his life, his own diligence practicing on that miniature golf course paid off, and he broke par at our club, at seventy-one.

This story, like the caterpillar crusade, signifies much of the depth of the judge's determination to "set things right."

The Medina Family

During summers Sam and I, as well as our daughters, had many occasions to enjoy the whole Medina family. Janet (Harold Jr.'s wife), Hope (Standish's wife) and I, with several of their and our children, boarded the Medina's small yacht and sailed out of their dock into Moriches Bay at the hour of the opening gun for the race each Saturday, about 1:30 p.m. To be a part of my husband's life, I especially wanted to spend time seeing Sam race those boats. Perhaps it was a bit boring, and sometimes too long and too confining, particularly for the younger children, but our husbands were having the time of their lives.

In addition to these races, Standish and Harold gathered as many small center board SS boats as possible at Apaucuck Point and organized five or six races for our children on Sunday afternoons. How lucky young people were to have instruction with such dedicated fathers/teachers.

Our daughters (Kathe was too young to participate) were mixed in their appreciation. Sharon never liked it, as she declared she was opposed to being cold, wet, and yelled at. Sam used to comfort her by telling her that he went through the same treatment at the hands of his skippers, and that it was all a part of the scene, but she never bought his explanation. Gilda seemed to love it and went on to crew for Jeremy Medina. Jeremy, Standish's son—who was at the Hill School, later at Princeton—skippered his SS in the Race Week which was held at a different harbor each day all around the tip of Eastern Long Island.

My mother was having a cup of tea in our kitchen during one "Race Week" when she found Gilda "ironing her money." Jeremy's SS had capsized so often she had been forced to return home midweek to get fresh clothes and "dry out" her small amount of pocket money. Mother gave her seventeen-year-old granddaughter a hug and said, "Gilda, darling, we've missed you. Don't you want to stay home for the rest of the week?"

Gilda's quick retort was ecstatic. "Granny, I never want to come home again!" The whole scene was intoxicating to her and so was Jeremy on whom she had an enormous crush!

Our children, who enjoyed the sport, developed good habits. Perhaps that was all that Harold and Stan expected.

It was Sam who interested the judge in celebrating July Fourth. He brought some fireworks from Washington one year, and we shared them with the Barclay Morrisons and the Standish Medinas off the waterfront owned by Polly Morrison's mother, Mrs. O'Gorman. (It is prohibited by law in the Hamptons to ignite any such things, except over water.)

Judge Medina, having enjoyed Sam's display, decided to express his love for his country by engaging the famous Grucci brothers to provide our community with some really **good** fireworks each July Fourth. We usually had buffet supper at Stan's and Hope's home and then walked over to the boat dock on the edge of Apaucuck Point as dusk was settling. We sat on blankets on the grass to watch this yearly spectacular. Many neighbors came in their own boats, and anchored a safe distance for the dock. The entire community turned out to watch, even though the mosquitoes would rise "en masse from Speonk," to quote Lee Davis, our local writer, "in holiday concert . . . while the technicians were eerily dashing back and forth with their scarlet, streaming torches." Families had difficulty keeping their children from getting lost or engaging in fisticuffs with their siblings or friends. The first explosion made all of us be still as mice, except for the oohing and aahing as each sensational bomb burst in air. "Exploding jewels moving into shattering chandeliers of stars," as Lee Davis described it.

This wonderful night of celebration was a gift of Judge Medina to his fellow townspeople and neighbors. He did indeed bring an adrenaline shot of life to us all by setting a standard of innovative energy, joy, and yes, "merriment" to his extended family. I still miss him. Judge Medina was on our side and we were very lucky indeed.

Notes:

1. See *Steamed Crabs and Cranberries*, by Meredith Medina Murray, Searles Graphics, Inc., Yaphank, NY, 2000.

2. Samuel Eliot Morison and Henry Steele Commanger. *The Growth of the American Republic*. (New York: Oxford University Press, 1930) 63.

3. Encyclopedia Britannica—(Southampton was the first of seven towns founded by the English in the seventeenth century. See also Peter Mattheissen. *Men's Lives: The Surfmen and Baymen of the South Fork*. (New York: Random House, 1986) 12.

4. Everett T. Rattray. *The South Fork: The Land and the People of Eastern Long Island*. (New York: Random House, 1979) 83–84 and frontispiece.

5. David H. Gilmartin. *Westlands at What Cost?* (privately published, 1982) Appendices IX, X, and XI contain facsimiles of the three deeds.

6. Mattheissen. Op. Cit., 14. (Ketchaponac and Wuno'hke are the transliterations of the Indian name given by Mattheissen.)

7. "World Documents. Judge Medina's Charge to the Jury." *Current History,* November 1949, 287–303.

8. Harold R. Medina. *Anatomy of Freedom*. (New York: Henry Holt and Company, c. 1959).

9. Lee Davis, various *Hampton Chronicle* articles.

CHAPTER FOURTEEN

Under the Shingle

*I have a high opinion of lawyers. With all their faults, they stack up well
against those in every other profession. They are better to work with or play
with or fight with or drink with, than most other varieties of mankind.*

— *Harrison Tweed 1885-1969*

When I re-entered the practice of law in 1962 and hung out my own
shingle, as scared as I was rusty, I could not imagine the joyous years
ahead of me. It was then that I began to build up a passion for my profession, and my cases became my adoptive children.

Only a few days after I was admitted to the New York bar, I received
a phone call from someone announcing himself as "an old friend slaving
away down at the Federal Court House." The way he introduced himself I
pictured a janitor at best. He added that he had learned of my recent admission to the New York bar and went on to say that he had a job for me.
He wanted me to handle the estates of two of his neighbors. Neither, he
stated, could afford to pay a great deal for probate services. I responded,
"Well sir, if I am to make a decision as to whether to take on these matters, I must know your name." Chuckling, he identified himself as "your
old pal Leonard Moore," and I nearly fainted.

Judge Leonard Moore of the U.S. Court of Appeals for the Second
Circuit was one of the best known judges of that high court. I had known
Leonard since my Washington days as assistant to Harlee Branch, Chairman of the Civil Aeronautics Board. Leonard had represented TWA before the board. Of, course I took on the assignment and learned a great

deal probating those two estates, primarily because Leonard's Brooklyn neighbors had fairly complicated problems. Soon after that assignment, I was offered more business than I could accept and checked with Sam before every move. That poor patient man came home after a twelve-hour, non-stop day only to become an in-house tutor. If it was a motion that I must argue, he would insist on hearing my opening statement. Bless his heart, he could always improve on whatever I had drafted. This could be either an opinion letter or one of the threatening variety. Frankly, I got to be pretty good at the latter, avoiding litigation whenever possible. Sam was an extremely versatile lawyer and able to handle any kind of case. He taught me much of what I needed to know.

First Cases

Not long after I began my law practice, I took a divorce case and handled it competently. At least I never heard of complaints. From that time on, the lion's share of my practice was in matrimonial law and collecting monies due my clients who were owners of small businesses.

I learned early on that there were certain cases that I did not want to handle. These were litigated, hotly contested divorces, that were invariably filled with acrimony, accusations, and just plain nastiness. I didn't want to spend my day involved in other people's bitterness. So I decided to handle only uncontested divorces. These are cases in which the respective parties' counsels hammer out a separation and custody agreement with which their clients can live. After execution by both parties, it is incorporated with the findings of fact into the final divorce decree, rendered in a special term of the New York Supreme Court.

All of my cases were not of the matrimonial variety. One was a heart-rending case for a male nurse whom I shall call Horace. How Horace found me I do not know. He was overweight, extremely distraught, and he blamed his physical problems on his former employers. He wanted to sue them—the Walter Kidde Company—for severance pay, plus an additional award for suffering. His problems, he felt, came as a direct result of his experience as a civilian nurse on a Kidde construction site in Vietnam, where the company was under contract with the Department of Defense. During the height of the Vietnam conflict, Kidde acted as a subcontractor, building service buildings, dormitories, and airport runways in the jungle near the Cambodian border.

Horace worked on this remote project for two and a half years. Life on the outpost was boring in the extreme. To complicate matters, the doctor assigned to this project proved to be an alcoholic, given to continual drunken bouts. He was incapable of caring for his patients. Horace, then, had to assume the principal job of keeping the carpenters, masons, and electricians on their feet and at work. Not surprisingly, however, Horace found the most serious ailments he had to treat were not fever, diarrhea, flu, or various tropical diseases but depression, anxiety, and tension. According to Horace, "I simply presided over barrels of valium and antibiotics and dished them out with abandon."

Horace struggled to carry this onerous load of being both doctor and nurse, a position for which, he realized, he was eminently unqualified. He had not been paid for this extra responsibility. Further, the company never satisfied their contract with him for severance pay upon completion of his tour of duty. I tried to negotiate with the proper authorities at Kidde to no avail, and we finally filed a lawsuit. Happily, before we went to trial, we reached a very satisfactory settlement. I was happy that I could help Horace. He provided me an insight into an aspect of the Vietnam War which was totally overlooked. He was but one of the many unsung civilian heroes to come out of the Vietnam conflict.

In the Field of Art

I've long nourished a love affair with the arts, begun when, as a full-time mother, I subscribed to museum lectures. Therefore, it was only natural that matters involving art became an integral part of my work. My first Bar Association assignment was with the Committee on Art to initiate a study of auction practices in the field of international art commerce.

It is the custom of most auction houses to make statements in their catalogs that each item listed has been extensively researched. Sadly, this is rarely true. As if to underscore the problem, I rode home after an art committee meeting with a number of young lawyers, also on the committee, whose expertise lay in art of the Near East. I asked if they were going to attend the Near Eastern art sale at Parke Bernet's (now Sotheby's) the next day. One spoke up and said, "Oh no, most of the items are not as represented by their provenance in the catalog, or really not even of the period."

The operative word in this sentence is "provenance." A provenance is the birth certificate of a work of art. It contains the artist's name, date of execution, and chain of ownership. It is essential to establish the value of the piece. A provenance is proof of authenticity and has been vital to understand in my practice.

Dealers

I later found that much the same situation existed in the field of antique furniture. I had been looking for a secretary desk for the bedroom of our youngest daughter, Kathe. We had just moved into our dream home, a duplex 14-room, 4-bedroom apartment at 830 Park Avenue. I really wanted to make Kathe's room so beautiful that she would not move out until she was married. The room was decorated around a Hepplewhite tester bed, in which we had slept our first ten years of married life. I felt such a desk was needed to complete the furnishings. I sought the opinion of a well-known antique dealer, Douglas Carson, concerning three desks, which were to be part of a forthcoming sale at Parke-Bernet Galleries. His opinion was that they were just pieces of furniture, nice reproductions, but not of the period as their provenance stated. "Wait until I go to England to buy for my firm (Stair and Co.)," he suggested. "I feel certain that I can find a really fine desk for much less."

He was true to his word. Sometime later, Sam and I were staying in London at the little mews house of Dame Moura Lympany, on Bruton Place, right off Berkeley Square. Lympany, a world famous pianist, always allowed us the use of her "digs" whenever she was on concert tour, as was the case on this particular occasion.

We returned to Bruton Place one afternoon to find that Douglas had slipped the picture of a fine Hepplewhite desk beneath our door. We fell in love with the photograph and immediately told him to buy it. I enjoy the desk to this day! We would not have had this beautiful piece had he not been skeptical of provenances in the auction catalog. Since then, my experience has dictated that if one desires a really fine piece of jewelry, furniture, or art, it is best to go to a reputable dealer. He, or she, will always stand behind the authenticity and value of his or her merchandise.

My first personal experience with provenance occurred soon after I moved to New York. I had taken several of Sam's foreign diplomas to a small shop called "The New Art Center" at 80th Street and Lexington Avenue to have them framed for his office. The dealer, Jacob Weintraub, who had recently arrived from Europe was suitably impressed. We immediately became fast friends, and I often browsed in his small gallery while pushing Kathe in her baby carriage.

It was about this time that I fell in love with a Toulouse-Lautrec poster with the figure of Misia Natanson in an ice skating posture. I had seen the poster in a 57th Street gallery and had inquired about the price. It was too expensive for me, but I asked the dealer if I might pay for it in three installments. He just laughed at me and said if he allowed that kind of thing, he would soon be broke. I regaled Mr. Weintraub with my tale of woe, and he offered to go down to the gallery, examine the poster to be sure it was not a fake and verify its condition. He explained that many posters by Lautrec and other artists had been plastered all over the fences and garbage cans of France in the mid-nineteenth century. They advertised everything from magazines to actresses playing at the Moulin Rouge. Many posters had suffered from the outdoor exposure, had lost much of their value and their condition was poor. To my delight, Weintraub offered to buy it himself and let me pay him on the installment plan. There was a catch, though. If it was in good shape, I must agree to pay him to frame it. It was, I did, and because it was so large, the framing was not cheap! I will forever be in that wonderful man's debt. How kind he was!

I had many pleasant experiences with the Weintraubs. Their famous gallery began as one of the "mom and pop" businesses that make New York so special. Much later, I bought a Matisse poster signed by the artist and another Lautrec poster of Aristide Bruant. This was after 1962, when my small practice was flourishing. Oh, if only I had thought of borrowing money and buying more art from Jacob Weintraub at those 1960 prices!

One day he said, "Mrs. Gates, whenever you earn some fees in your work, you seem to spend them in my gallery. I am very litigious and have a terrible cash flow. Can't we make some beautiful music together?" From that day on, I served as one of Jacob Weintraub's lawyers. Except for one case, I traded out what he owed me in art. I have bought numerous other pictures and sculptures on my own, but the things I have bought or traded out with this very wise and scrupulously honest dealer, I love!

The Giacometti Sculpture

Once I had a reasonable foundation in the legal complications in the authenticity of art, I undertook several cases for Jacob Weintraub. One was especially challenging.

Jacob, who wished to increase his sculpture inventory turned to Alberto Giacometti, one of the first Swiss impressionist painters. Alberto's first sculpture, a bust of his brother Diego, was completed in 1914 when the artist was only thirteen years old. In the early thirties, he used only a closely knit group of friends and immediate family as his models. Pieces from this period were extremely valuable to collectors.

When the canny Weintraub heard that a Giacometti, known as Tête de Diego, was to be offered at auction by a well-known London auction house, he called their New York representative and discussed what the piece might bring. Jacob offered $1,000 more than the high-side estimate, and was successful in his bid.

During this time, Jacob's wife Barbara was suffering from cancer, and he was taking her to Palm Beach for treatment. Prior to their departure, he made arrangements for the sculpture's transport from London to his gallery in New York.

In his absence, Frank Kent, Weintraub's gallery manager, and his employees uncrated the sculpture. They were ecstatic and quickly transferred it to a position of honor in the gallery's Madison Avenue window. Other dealers flocked to the gallery to view the prize, but several of them shocked Frank by telling him that it was a fraud. Unbeknownst to Jacob Weintraub, there had been questions in London regarding its authenticity, even before the auction. Unfortunately, none of these had been passed on to poor Jacob. When Frank relayed this information to Jacob in Florida, he became frantic! He immediately called the New York representative of the auction house, and then he called me for help.

He reminded me that the provenance had said "three of six—Pierre Matisse Gallery." Dealers knew that all odd numbers of the artist's sculpture were handled by Matisse and even numbers by the Galerie Maeght in Provence, France. At the time of the auction, Jacob told me he had tried to reach Pierre Matisse to verify the provenance of the piece, but Matisse was out of town. Jacob asked that Frank and I confirm the sculpture authenticity as quickly as possible.

Since Frank and I thought that the dealers who questioned the sculpture might simply be sore losers, angry because they had not been able to purchase it, we were determined to prove its authenticity. Several days went by before we were able to reach Pierre Matisse at his gallery. Jacob asked him if he had sold a piece known as Tête de Diego, numbered three of six. (Most sculptors make six castings and then destroy the mold.) He replied, "Yes," I sold that piece to Mr. Bonnier of the Swedish glass concern. Hold on and I will telephone him in Stockholm on my other phone." After several agonizing minutes, he returned with the terrible news that

Mr. Bonnier did indeed have the "sculpture three of six of Tête de Diego," that it was on his coffee table, and that he was looking at it during the entire conversation.

Now that we knew that Jacob's "Tête" was not authentic, we began an action against the London auction house to recover Jacob's money. I shall never forget entering the reception room in the law firm of Goldstein, Judd, and Gurfein—now non-extant—and bumping into one of the partners, Henry Hyde, an old friend. He held out his arms and embraced me with a big hug and said, "Darling Phil, what are you doing here?"

I replied, "Darling Henry, I'm suing you!"

A few months later, we prepared to go to trial, facing Edward Brodsky, a young litigator at Goldstein, Judd, and Gurfein and one of the finest New York trial lawyers. I cried "help" and Sam arranged for Jacob to hire Standish Forde Medina Jr., then an associate at Debevoise, to act as co-counsel. "Forde" was the son of Standish Medina, and grandson of the famous judge, Harold Medina. The first thing Brodsky did was file a motion insisting that the auction house fell under foreign jurisdiction. Forde, always the quick thinker, had already obtained catalogs and brochures from their New York offices which proclaimed ". . . offices in New York and London," or ". . . qualified representation in London and New York." These literally blew Brodsky's argument out of the water!

Judge Frederick "Freddie" Van Pelt Bryan who heard the motion, decided in our favor. After that ruling, we settled the case, although the settlement just about equaled Forde Medina's fee! Jacob had suffered a great deal of anxiety, spent a lot of time and out-of-pocket costs and, generally, felt that he had "lost." Truthfully, so did I, as I charged him very little for my time. Such is law, such is life!

CHAPTER FIFTEEN

Pro Bono

When I die I should be ashamed to leave enough to build me a monument if
there were a wanting friend above ground. I would enjoy the pleasure of
what I give by giving it alive and seeing another enjoy it.
— Alexander Pope 1688–1744

As I look back, the friends that I made in both the bench and the bar
are among those whom I hold most dear. This brings to mind an important facet of my legal practice—"pro bono." In its most literal sense this
term means "for the good," but to most people it simply means for free.

In Washington in 1947, I started my pro bono work by applying as an
attorney with the Legal Aid Society. I have a deep concern for those who
cannot afford legal advice, medical care, comfortable housing, educational training, and a host of other necessities at crucial junctures in their
lives. I don't want to live in a world where only the well-heeled can afford
a lawyer. For almost fifty years my small efforts to help provide legal
services for the poor have given me a real charge and greatly enriched my
life.

The Legal Aid Society

In 1876, public spirited lawyers formed a pioneer corporation to give
legal aid to indigent German immigrants. Twenty years later this nucleus
became the Legal Aid Society, and its service extended to all New Yorkers and later throughout the United States.

Our U.S. Constitution assures all persons accused of a crime a right
to counsel—a part of the Bill of Rights. "Equal justice under the law" is
inscribed on the porticos of most of our nation's courthouses. It is mean-
ingless unless every American has access to competent counsel. Before

Phil with Judge Simon Rifkind (left) and Chief Judge Charles L. Brient at a Legal Aid Society awards dinner in New York City.

the existence of the Legal Aid Society, if a judge asked a person if he had a lawyer representing him, and his answer was "no," then the judge would ask if he could afford to pay for counsel. If that answer was "no" as well, the judge would appoint an attorney from a group sitting in the two front rows of the court room—a hack, sometimes a drunk, but usually one who could not earn a living elsewhere.

I quickly realized the inadequacies of the assistance provided for the poor. Our Washington office of the Legal Aid Society, headed by Allan Fisher, a dedicated and able lawyer, handled only civil matters. We would receive ejectment papers from an indigent client, usually a parent with small children who had failed to pay his rent, about thirty minutes before the hearing for his case was scheduled. Studying pleadings on a quick walk to the courthouse was no way for me or any other volunteer to learn to litigate. As a result, the client had to settle, often after hurried and inadequate preparation of his case. A young lawyer, who contributed his time to poverty cases as a way to help others while gaining experience himself, found his opportunities to receive training inadequate to say the least. In addition his case load was three times heavier than those representing good paying clients. It was no one's fault. We had a tiny budget, too many clients, insufficient lawyers.

When we moved to New York, I became involved with the Legal Aid Society when Barbara Debevoise, wife of Whitney Debevoise, one of Sam's partners, asked me to speak to the society's newly formed Women's Division under the leadership of Fay von Wagoner. Fay had formed the Women's Division (now called the Civil Support Division) to raise funds to support the civil work of Legal Aid, not funded by the city, state, or federal government. It met at Mrs. Chauncey Belknap's robin's-egg blue penthouse in a building across from B Altman on Madison Avenue.

Chauncey was a partner of Patterson, Belknap & Webb. It depended then, as it does now, on private contributions. For the most part, these contributions came from the major law firms, generous foundations, and a dedicated group of lawyers' wives who worked hard to produce theater benefits, balls, lunches, and other fund-raising events.

Barbara Debevoise introduced me and spoke briefly about the volunteer legal work I had done for the past year and a half at the Washington office. I was so captivated by the earnestness of those women that I became a full member of the Women's Division.

Although I eventually argued a few appeals for the society after my admission to the New York bar, the majority of my efforts have been in fund-raising in the private sector, especially in initiating the Legal Aid Ball, a very successful fund-raising event still popular even today. I served on the Women's Division board for over twenty years, was a vice president for several terms, and later its chair. As an officer I was a member of the executive committee, which, in any organization, is where the action is and major policy decisions are made. I am proud even now, five decades later, to be a member-at-large.

Since the 1960s the Supreme Court has held that government must provide counsel for all serious criminal offenders and juveniles. During this period New York City adopted a plan requiring the Legal Aid Society to represent all indigent defendants, yet for a time public support included only criminal cases. By 1970 the society was receiving more than 200,000 requests for assistance each year. Funds, especially for the civil cases, came from law firms, individual lawyers, volunteer organizations, foundations, and trusts, and only a small amount from the city and state.

Our New York City charter indicated only those down and out and on welfare were eligible. Not included are the many, many deserving, hard-working people who desperately need a lawyer. Because they own a car (mortgaged) and a house (also mortgaged), they are ineligible for help from Legal Aid because of the "means" test. It is a crying shame that Legal Aid does not have the funds to provide these people with a lawyer, even though legal advice is of utmost importance to them, and they deserve to have it.

When Alexander Forger of Milbank, Tweed, Hadley, and Hope was president of the society, I used to move close to him at the lunch table meetings and show him the programs of the annual corporate dinner which I had started for the Girl Scouts. I told him how much money we had made and insisted that if the Girl Scouts could do it, surely we, with our connections with the corporate power structure, could initiate a similar corporate dinner to benefit Legal Aid. The result of this "pushing of the programs" over a few years' period was that Alex decided to make a special effort to initiate a "Servant of Justice" Award Dinner, now being held annually with good results. It is worthy of note that John J. McCloy was the first awardee—an altogether fine citizen. This event, with its honoree a former partner of Harrison Tweed, who had been president of the society and former head of the Association of the Bar of New York, gave credence to the award in the circle of New York's organized bar.

Over the years, I have become very involved in fund raising for the Legal Aid Society. The strong funding we have provided enables the society to employ lawyers with high professional standards who would represent a client's legitimate interests whether the case was civil, juvenile, or criminal. I have never swayed from the belief expressed by Supreme Court Justice Hugo L. Black during my law school days that, "There can be no equal justice where the kind of trial a man gets depends on the amount of money he has."[1]

The Girl Scouts

When people think of the Girl Scouts, they consider us "square" and "colorless"—even though our uniforms are green and designed by Halston! My enthusiasm for the Girl Scouts, nevertheless, has lasted until the present day. I joined because the organization was well known for its fine program, and besides I was in the girl business myself. Being a member of the Scout board has always meant a great deal to me. I served for sixteen years as chairman of the famous, nationally franchised cookie sale, a program begun in 1936. My responsibility was the five boroughs of Greater New York City which has raised a million dollars annually. Later I was president, then chairman of the board, and now serve happily as chairman emerita.

Juliette Gordon Low, from a well-established family in Savannah, Georgia, brought girl scouting to the United States in 1912. She had led groups of Girl Guides in England working in impoverished sections of London. Encouraged by the results of her work, she decided to form a similar organization, which she called the Girl Scouts, in the United States. Her first troop consisted of eighteen young women in Savannah with whom she worked on formulating a program and raising funds, most from her own pocket, for operations and personnel. Her first handbook, published in 1916, urged girls to become aviators, doctors, teachers, or whatever they wanted to be.

Mrs. Low's Savannah group was the nucleus for the largest voluntary organization for girls in the world. The Scouts' relationship with their troop leader is unique. She is not their mother, or their teacher, but a real mentor and caring confidante in their young lives. Each badge, approved by the leader, means that the Scout has mastered a special skill in one of dozens of fields, and has learned to be a competent leader and decision-maker.

Many of today's Girl Scouts are from one-parent families. As a consequence their troop leaders place special emphasis on teaching family values. It is a rare blessing for girls to have a continuing one-on-one relationship with an adult who does not impose unjust restrictions but instead provides a great deal of inspiration. Many of the 10,000 adults originally trained as volunteers, have gone on to extremely well-paying jobs. Their leadership training in scouting looks extremely impressive on a résumé! My own daughters say they remember well when I went to a church basement or community center to hand out "Thanks Badges." I would invariably return euphoric and proud of our Scouts, young and old! One very valuable lesson I and others learned in scouting: **One cannot say "thank you" too often!** Many wonderful fellow Girl Scouts taught me this and much much more.

The person who recruited me for Girl Scouting was Harriet Phipps. She told me that her mother had been a friend of Mrs. Low and said she had joined the Girl Scout board at the request of Mrs. Theodore Roosevelt Jr. She became so devoted to the organization that when Howard Phipps proposed marriage to her, she wore her Girl Scout uniform when she went with him to Tiffany's to choose a wedding ring!

In 1975, when I became president of the Girl Scout Council of Greater New York, Harriet became honorary president and promised to "hold my hand." At that time the city's membership stood at 60,000. We had plans to expand to 100,000 members, building among minority and handicapped groups as well as training more adult leaders.

With a history of illustrious leadership, it is no wonder that Girl Scouting was popular when I joined. The organization had attracted women of highest quality, some of whom were notables in the fields of art, music, writing, television, and Broadway. Their standards inspired the troop leaders and the young girls themselves. I made many friends during my scouting years. Among them was Ellin Mackay Berlin (Mrs. Irving Berlin), who joined our board.[2]

Ellin helped me in so many ways. She was completely down to earth and eminently practical. She once followed me out of a board meeting urging, "Phil, you are head of the cookie sale—we simply have to have kosher cookies for our Jewish troops."

My immediate reaction was that the cost of sterilization of the vats and the inspection of the ovens would wipe out the revenue for the Scouts. She said, "Nonsense, we'll talk the Rabbis out of some of the steps and costs. We just have to have at least one of the four kinds of cookies we sell made and baked in compliance with kosher laws so the synagogues will let us deliver them there."

Firm in her insistence, she went on, "You won't be able to tell the difference, Phil. I am a member of three minority groups. Irving is Jewish, I am Catholic, and I'm silver" (the minority metal controlled in part by her ancestors MacKay of the Comstock Lode). Needless to say, her argument was irresistible, and we were the first council in the United States to offer a kosher cookie. Now all of the councils offer kosher cookies. As Ellin said, "you cannot taste the difference and they are healthier."

Because of Ellin, we always sent Irving Berlin flowers on his birthday. On one occasion, I arranged for the Scouts to honor him as he was slowly driven through their midst in Central Park. On that chilly, but sunny, afternoon the girls had an opportunity to show their admiration for the composer who had articulated the American dream in "God Bless America," "There's No Business Like Show Business," "Blue Skies," and "White Christmas," songs they knew so well. I shall never forget his beaming smiles as he waved to groups of scouts along his path. That afternoon marked one of my scouting highlights.

Irving Berlin was among the best known patriots of his time. Ellin always said in public and private venues that being "Mrs. Irving Berlin was the greatest joy of my life." Irving Berlin had left his home in Russia, come to the USA when he was five years old, lived as a teenager in a boarding house for 15 cents a night, and worked as a song plugger, chorus boy, and singing waiter in Chinatown. Jerome Kern observed, "Irving Berlin has no place in American music—he IS American music. He absorbs the vibrations emanating from the people, impressions back to the world in his music, clarified, simplified and glorified."

At lunch, Ellin intrigued me with her memories of her grandmother, Louise Hungerford MacKay, a seamstress and daughter of a barber-druggist who married John MacKay. Ellin's story, as I recall, goes that John took young Louise down into the Comstock Lode, richest deposit in Nevada, and carried out the silver needed for the "memorable piece of a tiny pebble she had found which had a glint in it." They were married, and although there were initial periods of struggle, they eventually had an empire based on the Comstock Lode of silver and an international communications cable company. John MacKay died in London in 1902.

Ellin was a gifted writer. She gave me her book about her family, *Silver Platter*. Not until I began writing myself, did I realize what that aspect of her life had taken out of her strength. Ellin's grandmother had meant so much to her. She had lived in lavish castles and townhouses in London and Paris even after her husband's death. She had entertained the Queen of Spain, Ulysses S. Grant, and the Prince and Princess of Wales in high style. Ellin spoke often of her father, Clarence MacKay, who was known as Clarie and had a reputation as a playful and likeable man. It was he who had founded the communications company and was a fixture of Long Island's north shore society, giving parties for Charles Lindberg after his famous transatlantic flight. It was thrilling as a comparative newcomer to the northeast to hear her stories. Only by volunteering as a Girl Scout had I had the privilege of knowing and working with her.

When Irving Berlin died an era came to an end. Upon hearing of his death, I immediately went to my little chest on top of the bedroom desk and retrieved the five or six letters he had sent me thanking me for flowers I had sent him in the name of the Girl Scout Council. Since I had signed the cards for the council, I got the credit.

In untold ways Ellin Berlin's support for the Girls Scouts enlivened and enriched many occasions. Her name and financial standing and her illustrious connections opened wide avenues for me and my interest in the Girl Scouts.

Once Ellin did me the honor to ask me to lunch with Kitty Carlisle Hart, whose daughter Cathy was, I think, Ellin's goddaughter. Kitty, when I met her, was appearing on television in a popular show entitled *To Tell the Truth*, and subsequently starred on Broadway in a Marx Brothers' play, *A Night at the Opera*. Kitty was a loyal member of the Scout council during my tenure.

Ellin's friend, Iphigene, was married to Arthur Hays Sulzberger, owner

Phil, with Iphigene Sulzberger of the New York Times *at an award dinner.*
Photo by Nansi Bauman.

and publisher of *The New York Times,* positions their grandson, Arthur Ochs Sulzberger Jr., now fills. She was a most remarkable woman in her own right. The greatest pleasure was having lunch with Ellin and Iphigene. They would collapse into gales of laughter recalling the marvelous events they had attended (several visits of the Prince of Wales before and after Mrs. Wallis Simpson and of other celebrities). I would simply sit at their feet and have a marvelous time listening and finally ask, "Isn't this all written down somewhere, ladies?"

Iphigene not only headed the Park's Council of New York City but was schooled in the news business by being appointed by her father to the *Times*'s board of directors when she was in her twenties. She was his only child and the object of all his love. After her father's death in 1935, she continued as one of the three trustees of the Ochs estate which owns the controlling interest in the newspaper. She had been a guest of the heads of state all over the world and a guest of every U.S. president from Coolidge to Kennedy. Turner Catledge of the *New York Times* wrote of Iphigene, "She is a woman you instinctively love and want to please."

When we, at the Girl Scouts, honored Iphigene as our Corporate Achiever of the year not long ago, she accepted but only on the condition that she would not say anything. After all, she was about ninety at the time. Her daughter, Marian, now Mrs. Andrew Heiskell, came with her, sat in front of the dais and I introduced her mother. I thought she would simply receive the roses from a little Scout and say "thank you." Not at all. She spoke for about fifteen minutes, completely ad lib, in a charming and anecdotal way to Marian's and my total surprise.

I am an unabashed fan of the *New York Times*. Anywhere in the world, I scour newstands for a copy of my daily NY Times fix. A long friendship with the John Oakes family and casual friendships with other staff members have meant a great deal to me. Arthur Sulsberger's stroke and long illness took a toll on Iphigene for the last 10 years of his life.

The long strike of 1962-63 took an equally fatal toll on the life of Iphigene's son-in-law, Orville Dryfoos. We had met Orville and his wife Marian at various dinner parties, so it was a pleasant surprise when we were mounting the steps of the Palais de Papes in Avignon, France, to hear them call, "Phil, Sam." Orville and Marian were at the foot of the steps with Susan and Margot Jamieson (daughter of our friend Linda). They announced that John and Margery Oakes had just given birth to a son, John Jr. after three daughters. One of the daughters, Allison, was a bridesmaid in our daughter Kathe's wedding. This was the last time we saw Orville—the handsome, vigorous, and young *Times* editor—alive.

Iphigene kept her hand in the management of the paper, quietly, making her opinions known particularly in matters of education, women's topics, and parks. Just before her last illness when she was in her nineties, we had lunch at her apartment in my neighborhood. When I got up to leave, she asked me to tarry a bit, and I replied that I did not want to tire her out. She said, "Phil, I still have all of my original parts, teeth, bones, eyesight—all I need is better eardrums, so you don't have to repeat so often." Both Ellin Berlin and Iphigene Sulzberger were terrific role models for me. They were brilliant women, both had enormous class, and loved their husbands, children, and grandchildren and provided genuine sources of strength to all of them.

Another fabulous friend whom I met through Girl Scouting, is Jacqueline de Ribes, who lent her fashion collection, time, energy, and money to the Scout Winter Party one year. She walked into her showroom to discuss our benefit looking stately, radiant, beautifully groomed in a quiet stunning way. Instantly I knew I was in a **presence.** Her father-in-law apparently told her that her long slender neck, high bosom, and long

Phil, with two Girl Scouts and Countess Jacqueline de Ribes, whose designs were featured at a Girl Scout Council dinner dance.

waist made her look "half Russian empress and half lady from the Follies Bergère." She was born on Bastille Day, July 14. She lived the sheltered life of a well-born French child and says she never entered a public restaurant until she was married.

Jacqueline always adored clothes, but concentrated on **creativity**, saying, "**Fashion** was too weak." I was so proud of the show she staged for the Scouts that winter and bought two things from her, one of which I recently wore to my grandson Samuel Gates Williamson's wedding and which I will wear with pride all my life, knowing that they "do a lot for me." She lives in a house, one floor elegantly decorated, the other floor a workshop. Her collection is always in the best of taste, classically flattering, and wearable forever. Jacqueline has been aptly described as a "woman of substance." She is a French aristocrat whose lineage is traceable to the twelfth century. Just working briefly with this stunning woman was one of the real treats of volunteering. Jacqueline de Ribes has been a pivotal figure in international social circles as long as I have been reading fashion magazines. A French friend from my current traveling group, Les Amies Amercain de Blerancourt, said, "for the past 30 years one simply could not have a party without inviting her." Mimi de Romanov (formerly Countess de Nemesi) told a writer, "She was always so graceful that it was a joy to watch her do anything, take off a glove or waterski."

She didn't just design clothes, but ran the Ballet de Cuevas for years, raised its funds, and decided on its set and costume designs. She reported that until she was married she had never been to a hair dresser, worn nylon stockings nor makeup. Her long marriage to Edouard de Ribes has

Newspaper clippings from Phil's work with the Girl Scouts. Left, Phil with Mary Lindsay, wife of New York City Mayor John Lindsay, selling Girl Scout Cookies at City Hall in 1966. Right, Phil and Mrs. William Randolph Hearst, Jr. at the Plaza Hotel for a benefit fashion show.

Above, Phil at a Girl Scout dinner with Helen Hayes, first lady of the American theater. Left, Phil at a Girl Scout dinner with author Art Buchwald and Jane Freeman, president of Girl Scouts USA and wife of the Secretary of Agriculture.

been a devoted one on both sides. She says "if we had been Americans we would have been divorced ten times over, but that is not our way."

Jacqueline has created a villa of simplicity and great style on the island of Ibiza and still works and stays involved. Her luxurious Paris apartment includes one floor that serves as a workshop. She claims that she has done what she wants to do and life pleases her. That assessment so impressed me that ever since meeting her, I have tried to make quality out of every day, especially since lung cancer necessitated the partial removal of my right lung. Everyday is a blessed gift and part of that I learned from meeting and reading about Jacqueline de Ribes. She was a truly generous Girl Scout. What a woman! Meeting her was just one of the many thrills of volunteering.[6]

Grosvenor Neighborhood House

Another slot for time outside my home was my work with the Grosvenor Neighborhood House, committed to meeting the educational, social, and employment needs of families struggling to overcome environmental and emotional obstacles. It was planned to provide a safe haven for small children, teenagers, and their parents.

In 1915 stalwart New York City women raised money to buy two brownstone houses on East 49th Street near 1st Avenue. Their first board members installed a resident director and one or two helpers. The board members, themselves, read stories to the young, taught kindergarten classes, and served lunches to senior citizens.

In the beginning, most of Grosvenor's clientele were Polish, Italian, or other immigrant nationalities from Eastern Europe who were trying to find their way in a new and hostile environment. In those days, immigrants did not insist on a bilingual education. They wanted to learn English, and blend into their new country, a melting pot of cultures, races, and creeds.

After the United Nations settled itself in New York right in Grosvenor house's neighborhood, the character of the area changed completely. We found ourselves running services for middle-class families. This was not the founders' purpose.

As a consequence, Grosvenor House instituted a study with the help of the City Planning Commission to find a new spot for a settlement where "The Need Was Greatest." Meanwhile, we sold the two brownstone houses and rented a storefront in the eighties on Columbus Avenue. We served more people in need in that small space than we ever had on the East Side. After endless feasibility studies, we decided to build a house at 105th and Amsterdam Avenue, the first new settlement house in New York in many years. Through unflagging fund raising efforts, we were able to build a splendid house, which serves the neighborhood today.

Now there are over twenty settlement houses in the City. They continue to help immigrant families adjust to their new life. They offer tutoring in English, day-care for pre-schoolers, after-school programs for children, hot lunches for the elderly, and advice to aggrieved tenants. Bingo games and square dances, you name it, it was all there, a "home away from home" provided for hundreds of families.

At present, Grosvenor has more than 1,000 members who are primarily African-American, Latino, and Haitian. They range in age from three to sixty-five with 75 percent under the age of twenty-one. About 50 percent of the children come from single parent households and 85 percent are of families well below the poverty level.

Photo Copyright *Newsday*

Phil with William Casey, former head of the CIA and a Wall Street lawyer receiving an honorary doctorate at St. Johns University in New York.

New York Infirmary

It made me very proud that the first board of directors I joined in New York was that of the New York Infirmary. Peggy Talbott, wife of Air Force Secretary Harold Talbott, invited me to visit the Infirmary's chairwoman, Narcissa (Mrs. Frank) Vanderlip, during the first weeks of our move to New York. I had been suggested by my pal Dr. Khaki Brownell, a board member and wife of George, whose Christmas Eve suppers "made" our holidays. Ever bright, chic, and handsome, Peggy, a native New Yorker, had served as a dedicated volunteer for the Infirmary for many years. She called up to say "Phil, don't commit your spare time until I tell you about the Infirmary."

Who did she think she was kidding? **Spare time?** I had three children under seven and little domestic help.

Dr. Elizabeth Blackwell, founder of the New York Infirmary in 1853, was the first licensed woman doctor in America. Unable to gain admission to any U.S. medical school, she returned to the United Kingdom, where she was born, and received her medical degree from the University of Edinburgh in 1849. Peggy then told me that Dr. Blackwell began her career in New York in 1850, initially establishing a clinic on Bleeker Street, which grew into the New York Infirmary. She chartered both of these facilities for "indigent women and children" with an attending staff of women only because of her own difficulty in getting a medical education and later a hospital post. At the same time Dr. Blackwell opened the Women's Medical College and associated it with the infirmary in order to offer extensive training and clinical experience for women.

Despite Dr. Blackwell's many difficulties at the beginning, she succeeded in raising the stature of women in the medical profession. I shudder knowing that during this same period women law graduates were not being hired as lawyers at major law firms. It was wonderful to have such a fine hospital where women could have the opportunity of achieving full staff standing and even head a department.

Having given me a detailed background of the Infirmary's mission, Peggy drove me to Scarborough, where we entered the grounds of a huge white columned mansion. Narcissa Vanderlip waited at her front door to greet us and escorted us into her beautifully paneled library from which we could see the lush greensward sloping all the way down to the edge of he Hudson River. Legend has it that the towering beech trees were close to four hundred years old. A roaring fire and jasmine tea warmed us, and Narcissa did the rest.

I could not resist expressing admiration for Narcissa's salesmanship of her beloved Infirmary. I agreed to join the board and served as a trustee from 1949 to 1992. We later merged with the Beekman Downtown Hospital and moved from Fifteenth and Second Avenue to William Street. In 1992, we merged again, this time with the New York Hospital as our cash position was perilously low. Our institution is now called the New York Downtown Hospital, and it has entered a new phase presently allied with the New York University Medical Center.

After forty-three years as a trustee of the Infirmary, I resigned with regret. Narcissa Vanderlip had captured my heart, but she had died and Virginia (Mrs. Rush) Kress, her dedicated associate, had also retired as president.

Time marches on and the handsome Vanderlip estate has been divided into two attached, but beautiful country homes keeping the elegance of the architecture, the splendor of the interiors, and the advantages of the stately tree-filled lawn. One of these homes belongs to good friends, Joe and Clare Flom. Their dinner parties, which begin in their impressive library, include financial and intellectual leaders important to the New York scene, and I am always fascinated by their discussions. Joe Flom, an expert in corporate mergers, has been central to the success of his firm Skadden, Arps, Meaher, and Flom. Frank and Narcissa Vanderlip would rejoice to see the Floms enjoying the home they cherished.

The Infirmary, the Grosvenor Neighborhood House, and the Junior League—all three—had for many years staged large, income-producing benefits, including debutante balls, to support their projects. During World War II, any lavish private entertainment would have been not only in bad taste but downright unpatriotic. Even the private "coming out" parties, a custom to introduce one's daughter to one's friends and eligible bachelors in town (a fashion during Edith Wharton's New York), did not go out of style until well after 1945.

The Grosvenor Ball, which presented only twelve girls each Year, flourished from the 1940s to the 1970s, but no longer exists. The Grosvenor Ball gave Sam three great thrills in his life—to waltz with each of his daughters all by himself in the Plaza ballroom with his white tie and tails flying and eyes slightly closed in rapture.

The other two balls are still popular and prospering, and our girls

Sam dancing with his daughter at the Grosvenor Ball.

participated in all of them. The Junior League holds its ball at Thanksgiving and now presents the League's provisional members who will thereafter serve as intelligent, dedicated community volunteers. The Infirmary, known as "The Debutante Cotillion and Christmas Ball," is larger than the League. Initially our daughters balked at attending until I convinced them that they were extremely lucky to be able to dance so others not so fortunate could afford to be hospitalized, thanks to the money earned at the ball. In the end they obediently "came out" at these parties and had a very good time.

Only my oldest granddaughter, Katie Wray, "came out." She phoned me, "Goggi, I'll do the Infirmary for you, the Junior League for mother, but I'm not even going to that old Junior Assembly. Its not for the benefit of any charity." The Assembly is the most exclusive of all—my own daughters were thrilled to attend. What a difference a generation makes.

The Rewards of "Pro Bono"

Pro bono service has included membership on the boards of organizations I have mentioned, as well as of the Southampton, N.Y. Hospital, the President's Council of the Museum of the City of New York, and Florida State University. All of these administrative bodies have kept me very busy. As a result, most of my thoughts are about other people and other things—surely not myself.

Town and Country Magazine had an article in the late sixties featuring New

Phil was included in a Town and Country *article on "Volunteer Executives" in the 1960s.*

York women who, if they were to get paid for their time, would be earning in the six figures. I was proud to be included in the group.

Most people will say that there are many advantages to volunteering one's time other than the inner reward of knowing that your world is a better place because of the time and commitment you made. Wise development offices of charities, always on the lookout for able volunteers, know that they must offer some "goodies" to recompense for all the unpaid hours they are requesting. One such "goody" is the friendships one makes while planning fund raising events. The staff helping the volunteer is usually able and dedicated, so one makes new friends with those paid, usually poorly, to do the work which supports volunteers. The other goody is the chance to get to know such wonderful people I have described, who have so enriched my years.

The old Girl Scout adage is for me: "The greatest joy you keep is what you give away."

Notes

1. *Powell versus Alabama,* 287 U.S. 45, quoted in *Betts versus Brady,* 316 U.S. at 463-64. (See Robert Hermann, Eric Single, and John Boston. *Counsel for the Poor.* Lexington, Massachusetts: Lexington Books, 1977) 20.

2. Ellin Berlin. *Silver Platter.* (New York: Doubleday and Company, 1957)

CHAPTER SIXTEEN

Travels with Sam

Much have I travell'd in the realms of gold,
And many goodly states and kingdoms seen;
Round many western islands have I been
Which bards in fealty to Apollo hold.
— Sonnet: John Keats, 1795–1821

Too much of a good thing is marvelous.
— Mae West

As a result of Sam's outstanding performance as a litigator, he was often invited to attend a variety of organizations that dealt with international air transport. Among those who sought his presence were the Council on Foreign Relations, the U.S. Defense Department, the North Atlantic Treaty Organization, and the even the United Nations when it was establishing its role in peacekeeping and peacemaking.

Sam's interest in all of these organizations emanated from his Civil Aeronautics Board and wartime Air Transport Command years, as well as from his counseling of American Airlines, SAS, KLM, and other carriers. It was this linkage that made it possible for us to see almost every corner of the world in grand style. Sam and I often pinched ourselves and wondered why life had dealt us such a good hand. We were able to go everywhere as a part of Sam's professional life, spending a fraction of what it costs others.

The wonderful memories, now in scrapbooks and logs, recount our times in Lebanon, before its troubles. We stayed at the Saint George Hotel where politicians made deals at the bar, just as they did when we were in Athens at the famous bar of the Hotel Grande Bretagne, which had seen its own share of gunfire. I still taste the great souffles at the Goldener Hirsh in Salzburg, the tortes at the Sacher and the venison at the Drei Hussars in Vienna. We were captivated by the stunning harbor views of Rio, of Hong Kong from a top floor of either the Peninsula, Mandarin, or Regent hotels, and of Acapulco from Casa Carlena. We savored the mystique of the Oriental Hotel in Bangkok and the Shangri-la in Singapore. We were dazzled by the flowered carpets and embroidered sheets at the Ritz in Madrid, just across from the Prado. We delighted in the elegance of the Crillon in Paris and the Connaught in London where every footman remembered our name. (How in the world do they ever do that?) All service in those places was quite different from that of the Okura in Tokyo, where there was no personal touch at all. We also stayed at the Cipriani, intimate and warm, at Asolo in northern Italy, and the Cipriani on the Venetian Canals, now too chic and full of the nouveau riche.

My most enchanting night was on the shores of Lago Maggiore in Stresa, Italy. The dusk was just beginning. I walked out on our balcony at the Hotel del Isles Barromea. The lights around that great lake began to flicker like a fairy tale or an extravagant stage set. I screamed for Sam to stop his unpacking and come to look. I think I said, "Just shoot me now, for I never want to see anything more exciting in my life!" Fortunately, he did not follow my instructions as I lived to see so much more. I hope there are a few sights left to see in my old age! When I close my thirty overstuffed scrapbooks, I think of Sam's and my charmed life. While we had many wonderful trips together, I will recount a few of the most special.

Guests of the Government of Mexico, Spring 1942

Our first trip to Mexico in 1942 was when Colonel Alberto Salinas Carranza, head of Civil Aviation in Mexico, arranged to have the President of Mexico invite Sam and me for an official visit to his country. While there, Sam's obligation was to write the rules and regulations for air, rail, and bus transport, across our borders so that pilots, engineers, and truck drivers would have to know only one set of rules. Sam met all day every day with his counterparts at the Mexican Civil Aeronautics Authority, and I listened to the proceedings, an opportunity that supplemented a practical aspect of my law studies at George Washington.

In the course of his work, Sam flew on about eleven separate domestic air carriers, loaded, as he told me, with goats, pregnant women, children, and laborers.

We did find time, however, to celebrate our first wedding anniversary in Xochimilco, a little Venice with floating flower-covered gondolas, outside of the nation's capital. All of the presidents of the domestic carriers gave us a festive luncheon and signed its menu, which still hangs framed in my New York kitchen. After seeing Puebla, Cuernavaca, Oaxaca, as well as the Aztec Pyramids, I concluded there was, indeed, a lot to be gained by Sam's "hitches" abroad.

On Business in New Delhi

Sam and Phil in Xochimilco, Mexico's Venice, on their first wedding anniversary, 1942.

Another memorable trip was to New Delhi in 1951, where the International Air Transport Association (IATA) met. We had the pleasure of meeting J.R.D. Tata, India's first pilot and founder of Air India. Members of Mr. Tata's family were and still are the most important industrialists in that nation. Almost every bus, train, airline, bicycle, steamship—yes—every atomic energy component had the Tata logo on it. For weeks before our arrival, Mr. Tata had worked hard to persuade Jawaharal Nehru, then prime minister and father of Indira Gandhi, to meet with us. When we said we had intended to leave during the first weekend of the conference to visit Kashmir, Mr. Tata persuaded us that having lunch with Nehru was much more important. Sam agreed, and with memories of that fascinating lunch still vivid in my mind, I am glad that he did.

A Side Trip to Kashmir

Twenty years later, we had an opportunity to visit Kashmir, our one and only opportunity to see this historical region northwest of India. In the autumn of 1971, Sam and I spent four weeks in Asia and India, a trip full of business obligations for Sam but afforded him some time for adventure. Our companions were Jock and Carlene Lawrence. While Carlene made the principal reservations, they delegated to me the reservations for a houseboat sojourn on Lake Dal, Srinagar, Kashmir. After inquiry I learned that all travelers of any note stayed on one of four houseboats owned by a Moslem gentleman named G.M. Butt. I wrote to reserve our space. No answer! At each stop, To-kyo, Hong Kong, Bangkok, and New Delhi, I tried to confirm our reservations—no answer! This was my only responsibility on this extensive trip and so far, I had nothing to show for my work. The time to arrive in Srinagar was drawing per-ilously close.

Finally I sought the help of the concierge at the Oberoi Hotel in New Delhi.

Sam and Phil at Tsavo Camp in Africa.

We received a brief reply that Mr. Butt knew we were coming and would have a car to meet us. As we deplaned in Srinagar, a very remote and exotic place, my uneasy feel-ings were not soothed by the appearance of our driver, a shabby fellow in tattered clothes, and his dilapidated 1930 vintage car. I just about held my breath the entire 30-minute ride. My sophisticated traveling pals said little or nothing. In fact they tried to avoid me!

We climbed out of the "tin lizzie," pointed out which bag belonged to which person, and entered a small room which contained a reservation desk of a sort. While we all registered, I glanced over to the right-hand wall, and what did I see but a framed poem signed by a friend of ours, Mary Tweedy, and dedicated to Mr. Butt! Mary and her husband, Gordon, lived in New York and their girls were our daughters' classmates. Mary had worked at Time, Inc., and I had often heard the story of how, when she was four months pregnant, she covered the "over the hump" opera-tion of the Air Transport Command and went off to join her husband for a belated honeymoon in India. Something went wrong with her plane, and Mary had to parachute into the snowy mountains of the Himalayan re-gion on the Kashmir border. Sherpa guides, who worked for Mr. Butt, rescued her and brought her back to Srinagar, where she was nursed to health. When I saw her poem in Mr. Butt's office, my heart leapt with glee. I showed it to Sam and the Lawrences, and, with a sigh of relief, I walked confidently into the beautiful gardens on the banks of Lake Dal, which harbored the Butt houseboats.

We were met by a small gentleman in white turban and long, white Arabian robe with his hands clasped, saying greetings in Hindu—*namaste*. "Is the poem framed in your office signed by my friend, Mrs. Gordon Tweedy of New York and *Time Magazine?*" I blurted out without even introducing myself. "That is Mary Parachute Tweedy," he replied. For me, all seemed right in the world at last.

We looked out on a crisp, cloudless sky and a beautiful Dahlia-filled garden, bordered by glorious chrysanthemums, seemingly planted just for Sam. When we went back into the office, I noticed numerous pictures and tributes to a beautiful stay there from the likes of Chester Bowles, Dean Rusk, Lord Mountbatten, Anthony Eden, and various other international figures. I now knew for certain that I had chosen wisely.

We were shown to our boat, which had a lovely living room, four bedrooms, all decorated with Chippendale furniture and exquisite crewel-embroidered upholstery and draperies. Walls were hung with Mongol miniature paintings. After unpacking, we were served a delicious luncheon in the sunny October garden while Mr. Butt trotted out guest book after guest book full of tributes from people; about one-half of whom we knew and many whose name we recognized.

During lunch, Carlene Lawrence kept saying how staying on the houseboat was the most special part of the entire trip. I'm glad it was so special. We were treated so royally that we began wondering what this splendor was going to cost us. I had never been quoted a price, so we were steeling ourselves for the worst. Shortly after lunch, a most attractive couple sauntered out of the smaller (3-bedroom) boat moored next to ours and began chatting with us. They were in the Swiss foreign service, and they told us that the mountains in the distance were a great deal higher than their Alps.

After a bit more conversation, I could bear it no longer. Still feeling responsible for this segment of the trip, I ventured, "Could we be so bold as to ask what the daily rate is here?" Knowing it was on an American Plan, with three meals a day included and masses of servants swarming around us, I held my breath. The rate was, in the 1971 dollar, about $20 a day, per person. It was a bargain never encountered before or since. From then on we relished each day.

Alas, Carlene soon caught the flu, and the Lawrences had to return to a Delhi doctor. We were quite lonely in our vast accommodations, but we had many unforgettable days there, each offering a new excursion. We especially enjoyed golfing at a nine-hole course, miles up in the snow-covered Himalayan mountains. The last day we were to be on the lake, Mr. Butt paid us his morning visit to see how we were doing. I had given him one of my asthma inhalers as I, a fellow asthmatic, saw him struggling for breath and recognized his misery. He reported that he had slept well the night before and felt better than he had in months. He wanted to do something nice for me but sadly, he could not include Mr. Gates. The kindness was an invitation to his house at the end of the feast of Ramadan, a fasting period similar to our Lent. If he were to include Sam, he explained, his "women" would have to wear purdah (veil) and would not have the freedom for fun; whereas, with me, as a woman guest, they did not have to cover their faces.

Sam said I should jump at the chance to see this family on such a special night, that he would happily dine alone and finish his book. Only two or three of the thirty or so family members at this gathering spoke English, so we communicated in sign or body language. We had murky, too-sweet tea and what they described as sweetmeats—very, very sweet cookies and candy. No furniture to speak of was visible anywhere in this four-story home, except beds. One daughter-in-law had just had a baby so I climbed to the third floor to greet her as she rested. I could peek at the various rooms on my way downstairs. We sat on cushions and rugs with pillows at our backs. Every room was lit by candlelight. I saw no evidence of any electricity.

We found it difficult to tell Mr. Butt how much we loved a glimpse into his "world." Sam, who was not much of a shopper, spent over $400 in twenty minutes in his shop, a very rickety building on a side street (all of Srinagar seemed about twelfth century). We bought lovely crewel drapery and upholstery materials, tiny embroidered featherweight shawls and bathrobes, and a lovely petit point rug, which still graces my country living room. We gave away most of the linens as gifts. I still have eight gold-encrusted placemats which I use weekly. After twenty-five years of use, their bright colors and gold tracery look brand new. Now that Mr. Butt is no longer with us, his sons are continuing his export business. I think of him often. My dream, and Sam's too, was fulfilled on his lake in Srinagar.

Even yet, I have dramatic thoughts of the Vale of Kashmir. Nehru said it "whispers its fairy magic to the ears, and its memory disturbs the mind." While we were there the armies of India and Pakistan were fighting on its borders and they still are. Yet the lofty Himalayan peaks towered over us, seemingly enclosing us from danger. My dream, and Sam's too, were fulfilled on Mr. Butt's lake in Srinagar.

New Year's Eve in Red Square

In the winter of 1977–1978 we had two weeks in Russia, a nation I had visited on the eve of World War II under very different auspices. After hearing of my trip, Sam yearned to go with me, but he only wanted to visit there in the snow. We went, thanks to Pauline Frederick, my colleague in Washington, who covered the United Nations for NBC for many years. She arranged our trip through her connections with the Soviet delegation's public relations office. We were accompanied by our friends, Al and Carol Fehsenfeld. We had great fun celebrating New Year's Eve in Red Square, drinking champagne provided by the U.S. embassy. To Sam's great delight, we rode through Russian forests in a troika drawn by three grey horses covered with a mangy, fur rug over us, with beautiful snow falling softly about us. We were fulfilling one of Sam's long-delayed desires made possible by my old office colleague at the Federal Register in Washington.

We learned that Moscow was a tiny village surrounded by wooden walls in 1156. Situated on a river system with access to the Volga, it grew rapidly into a center for trade, despite being ice bound in the long winters, with biting Baltic winds flogging its inhabitants.

Half a millennium later, in 1703, Peter the Great founded St. Petersburg. According to legend, during his campaign against the Swedes, he is said to have cut two pieces of peat, laid them crosswise and declared, "My city will be here." He then captured a small fort on the edge of Lake Lagoda and called it St. Petersburg. This tiny stronghold, surrounded by salt marshes, was soon built into his capital. His enormous statue with its great Bronze Horseman, erected by Empress Catherine II eighty years later, dominates the city. no longer called Leningrad since the dissolution of the Soviet Union in 1991.

The glories of Leningrad, as the city was known when we were there in 1978, with its canals, pastel-colored palaces, and magnificent art collections, were especially appealing to Sam who was making his first visit to this cultural center of the Soviet Union. (During my 1938 visit, there was not a single color on any building in Leningrad.) Many critics say that Peter's equestrian monument is a better symbol of St. Petersburg than the Winter Palace, known as the Hermitage.

Holland, Our Favorite

The last country I'll mention was Holland, where we made lasting friendships. As counsel for KLM, Sam's work for that company afforded us many visits to Holland and the opportunity to make friends among those marvelous Dutch people. We were there several times a year, principally in The Hague. Our good friends in that city were, "Tous" Steenstra-Toussaint and his lovely wife Meis. After being an officer of KLM, Tous became the first chief executive of the famous Bols Company, who had not been a member of this famous family since it was founded in 1492.

The Dutch had suffered so much during the German occupation of their nation in World War II that Tous and Meis could not allow us to park our German-made Mercedes-Benz in front of their home when we visited them. It took ten years before they not only changed their minds but bought their own Mercedes.

Anne Frank and her family had not been the only people to hide from the Nazis. Many of our non-Jewish friends, such as the Toussaints, had hidden, as well. When the Gestapo knocked on the door, the husband would quickly go to the "hiding place" and the wife would toss the bed covers back to chill the bed. It was the first place the security police inspected. If there was any evidence of body heat, they would search the whole house thoroughly.

We had many visits with Tous and Meis Toussaint in their comfortable home in the center of The Hague—its great living room "giving out" on a fine garden. We toured in their sailboat and car through the quaint and beautiful sixteenth century harbors in which that country abounds. We stopped to sightsee and lunch in many tiny harbor towns, with their ancient town clock towers. Alkmaar is especially picturesque with its huge market of red, round, wax-covered Edam and other cheeses piled on carriers or being weighed on ancient scales, just as Breughel depicted in his paintings.

During our long friendship, Tous occasionally found it necessary to come to New York. Our children, when possible, joined in our visits. When Robert Plessman, the older of the two sons of Meis Toussaint and her first husband (killed in a World War II air crash) came to stay with us in Westhampton, it was at the request of his stepfather. Tous telephoned Sam, "Eh Sam, Robert (aged 16 or 17) is spending a week on the Donald Douglas's (of Douglas Aircraft) yacht. I just want this boy to know that, in the United States, everyone does not live as lavishly as the Douglas tycoon. Will you and Phil take him for a week in Westhampton so he can see American people, who live as his parents do?" We agreed enthusiastically. I met Robert, a handsome, six foot-three-inch, blond, athletic Adonis at Kennedy Airport and drove him to Westhampton.

After we chattered for a while—he was especially amazed at how large American autos are—he asked me what was really on his mind. "What is the average Westhampton day?" I replied that if he did not come down from his bedroom to the kitchen by 9 a.m., we would leave eggs, bread, and fruit on the counter for him, and he could make his own breakfast. We would also leave a brown paper bag with a sandwich, an apple, and a hard-boiled egg for his lunch. We would assign him a bicycle for his exclusive use during his visit. He would have to be either at the Quantuck Beach Club or the Westhampton Country Club for tennis or golf, or he must leave a note on my telephone stating where he would be, for I was responsible for his safety and his parents were depending on me.

"A sandwich?" he asked and I countered, "Don't you like sandwiches. Most of our children do."

He said, "I'm used to five!" That threw me slightly off base, but I quickly promised "Your paper bag will have five, Robert." I later discovered that since he liked his sandwich Holland-style, which is open-faced— he simply threw away the tops!

Another question followed, "Do you kiss a girl on the first date?" I replied, "Ask my daughters, they can answer that much better than I!"

Robert was a great help, a fine house guest, and we did, and do, adore him.

Some years later, the highlight of our Dutch friendships was the marriage of my "adopted" Dutch daughter, Patricia Slotemaker, to Philip van de Veen in a large Catholic church in The Hague. We had cocktails on the eve of the wedding day with Tous and Meis, as Patricia's mother, Tessie, had died and her father, Bert, was on his way from Switzerland to host the wedding. It was Bert who was responsible for Sam's representation of KLM, his wife Tessie who had enlivened our lives, and their daughter and Philip who came frequently to see us. We celebrate their children's and my grandchildren's weddings together. They are fabulous. Later we went to dinner without the betrothed couple, at the four-star private club called the *Jagertje*, located in a picturesque sixteenth century house built on a small canal.

The dinner for sixteen was a two-family affair, hosted by Tous and Meis. Four of the Toussaint/Plessman sons came to dinner with their beautiful wives. Our children, Kathe and Edwin, who were living in London, and Gilda and Cecil, who were living in Paris, joined us. Tous and I were seated at one head of the table, Sam and Meis at the other. About half-way through the dinner, I leaned over to Tous and said what a thrill it was, after fifteen years of transatlantic visits to each of our homes, to have our children grown up and with us. I remarked that it was a reward for parents to see their children so successful in their studies, their careers, and their choice of mates. I added, "I shudder to think of what this evening is costing you!"

Tous replied, "Phil, nothing in the world would be too much to spend on this special evening together with our children, who have built such extraordinary international friendships with one another."

Tous was right. As I end these notes on our most memorable travels, I cherish the sites we saw, but most I cherish the friendships and all the extraordinary people we were privileged to meet on our way.

CHAPTER SEVENTEEN

Sam

Life engenders life. Energy creates energy.
It is by spending oneself that one becomes rich.
— Sarah Bernhardt, 1844–1923

A wise old pundit points out that we spend a lot of time being educated to make one important good judgment in our lifetime. My one un-
impeachable judgment was to marry Sam Gates. From my vantage point,
and now eighty plus, I believe more firmly than ever that the most important decision in one's life is to choose one's life's partner. All resources
must go into that judgment if the future is to develop according to one's
dreams.

Sam Gates was a very rich man, but not at all in a money sense.
Neither of us inherited anything except wonderfully supportive love from
our parents. He paid 70 percent of his income in taxes during his prime
earning years at the law. World War II took five important earning years
out of our lives and demolished what little savings we had. Lawyers did
not make the huge amounts successful name partners do today. However,
Sam was rich in being a very happy and contented man.

Sam's sources of happiness and contentment stemmed from his love
of family and his satisfaction with his chosen career. He undertook a variety of professional activities and thrived on them all. I dare say he could
perform almost any kind of legal service, was the most versatile practitioner in his firm, and he ended his career as a trial lawyer, a master of his
craft. He was selected as a Fellow of the American College of Trial Lawyers, a professional society whose membership is limited to the very best

Sam receiving his DSM from Lt. General George in 1945.

litigators. He was chosen by his peers as one who met the highest standards of professional ability, industry, and integrity. In 1974, after his election to the college, he headed the committee concerned with the most complex litigation. According to its past president, Thomas Deacy, Sam brought his knowledge, skill, wit, and wisdom to help shape the course of decisions and events in all branches of judicial administration—the courts, the Department of Justice, and the Congress. Through his warmth and leadership and his skill in bringing people together, he attracted other able colleagues to those endeavors.

Launching a Post-War Career

When Sam first joined Debevoise, Plimpton, and MacLean in 1948, he had not practiced bona fide law since mid-1942, when he enlisted in the Air Force. While he had been deputy chief of plans with the Air Transport Command, helping to run the biggest airline the world had ever known, his work was quite different from writing a debenture, which I recall was one of his first post-war assignments. Sam was frantic! With all of his education and experience, he was not in his area of expertise, and no amount of foreign diplomas or memberships in international organizations could help him write a **debenture**! Neither one of us slept much the night before that document was due to be executed. His work, which I helped him edit until 3 a.m., went into six drafts.

One day shortly after getting settled at 20 Exchange Place, where the firm was then located, Sam was asked to defend a law suit brought against one of the firm's biggest clients, the National Starch Co. The firm was accused of selling defective glue to a furniture manufacturer in Tennessee. Sam worked day and night (not having been in a courtroom for six years) preparing for the opening of the case in Memphis. Not one of the Debevoise partners expected him to win, but their important client needed a vigorous defense.

Sam assigned Bret Carlson, an associate who later became chief of the tax division at Debevoise, to write the trial brief. When Sam read what Bret considered his final draft, Sam said he could not understand it and a judge would certainly not be persuaded to vote for the firm's position because of it. He sent Bret back for one, two, three more drafts. Finally, according to Bret's letter to me later, Sam said, "I'm going to take this draft home to my wife. She is a lawyer, and she has learned a lot about this case from me. I'll see if she understands it and is persuaded by your argument." I wasn't. After two more drafts, Bret produced a superb brief.

Every day for about four weeks, Sam walked into the courtroom filled with broken furniture that had come apart because the glue had not held. Contrary to what everyone had expected, Sam won the case. He was able to prove that the manufacturer had stored the furniture in a warehouse with below freezing temperatures—contrary to National Starch's explicit instructions for the use of the glue. This triumph in a supposedly un-winnable case established Sam with his partners as an unbeatable litigator and launched his career. In time, his specialty became complex multi-district federal cases and stockholders' derivative actions, including antitrust.

Sam's practice at Debevoise, Plimpton, Lyons & Gates was as varied as it had always been even though he represented American Airlines, KLM and National Starch Co., as well as the group of Ivy League Universities in their troubles with Equity Funding and on and on.

The most "fun" client he had was the 200 tournament golf champions who wanted to leave the Professional Golf Association. The office was buzzing one day when he returned from lunch; all halls leading to his

Newspaper clippings on Sam's legal career.

corner office were filled with stenos whispering. As he neared the door of his inner sanctum, there sat Jack Nicklaus, Arnold Palmer, and Gardner Dickinson, all well known golfers as the tournaments were beginning to be televised. After Sam waved them in, he asked "How did you fellows get here, to me." It developed that some opposing counsel who had appeared with Sam recommended him, which was a very high compliment indeed. There began a three year exercise in motion practice and negotiation leading up to the formation of an independent Tournament Players Division within the PGA. As it had all become a multimillion dollar business with TV rights, most of which Sam ran out of his law office for months until they persuaded Joe Dye of the USGA to assume its chair, we did see a lot of its principals. Additionally, we were able to attend many famous tournaments, including the Ryder Cup at Muirfields in Scotland.

Sam had a very high handicap (much lower than mine), but he had deserted tennis for golf after 50 and therefore had an erratic, if enthusiastic game. He loved to quote Winston Churchill, "Golf is a game it is to hit a very small ball into an even smaller hole with weapons singularly ill-

Sam and Phil at the National Golf Links in Southampton, Long Island, 1978.

designed for the purpose." The law, especially litigation, demands that one knows more about one's client's business than he knows himself. This was one client of which that was not true. When Jack Nicklaus used to ask Sam how anyone with a 26 handicap could keep playing golf, Sam always replied. "I'm thinking too much about your legal problems, Jack, and not enough about how I am going to hit the ball to be any good." The Nicklaus's were a wonderful family and one of Sam's best memories was putting their new colicky baby to sleep with his lullaby when he was visiting them in Florida.

From then on, part of the excitement which seemed to pulse through Sam's practice, as a young lawyer, was his exchange of experiences with men who became giants of our profession. In the late 1950s and 1960s Sam's "gang" was known as the "Wall Street Lawyers," who handled the biggest cases and in so doing charged the biggest fees—by today's standards these fees would seem paltry. They boasted legal craftsmanship of

Sam and Phil at the American College of Trial Lawyers meeting in Phoenix, Arizona, 1978, when Sam was installed as President-Elect of the College.

the finest order and could assign whole squads of associates and younger partners to handle complicated antitrust cases.

During one thirty-day period in the fall of 1957, Sam's gang of Wall Street lawyers was instrumental in the following: analyzing and approving an important antitrust consent decree for Combustion Engineering, Inc.; representing American Express in the organization of an international car-rental system owned jointly with Hertz; handling the $11 million stock swap which involved two of New York's largest hotels, the Ambassador and the Sheraton-Astor; giving opinions on the culmination of the merger of Climax Molybdenum and American Metal; defending the attack on the merger of Bethlehem Steel and Youngstown Sheet and Tube by the Department of Justice; and, lastly, preparing major corporate security issues, including a $288 million common stock offering! This legalistic legermain seems pale compared to today's billion dollar deals, but they were top of the line in the practice of corporate law through the 1950s and 1960s.

In today's world of mega-mergers and acquisitions, these Wall Street lawyers' accomplishments are still impressive, but in 1958 they were more than stupendous. Over the years this corps of Wall Street lawyers also became very active in pro bono work. Many took temporary leaves of absence from their partners and served the government. Edwin Weisl, a close friend, was at the president's call during both the Roosevelt and Truman administrations and served as counsel to various Senate committees during the Johnson administration. The public service record of John Foster and Allen Dulles at the State Department and the CIA are well chronicled. They served on such august bodies as the Carnegie Corporation, Rockefeller Institute for Medical Research, and the Ford Foundation. During our first ten years in New York, many of the country's major corporations were headed by former Wall Street lawyers. Two of Sam's partners later headed Phelps, Dodge Copper. Other firms sent their partners to direct Chase Bank, J.P. Morgan, Chrysler, and Chase Manhattan.

Sam Suddenly Stricken

During the first weekend in March 1979, we attended a ball at the Kennedy Center in Washington, D.C., to celebrate the birthday of Pat Hayes, founder of the Washington Performing Arts Society.[2] Sam was to return to New York, then fly to Boca Raton, Florida, for the spring meeting of the American College of Trial Lawyers. He was looking forward to taking office as president-elect of the college, for he felt that this presidency was the highest honor he could receive except a place on the U.S. Supreme Court. I was to stay at my sister's home in Alexandria, Virginia, and then fly to Orlando to nurse my mother before joining Sam in Boca Raton.

As Sam began to drive back to New York, after our gala weekend, he was taken suddenly ill, stricken with a rupturing aorta, and rushed to the Thomas Jefferson University Hospital in Philadelphia. After hearing of his collapse, I rushed to join him. As soon as he was able to speak, he dictated to me a memo he wished me to send to the fellows of the college, regretting that he would not be able to attend the program. Sam's words, as I recorded them, are:

> "Mr. President, Messrs. Past Presidents, Regents, and Fellows: Through a spokesman, I rise to a point of personal privilege. I have learned that within the last few days a baseless and vicious slander about me has been circulated within the ranks of the college by some Midwesterners who should know better. I am surprised that those who have passed the rigorous requirements for fellowship should engage in such efforts. The calumny to which

I refer, is that in order to avoid the possible loss of a few bucks on the golf course, I elected to spend roughly two weeks at the Thomas Jefferson University Hospital in Philadelphia recuperating from a six-hour operation, during which I had a ruptured aneurysm of the right aorta and lost one of my kidneys.

The medical facts are correct but the alleged motivations have no support. I pay tribute to the medical staff of this hospital. They saved my life and I owe them a real debt of gratitude. I add parenthetically that I won the weekly Purple Heart Award from the Intensive Care Unit.

Unfortunately, the doctors have unalterably forbidden my attendance at the Boca Raton meeting. In a real sense, this is an enormous disappointment. I learned only after my election as President-Elect last August that I was responsible for arranging the programs for the Spring and Summer meetings. I think that we have an outstanding program and hope you will enjoy the fruits of the labors of all of those who participated in putting the program together. I thank each one of them by this brief message.

Phil and I will miss your fellowship and being with you. We, also, thank you from the bottom of our hearts for your many calls, telegrams, prayers, and flowers during my illness. Have a great time. We look forward to seeing you in August in Dallas. I should add that the Chandler Memorial Trophy which I won in Phoenix is on its way. I especially anticipate the pleasure of dancing with the beautiful wives of my colleagues. So, until we meet in Dallas, even if it means a continued subsidy to the likes of Mattson, Eidmann, Deacy, Jennings, Baker and LaFitte and all of you sterling fellows, please count on my full support. Love, Sam

As Sam left the intensive care unit for his own private room, he received a telephone call from his friend Leon Jaworski, who had finished his job as Watergate prosecutor and was trying to persuade Sam to take over the Korea Gate.

Leon said, "Sam, I've had a bypass operation. You must take it easy now, I know."

Sam jokingly replied, "Look, Leon, anything you can do, I can do better."

Tragically, this time Sam's optimism was not to be. He died a few days later on March 8, 1979.

Since the rector of our own St. James Episcopal Church would not allow eulogies, we held Sam's memorial service at St. Bartholomews at 50th and Park Avenue. Tom Deacy, who spoke at the service, said "I had the pleasure of working with Sam, sharing victories and defeats. But it was not all labor without repose. I shall remember Sam, the golfer—not a professional in this, by any means, but a splendid companion who so enjoyed the game that he added to his friends' enjoyment of it."

Henry Harfield, a great friend, partner of Shearman and Sterling, followed Tom with these words: "Sam was indeed a man of parts. As a counselor he had a keen and perceptive mind. As an advocate, he had a facile tongue and persuasive voice. As a dancing man, he had nimble feet and tireless limbs. But, I shall remember him most for a less conspicuous characteristic. Sam had a green thumb. He made things grow. The dahlias that he grew, among his other flowers, were a source of pride to Sam and a source of pleasure to those with whom he shared them so generously.

"His garden was not markedly different from those of his neighbors. The earth, water, sun, seeds were all common to all. But Sam's garden was nourished by his special warmth and vitality. He strengthened plants as he sustained people. Those whom he brought into his garden came away refreshed. None of this means that Gates at any time epitomized meekness, nor even that he suffered fools or knaves gladly. Like the gardener that he was, Sam knew that acid is frequently necessary to ensure the fertility of soil. He had a good store of acid, and he knew how to use it. There are young lawyers among us who stand taller and straighter for having had their early growth severely pruned by Sam. He went out to meet life physically, mentally, emotionally. Yet, he was a gardener, and in his relation to people he was more than a gardener, he was a cultivator. He brought people to fruition. Beyond his family stand a multitude whose lives were enriched by his teaching, his patience, the understanding, the tenderness that Sam displayed in his garden of people and flowers."

Oscar Reubhaussen, his law partner, seemed to put the essence of all of Sam's colleagues together for me. He said: "Sam came to us with a solid record of achievement behind him—as a lawyer, author, public speaker, civic leader, legislative draftsman, pioneer in aviation law, public servant in Washington, and recipient on the Distinguished Service Medal for his wartime service which culminated in his leaving the Air

Force as a full colonel. No need that Sam perceived was left unmet. No client interest was left unserved. No hours were too long when there was a problem to be solved or a job to be done. He loved his work. But Sam also loved life, people, and action. He could play as vigorously as he could work.

"At our annual office outings, he was a participant in every event from the opening round of golf to the last hand of poker, with stops on the pitcher's mound and the tennis court along the way. As a dancer, he was a joy to watch. His waltz was smooth, his Samba stylish. He was out on the floor for every number, giving pleasure to others, and enjoying himself enormously. His practice was diverse indeed. He practiced the whole spectrum of the law. His clientele ranged from airlines to banks, from professional golfers to pre-eminent scientists. Yet, there was a strong, unifying rhythm to his entire legal career. The central theme was oral advocacy. A college debater himself, he actually taught public speaking and debate for several years in a junior college and remained a teacher all of his life. As an advocate, Sam had rare qualities—he was never hostile; he was never thorny; he never personalized; he was always warm and friendly. The legion of his friends bears witness that his own great capacity for friendship was fully expended and his personal warmth fulfilled his life."

Rick Stearns, our son-in-law, gave a superb perception of Sam— husband, father, and grandfather—following the beautiful verses of the Prayer Book. Rick said:

My name is Rick Stearns. I am one of Sam Gates's three sons-in-law. I am here to say a few words about Sam Gates on behalf of our family—Mom Gates, their three daughters, and my two brothers-in-law. I hardly need say that your presence here in tribute to Sam Gates is very touching to all of us.

Thinking of him and of the times we shared, and realizing they won't continue, obviously is sad. Yet the memories are joyous, some amusing, and all filled with affection and love. And thinking of those wonderful times together, we realize that his energy, personality, and interest in people assure a continuation of his ideals through those he loved.

There are many facets of his journey through life. I would like to limit my comments to two of them—his interest in young people and in his family life.

Young People: In selecting his interest in the young, I don't intend to overlook his enjoyment of all people or the enthusiasm with which he sought out their friendship. Yet, he had a special interest in the young, perhaps because he lived such a full life that he wished to share with younger generations some of what he had learned.

He also had the rare ability to relate to young people on their own level, not as a superior or remote adult but as one genuinely interested in them. To most young people, he was simply—Sam— a friend to whom one could speak any time, whether a young associate in his law firm, his children's friends seeking guidance on a career or a neighbor inquiring about his other specialty, gardening and growing beautiful dahlias.

There are some young people who were truly special to him, his grandchildren. I would like to share with you some of their recollections of their grandfather.

His namesake, Sammy Gates Williamson, aged seven, would frequently refer to him by saying, "Grandfather certainly has high standards." Indeed he did. Hopie, a granddaughter, at age five, has a different perspective. She remembers grandfather as the friendly person who would sneak her gumdrops after her mother had cut off the supply.

His oldest grandchildren, Christopher and Katie Wray, remember the interest he took in their studies and in helping with their homework. Also, a few months ago, when visiting them in Paris, he spent several hours as they tried to teach him what they called "real" disco dancing. There he was, seventy-two years old, coat off, tie flying, trying to shake those solid hips with the same suppleness as his pre-teenage grandchildren. This was only last Christmas. Christopher and Katie also recall the vacation bedroom they shared with him a few years ago when his loud and persistent snoring kept them awake until he realized it and moved to the bathroom to sleep in the bathtub.

My son, Owen, aged seven, after learning of his grandfather's death, came to me and asked sadly, "Daddy, who will help me now with my garden and with grandfather's beautiful flowers?"

Sam Gates was not an aloof figure to his eight grandchildren. They would curl up on his lap for a story, or eat his homemade

popcorn, or ask questions—frequently about his plants and gardens. Grandfather was very much a part of their young lives.

Family: Sam Gates's special joy in life however, was his own immediate family—his talented, beautiful, and devoted wife and their three wonderful daughters. He cherished them and called them his "harem."

I will always be able to picture him dancing with one of the ladies of his family. He was a superb dancer. Dancing with one of them his eyes glazed over or totally closed, his face turned upward, with a big smile—he was completely oblivious to anyone or anything except his partner. That was pure joy for him.

I will never forget the day I first called on him for a very personal appointment. The topic, now acknowledged, but known to us both, was my wish to marry his second daughter. I envisioned a brief discussion, his acquiescence, then a few drinks and some fellowship. I was wrong. He wasn't going to let this moment pass without letting me know his family was very important to him. It was an extremely awkward meeting for me. He didn't offer me a drink. He didn't even make it easy for me to bring up the subject. When I finally blurted it out, he said: "What do you know about her—she's very special to me?" I made a wholly-inadequate response. Then he said: "What do you love about her? What are her strengths and weaknesses? How would you handle this or that situation?" Later he turned to me—courteous yet persistent. What was my background, my job, my future? Could I provide for his daughter? What was my salary and how much had I saved? This went on and on. I wondered if Sharon had really spoken to him in advance. Then suddenly he came to me, embraced me and tears came into his eyes. It was over. He had made his point—his family was a very important facet of his being. I also realized how hard it was for him to see his daughters leave his nest. This was not the last time I would see his sometimes gruff exterior turn to incredible softness over someone of importance to him.

Later I understood, as he and I referred to that day, that he had thoroughly enjoyed watching me squirm. He wasn't going to let one of life's traditions and customs pass him by without putting a prospective son-in-law through his paces. After all, he loved being a litigator. And, as the only son-in-law who was not a lawyer, I was a particularly tempting target.

These events reflect much of his character—deep pride in his family, a demanding toughness for high standards, tempered by incredible tenderness and a thorough enjoyment of life's experiences.

As a man with enormous energy and capacity for love, his personality and ideals had a great influence on his family. This influence and this spirit will continue through all of us who remain.

The "high standards" for which Sammy Gates Williamson remembers him, will be maintained by his family and his friends; Owen's garden will be planted again, as will Dad Gates's beautiful and famous flowers. Each of his grandchildren will reflect him—each in his or her own way.

Speaking on behalf of our family, our love and memories of Sam Gates shall always live.

(Little did we know that just short of Sharon and Rick's 25th wedding anniversary, we would be preparing a memorial service for Rick, who died from cancer of the bladder in 1993 at the age of fifty-three.) Sam loved to see new places in the world and revisit old, as most of us do. Thanks to C.R. Smith having us represent American Airlines for about fifteen years, we saw the world on a red carpet. From the castles and museums at the Hague, to Scotland and the great Manor houses there where we did the Highland Fling, to the castle of Chillon singing in candlelight at the beautiful lake of Switzerland, to Madrid where we luxuriated at the splendid Ritz Hotel and went to the Prado every day, ate at the Jockey club at night when we weren't in the banquet hall of the palace, to Delhi and Agra where the tents were so ornate that one thought one of them WAS a palace and where J.R.D./Tata, Mr. India, who had died this 1993 year, opened up the world to us and arranged for us to have lunch with Nehru; and Paris with dinners at the Hall of Mirrors at Versailles trumpeted up by the Napoleonic Guards—oh it was all wonderful. Sam went to Tunisia and Casablanca during the war without me but we had so many marvelous trips, safaris in Kenya, Tanzania and Uganda.

Lingering Images

Some of my favorite glimpses of Sam: in his garden tying up his dahlias to the stakes, hanging up the Christmas stockings knitted by his mother with each of our names purled into the cuff, wrapping each little gift with Christmas paper with his stubby fingers, talking to the doorman about his ill wife. He loved passing out candy and chewing gum to the little children at the Kirov Ballet Marinska Theater in Leningrad, or making ten or twelve large floral arrangements from flowers in his own garden for the funeral of his black gardener, William Morris, and remaining through the service to hug his wonderful wife and relatives. He shed many tears on sad occasions and sometimes sobbed as though his heart would break. These acts of kindness are all so typical of this unusual man with whom I shared forty years.

I was touched at his diligence in buying Christmas presents for me at Bonwit Tellers, dragging seven-year-old Sharon with him and watching the mannequins model the "at home" gowns he chose while he sipped a martini and Sharon a Coca Cola.

I love remembering his singing in the Father's Chorus at the Brearley School's Christmas assembly and their Last Day ceremonies, even though he couldn't carry much of a tune. I can see him walking us to the 9:30 service at St. James, where we had a perfect attendance at the Lenten services for years. I used to watch him from our dining room window at 970 Park, dressed in his Homburg or derby, walking Kathe up to her kindergarten at the Brick Presbyterian Church, seven blocks north. He was holding her hand and leaning over to hear her comments. He later reported to me that those seven blocks each weekday morning caused a permanent crick in his right side from leaning over so far to catch what tiny Kathe was saying above the loud noise of the traffic.

So many sweet and thoughtful acts will always remain with me. His surprise birthday parties for me, the cute stocking presents in my Christmas loot, the unexpected compliment as we got in the elevator to go out. He fought his paranoic temper every day of his life. It was a Gates family trait. No one ever knew what caused it to explode, but no amount of apologies for something one did not do would abate it. As the years progressed he suffered it less and less, but until the year he died, he would occasionally explode. He could never say he was sorry but his other qualities of ultimate integrity, honesty, responsibility, dependability, caring and loving us, far outweighed those occasional tempers. Once I understood that they had no rhyme or reason for being except a chemically unbalanced moment, I could forgive and forget them.

One episode did trouble me for some time. I had thought that we should sell our dream home, a fourteen-room duplex apartment at 830 Park Avenue. We had enjoyed it for fifteen years but we did not need that much space any more. In 1978, after two years of having the duplex on the market, I finally received a bid, and I telephoned Sam to tell him. He exploded, "Darling how in the world are we going to do that when we are leaving for Paris in the morning?"

My reply was, "Come on Sam, you promised. We don't have to be here to conclude the deal. You have several real estate partners in your firm, give them a power of attorney. We are not going to outer Mongolia." In the end, Sam arranged, as head of the building's board of directors, to recuse himself from a decision with respect to the approval of the buyers. He carried this in his mind and mentioned all over Paris that by selling our apartment, I had "détruit la qualité de sa vie."

This was a serious accusation, I felt. I told him he was unfair because he had agreed to the sale of the duplex. For my part, I told him, I was not destroying but contributing to the quality of his life by moving fourteen blocks uptown to be nearer to our children. In response, he winked at me and said, "You should know I was just teasing you. I am certain the board will never approve that purchaser. He was wearing Gucci shoes!"

Only then did I realize that he was simply associating my sale of our duplex with his lack of respect for people who sported "name brands." He even cut off the Izod alligator from the tee shirt he wore to play golf. Perhaps I should have stopped worrying earlier, but I didn't.

Weeks later we received a telegram at our hotel in Leningrad that the building's board of directors, despite the Gucci shoes, had indeed approved our buyer. Immediately upon our return to New York, we began an apartment search, and we found a great smaller one in which I now live.

In Retrospect

Although my main role in our marriage had been caring for the children, as well as managing our home and travel life, I never forgot the teachings of my own parents—honesty, fairness, and willingness to work hard.

As for child-rearing, Sam left 90 percent up to me, yet his own standards of ethical and moral behavior were well articulated to our girls during in their most impressionable years. In their senior years in both high school and college, he told each one, "You have only one job. Your beds are changed, your food is provided for you, your clothes are bought for you. Your big job is to make the best grades you can. If you can't make any better ones, I'll understand. But you've got a lot of brains and you've got a lot of energy and good health and there's no reason in the world that you can't do excellent work." In hindsight, perhaps, that was too much to be expected, too high a standard.

When our first daughter, Gilda, came home with a "B," we noticed extreme disappointment in his face. We all hoped, "Oh my Lord he's not going to make a point about that B." He didn't but she felt it. I felt Sam had put too much pressure on our children, and yet I realized they should know, privileged as they were, that they must do their best.

When our oldest granddaughter, Katie, was graduating from Princeton, she knew she was graduating with honors. She told me she went to look at the Princeton honors bulletin board and she did not find her name with the Cum Laudes. She was getting a little angry then she looked at the Magna Cum Laudes and her name wasn't on that list either. She said she was about to explode. Finally she looked at the Summa Cum Laudes and found her name on a very short list. Of course, she was terribly excited and she ran over to her parents and told them. Of course, they were thrilled. Then she said "But I didn't get Phi Beta." And her Mother said "Come on, Katie, look how fabulously you've done. Who cares whether you're a Phi Bet." She said "Daddy does, and his Mother and Father and brothers were Phi Bet, and I care."

Then Gilda said, "I wasn't, and my Mother and Father weren't either, and I think you're absolutely ridiculous to worry about it."

But, she did worry about it and the next morning the letter came under her door asking her to be a Phi Beta Kappa!

So often I think of Sam's general influence on our children. He did not put pressure on them in a mean-spirited way, but he simply expected a lot of them. The only one who probably didn't do her best in college was Kathe, our youngest daughter. She's excelled ever since then, however. She married a wonderful man and has learned a lot more about life. She insists that she really didn't know her Father until she was in college because he had so little time for her in her younger years. I think she's a little unfair about that. Sharon and Gilda, her two older sisters, probably saw more of Sam than did Kathe. To me, their extremely prejudiced Mother, I think all three of our daughters are just about as perfect as they could be, as wives, mothers, friends, and caring members of their communities. Sam deserves a lot of credit for his fathering.

You can tell a lot about a man by the happiness of his wife and the respect given him by his children. These are my thoughts of Sam as my husband, lover, companion, and friend. My wish is that each of his children and his grandchildren will reflect on what his friends, colleagues, and I have said of him. In this way, it is my hope that memories of Sam Gates will live forever in our family. His every instinct was to do each task to the best of his ability. He expected this kind of performance from us and I know we shall all try to not let him down.

CHAPTER EIGHTEEN

On My Own

*One of the oldest human needs is having someone to wonder
where you are when you don't come home at night.*
— Margaret Mead, Anthropologist, 1901–78

My post-Sam life has been fulfilling and often not "alone," but the
desolation I felt after losing Sam sometimes made my hours of solitude
unbearable. My friend, Carlene Roberts Lawrence, described the condition, "We need someone to feel sorry for us if we have a bad cold."

My pain has been eased as I have been able to travel widely and with
many cherished friends. My travels have taken me to Bombay and New
Delhi, where I saw the Taj Mahal at midnight; to Santiago de Compostella
in Spain, to Egypt, Hawaii, Kuala Lumpur, Taipei, Mainland China, Cambodia, Vietnam, Burma, Thailand, Chile, Argentina, Brazil, and many
places in between.

While I saw so many wonderful places, as I traveled throughout Europe and Asia, my home-away-from-home, soon after Sam died, was
Acapulco, a world famous resort on a glittering bay on the Pacific Ocean
shore in the Mexican state of Guerrero. My beautiful home in Acapulco
came about through my friend Carlene Lawrence. One day she phoned to
say, "We are going to sell our house in Las Brisas, Acapulco. I cannot let
Jock (her husband) have another illness down there where he has suffered
so much."

I almost screamed over the phone, "Carlene, but you must sell that
house to me, I have had a right of first refusal ever since, as your lawyer,
we closed your purchase of it in 1965."

She went on to say she had completely forgotten about our deal and didn't think I would be interested because Sam had just died. I reminded her that she had bought that house when she had just been widowed. She said nothing would please her more than if I DID buy it, but she already had two outstanding offers from Texans. I persuaded her to give me about forty-eight hours, until I could discuss this development with my three married children, their husbands, and my financial advisors.

With general approval from everyone, I gulped at the current price, about ten times the amount I knew Carlene had paid. I could have bought, at that time, Frank Sinatra's house next door for $35,000. In any case, I made the purchase, and I never regretted it. The property is surrounded by an enchanting Pacific bay and is in the most desirable residential area in all of Mexico. I borrowed more money than I ever thought I could afford in order to make Carlene's house *Casa Filomena.*

I was very comfortable making this purchase because my neighbors were special friends. One was Frank Brandstetter, who conceived of and managed Las Brisas, a luxurious hotel on seven hundred acres overlooking the bay. Las Brisas is my version of Paradise in this hemisphere. My other cherished friend in Acapulco was Marianne Rivas, a gifted beauty from Dallas who had divorced her Mexican college sweetheart and was the real estate guru and social arbiter of Acapulco. I always told her that none of us gringos would remain in Acapulco if she were not there. She died in 2000 and I shall always miss her and cherish her sharing our stateroom from Chile around Cape Horn to Buenos Aires in 1998. Enrique and Sandra DePortonova always invited me and houseguests to their fabulous Moroccan palace on the bay.

Casa Filomena did more to pull me out of my grief after Sam's death than any other undertaking. I knew how much Sam loved that house where we had visited for about ten years, and would so approve of my having it. (I used to talk up to the sky to him all the time I was down there, wishing he were with me.)

For almost twenty years I found comfort in my home in Acapulco. Jim Baker, Gould Jones, Henry Ehrlich, and Bill Draper, my good friends and wonderful traveling companions, as well as many others visited me there. We had gourmet food cooked by Lupe, whom I had taught a delicious "American-French" cuisine. She made a fine coconut soufflé, our house specialty.

Our adoption of Mexico as our second home country began the first year of our marriage, when we spent seven weeks there as guests of the

Phil at her Casa Filomena, Acapulco, Mexico.

Mexican government. Sam, as international counsel for the Civil Aeronautics Board was invited to write the transportation rules and regulations for the Mexican government, then headed by President Manuel Avila Camacho so that airline pilots, railroad engineers, bus and truck drivers would not have to learn two sets of rules when crossing the long undefended border between ourselves and our neighbor to the south. During those seven weeks we celebrated our first wedding anniversary in Xochomilco, then a beautiful public garden with lots of canals with gondolas festooned with flowers.

Having done the legal work incident to the purchase of a lovely villa, Casa Carlena, in Acapulco, we traded out my fees in its occupancy for as many winter holidays as Sam could take, always traveling throughout Mexico to see its many wonders. Only after Sam's death, did I buy that lovely hillside home overlooking spectacular Acapulco Bay and made it Casa Filomena. Since Sam's death in the company of my friends Gould Jones, John McKesson, and Henry Ehrlich; and later my daughter and granddaughter, Kathe and Bess Williamson, we've seen the villages around Guadalajara, Ijiji, Tonala, Chapala, as well as Oxaca, Palenque, Chichenitza, Ixmal with their marvelous Aztec and Mayan ruins.

When the time came in 1993 to sell *Casa Filomena*, my investment had rewarded me well. The house had not only soothed my spirits, but it had cost me little to own for I was able to rent it when I could not be there.

During all my visits to Mexico, the most exciting time was finding myself on New Year's eve 1994 one block away from the explosion of the Chiapas revolution. Even with the most recent change in 70 years of PRI Party rule with its new PAN President Vincente Fox, Mexico has not found a way to settle the Chiapas problem.

After fifty-two years of being in and out of Mexico, I had never before January 1, 1994 heard of a town called San Cristobal de Los Casas in the State of Chiapas. But, John McKesson, former ambassador to several African countries and a great friend of mine, wanted to go to Palenque, as well as the Yucatan to see Chichen Itza and Uxmal. We wanted to see more of the Mayan culture and a charming, private guest house was recommended to us in San Cristobal called "La Jacaranda" near the town of Tuxla La Gutierrez. We were to fly to Tuxla, the capitol of the State of Chiapas. Mexico is a federation of states, organized as is the United States. Chiapas is the southern-most state in Mexico, bordering Guatemala. The Mayan culture is evidenced throughout in villages, churches, handcrafts, and their costumes. Most men wear fuchsia-colored tunics and the women elaborately embroidered blouse called "Huilpels."

My friend and I both put down a hefty deposit for five days for our stay in that lovely place and planned a fascinating trip. At the last minute, John developed a bad case of the flu and couldn't leave. I proceeded to eliminate the Merida part of our trip and decided to go by myself to San Cristobal. John called me on the 15th of December when he was to be my escort at a ball that was honoring me in the Grosvenor Neighborhood House and said, "Phil, I'm coming. I know you can't get anybody to take you at this late hour, but I have the flu. I have a fever and a sore throat and I feel like Hell." He said, "I will take you but I won't be fun and games. I really feel lousy." I said, "Oh, poor you. I will make some calls. If anybody I know happens to be available" —of course for six weeks in November, December, and January, New Yorkers are booked up almost solid every night. I called him back, "Poor you, but I think you're going to have to take me after all." He bravely replied, "Of course, I'll pick you up." We went to the University Club where the dinner dance was to be held. As soon as they had made their speech about me and I had made my speech about the wonderful work Grosvenor had done for 50 years, we went home. "John, you have to get healthy. We have our trip coming up in about 10 days," I cautioned, as he said goodnight. He said, "I know it. I know it." Well, four days before we were supposed to leave he called to say, "There's no way I can make it. I've got the flu and the last time I had the flu it took me five weeks to get over it. And the best thing I could do is try to meet you in Cuernavaca." The bottom dropped out of my life. I thought, "How can I recoup this trip?" We had a car and a chauffeur hired.

I was picked up by a taxi from the Tuxla La Gutierrez airport and was swept through two hours of dangerous curvy roads winding through the mountains of southern most Mexico. I finally arrived at the gorgeous guest house, "Jacarandal," actually a folk art museum with English style gardens, Spanish patios, handsome bedrooms, and inviting public rooms. An attractive, bright host and hostess operate it as though one is their personal friend and guest. One quickly forgets that one has paid for it! Our host and his wife had retired to Mexico, but lost a great deal of money in the first devaluation of the peso, making it necessary that they take in paying guests. One feels immediately as though one is their personal friend of long standing.

I arrived at La Jacaranda on the night of December 30, 1993. Dr. Percy Woods was waiting for me in front of his blazing Colonial fireplace. The rest of his guests and his wife had gone to a party in the neighborhood from which they all soon returned. We had a charming dinner, followed by port before a roaring fire as it was quite chilly. Later I wrote my friend, John, how much I missed him, was sorry he wasn't there as I felt that I had died and gone to heaven; it was that exquisite. The next morning offered blazing sunshine, crisp and cool weather—a sparkling day in every way. The Woods set out to take us sight-seeing in the neighborhood town of Zinacantan. Most of its citizens were in the fields tilling corn and coffee beans and attending their animals in the farms. Most are very poor. Their faces look as though they have just popped out of the Friezes of some of the B.C. pyramids that one sees in that part of the world. The natives speak Mayan, not Spanish. Some who have been lucky enough to go to school—especially those who have worked in households such as the one where we were staying—speak Spanish. After admiring the charming English garden of Mrs. Jane Taylor, an English woman who lives there all year, we went back to the house —four other guests had gone horseback riding with Dr. Woods. We were all included in the daily mountain horseback ride should one want to do it.

In the afternoon we visited a museum-type exhibition which sold the intricate, distinguished embroideries and weavings of that area. These are unique, meticulously executed, and typical of the area. They are of museum quality. One of the other guests, Marion Goodman, owner of a 57th St. New York City art gallery, and I wandered around the town square. On our return we were told that we were all invited for a New Year's Eve party supper and buffet at the home of local anthropologists! A number of younger couples all live in Chiapas doing a variety of jobs. Ornithologists, environmental, and national park experts would be there.

We went after seeing the assemblage of about 10 children, belonging to the guests, in the patio pounding the Piñata (a clay animal covered with huge ruffles of crepe paper in the form of donkeys and geese and stars and dolls). Inside, the piñata is filled with puzzles and presents. It is a traditional party Mexican custom to hang this apparition on a tree or other suspension and let the children, blindfolded, flail at it with batons and sticks. Sooner or later it breaks and all the presents fall down at their feet. They, then, are permitted to remove their blindfolds and scramble for the fallen presents and goodies. After all that was over, we had supper, and it was nearly 11:30 p.m. The guests at Jacaranda suggested that while the Woods knew everyone there, we didn't, and perhaps it was time for us to go home. There were nine of us from the Jacaranda including our host and hostess. We climbed into the van. There were two cars and a mini-van in which most of us could fit. We were aware of quite a lot of young people on the particularly dark street where our host lived who were lighting firecrackers going bang, bang, bang. We figured it was getting close to midnight, and it was their way of celebrating the ushering in of the New Year—1994.

At home we lit fires in our various bedroom fireplaces, a cozy aspect and a cheery sight to sleep by. We continued to hear such noises, during the night, as we were awakened from time to time to hear bang, bang, bang. Naturally I assumed, as did everyone else, that it was firecrackers. Believe it or not, there were 2000 or 3000 persons organized throughout Chiapas who had carefully planned a revolt—a revolution if you will. All wore ski masks, carried guns and had taken over the City Hall, quite a beautiful Spanish Colonial building on the town plaza, probably built around the turn of the century. They had smashed out all of the windows of the City Hall and thrown out on the square all of the property deeds and files which were housed there, records of property owned by the people in the area as well as other official records.

Jacaranda, where we were staying, needed about seven servants to manage it. Only two showed up that morning—January I—shaking, crying and hysterical. I walked into the hall as our hostess was saying, "You go right back home and take care of your children. You don't want them caught in any of this crossfire." We assumed, correctly of course, that we were under a kind of self-imposed house arrest. We didn't dare leave the house; the radio cautioned against it because we might get shot! All of the shooting was happening within a block from where we were, around the Central square where the Cathedral and the Municipal Building were located.

That night, when we had been in all day trying to figure out what was happening a block from us on the square, I asked my fellow host apologetically if I might see the Orange Bowl football game. I had not seen a TV set in their house. Recently, I had accepted a job as co-chairman of a $200 million dollar campaign for my university, Florida State in Tallahassee, Florida. I had spent four very happy years and learned quite a lot there. In taking on this responsibility, I have become extremely interested in the university. Its most public posture at that time was as national college football champion. The teams' star quarterback was a very fine young man named Charlie Ward. He won the Nobel Prize of football that year, the Heisman Trophy. I plaintively whispered to Dr. Woods, "I've got to see this game. Our team has made the Orange Bowl and they're playing Nebraska to whom they had lost the week before." Dr. Woods, a football fan of types, said, "I think I can get CNN and the game." What else to do when shooting was erupting outside! Their satellite dish could get a number of stations, and indeed, he was successful in finding it. As he turned it on, I crawled up a circular wrought iron stairway to their master bedroom—which sported a huge, king-sized bed. Sitting alone at the foot of it, I was pretty soon joined by Dr. Woods and then up struggled a couple of other guests. It ended up that most of the eight of us were up there on a king-sized bed looking at the Orange Bowl game, which was, indeed, a cliffhanger. In the last 24 seconds of the game, when Florida State was two or three points behind, our Seminoles kicked a field goal and won by a point or two! Most of us on that bed said that it was one of the most exciting football games we had ever, ever seen. Before the field goal was kicked by the opposing team, which put them ahead the last minute of the game, some people on the sidelines were pouring ice water all over FSU Coach Bobby Bowden's head. This was, of course, a premature victory celebration because the other team then scored ahead of us. And it was only in the last 24 seconds that Florida State won the game. It seems amazing that we were able to focus on a college football contest when we were one block away from an important uprising of peasants which is still destabilizing the government of Mexico.

After three days of becoming rather stir-crazy and housebound, my fellow houseguest, the art gallery owner, and I managed to persuade a fearless taxi owner to take us to the Tuxla airport, braving what gunfire might occur. Tuxla was the nearest airport from which we could fly to Mexico City.

Only just recently I have been to Tallahassee to a meeting of the Campaign Committee for our Investment in Learning Campaign for $200 million dollars. The President of the University gave a dinner party the last night of that weekend meeting on the patio of the Law School. I was privileged to sit by Coach Bowden and heard even more personally his own recitation of the last moments of tension he was enduring in those last 24 seconds of the game to make our team the National Champions.

In addition to Chiapas, I wanted to add to my account of the beginnings of the revolution there January 1. All the people that I met and questioned in the area were extremely sympathetic with the peasants. The peasants, forgotten by their Federal government, had suffered an extremely corrupt governor who was building a theater on land owned by his wife's family—a project which gave him, of course, a great big and unconscionable profit. A theater the peasants needed like a hole in the head. The farmers need schools, hospitals, and social services. They certainly don't need a theater that would probably turn into a disco. The people in Chiapas did kick out one governor and President Salinas finally fired the other, a disaster and one of the causes of the revolt. I hope the revolt will produce some benefits for the people there. The Mayans yearn for reform, but until the Mexican government cures itself of some of its innate corruption, it is going to be a very difficult partner for NAFTA. I worked very hard lobbying Congress for NAFTA. This uprising has, in a way, been a very good thing, albeit a disaster for the tourist business and the farmers, who were hidden in the hills and unable to plant their coffee and corn in time for the current growing season, and the whole Mexican economy. Chiapas is still at war, tanks are barreling through their villages, government troops are rounding up farmers.

The war, as I now write, does linger on. The PAN party is in power, with a competent Vincente Fox in office, and has finally agreed to sit down with Marcos, their leader. Most, including Marcos, of the Zapatistos have insisted on wearing ski masks, this making the negotiations nigh on to impossible. How can one talk face to face with an adversary and work out a meeting of the minds when one's adversary has no FACE? As of this writing, Marcos is still masked, but the tanks are still and the populace is less terrified. Many have been jailed and tortured, who really were only bystanders.

As formerly stated, most residents of the area, particularly the Americans and Western Europeans who have claimed it as a residence, are sympathetic to the Zapatistos. Zedillo, Mexico's past President, who was elected after Colossio, the party's candidate was murdered—many believe by his own party—tried to negotiate. I so love the Mexican people and feel that they must be able to extricate themselves from the misery of their poor and the corruption of their rich and powerful. Both have interests at stake and both will, with proper mediation, be able to achieve some of their goals. Population control is indispensable, and not as yet properly dealt with by the government. That is not easy to achieve. It seems only yesterday in India, when walking through their villages much poorer than their Mexican fellows, asking mothers with six or seven children why they continued to breed children when they had only one brass, round bowl to their name and only the sand beneath them with which to scour it. Their answer was "will you take away the only pleasure I have in my life, my children?" One is likely to receive the same answer from the poor Mexican mother of today. Ruthless birth control such as has been practiced in China must ultimately prevail, as painful as that is to administrators and citizens alike. No economy can grow fast enough to feed a population increasing at the rate of Mexico's growth today. Mexico is my second home, Spanish my second language, and I simply pray for some light at the end of their troubled tunnel.

After finding one of the last seats on the plane from Tuxla to Mexico City, Marion Goodman and I found ourselves in the safety of Mexico City, with its exquisite museums, its bustling energetic people and the artistic and entrepreneurial energy bursting forth from each street corner. Friends and friends of friends kept me busy for lunch and dinner, and after four days, I flew to Guadalajara to visit my friend, Jack Conner. When John McKesson became ill and unable to take our trip, I had phoned Jack in Tlaquepaque, an arts and crafts enclave near Guadalajara (Mexico's second city). "Jack, I'm suddenly flapping around by myself with car and driver waiting to take me to Morelia from your town. Can I come and stay a couple of days with you?" He immediately shouted, "Come stay a couple of weeks with me." I could only do two days, but told him that my great friend, Gould Jones from San Francisco, had agreed to join me and continue the trip with me, and I would like to bring him with me. Blessed Jack met us in the airport and took us lovingly to his gorgeous town palace in Tlaquepaque, where we luxuriated in that splendor created by him and his departed famous decorator friend, William Pahlmann. I had been their houseguest several times and pined to see their treasures one more time. We had a sublime luncheon at Lake Chapala in the area and saw many of the new ateliers in the area, increasingly a showcase for artisans.

Our driver picked up Gould and me at Jack's the third day and we waved him "Adiosito" and off we drove to Morelia. Again Mexico has so many fascinating cities to visit. In all of my years in Mexico, I had never been to that famous Colonial city, with its great University (said to be the oldest in our hemisphere), Aqueduct, from colonial times and its most elaborate cathedral.

From Morelia through many other lakes, forests and art cities, we arrived for four days with former Ambassador to the Philippines and our last to Iran, Bill and Marie Sullivan. A most handsome brilliant foreign service couple who met while they were both preparing for diplomatic service at the Fletcher School of Diplomacy at Harvard. Marie's background was Mexico, so retirement in Cuernavaca was a natural finish to their distinguished diplomatic career. We left them with much regret having had a great series of soul searching evenings about "whither U.S. foreign policy." Then we returned to my old house, Casa Filomena, in Las Brisas, Acapulco, which I had sold the previous year. We three couples had rented it from the Mexican owner who had bought it from me the year before. One cannot go home again. He had fired my fabulous cook, and while our week was lovely, to me it was not satisfactory because blessed Lupe was not in the kitchen. Mexico remains for me an enchanted land and I hope never to lose touch with it, through its trials and successes.

Two months later, when John McKesson was able to make the trip, we returned to the gorgeous La Jacaranda and felt it still one of the highlights of a journey to Mexico. We were able to see Palenque and then fly to the beautiful city of Merida with much colonial history and art and its neighboring sites of Uxmal and Chichen Itza. Later we flew to Zacatecas. Again, a city after 50 years of Mexico I had never heard of! Mr. Misrachi of the famous art dealership in Mexico City had advised me to go there. He had just attended the dedication of the Colonel Museums, two brothers who both have museums dedicated to their works and their collections. I had mentioned to Enrico Misrachi that my friend, John, had a distinguished collection of African and Southeast Asian art, and many masks. He then counseled me to see the Rafael Colonel Museum in Zacatecas. The Anthropology Museum in Mexico City had 100 masks, the Zacatecas Museum had more than 1,000. So off we went. Not only were the churches and museums worth the trip in the northern city, but the hotel was indeed splendid. It is built around the oldest bull ring in the Americas and spectacular. We were driven by a fine archeologist friend of mine through the haciendas, old colonial times now disintegrating, en route to San Miguel de Allende, where we spent a lovely evening with Florence and Gerard Van de Kemp (curator of Versailles and Giverny) and the Bleysteens. Always in mind was the great book about all of that area, *Mexico*, by the best story teller of all, James Michener. It is superb.

In my years without Sam I have been sustained by my friends, by travel, and also by my involvement in various councils and associations. Quite by chance one evening in New York, I met a trusts and estates lawyer whom I had known casually. He said, "Phil, you should become a member of the Thursday Evening Club, and I would be delighted to propose you." Within a half an hour, he had rounded up a seconder and the appropriate number of sponsors. Years ago Sam and I had heard of this club, but we thought it was for "people who have lived and grown up in New York." At that time we considered ourselves outlanders from Florida and California. Needless to say, I became a member.

At the club's 129th winter party, the president, Lynn Mehta, (the beautiful daughter of Bill and Kitty Carey) spoke about its founding in 1878. During her remarks she mentioned that on February 25, 1928, *The New York Times* headlined the occasion as the "Club of Famous Wits Rounds Out 50 Years." The club still flourishes, the *Times* said, as a "meeting ground of intellectuality and affability, bringing together kindred spirits interested in arts, music, literature, and science." In 1928, members gathered at the home of Frederic Delano Weekes, 10 Washington Square North near 22 Washington Square North where they had held the club's first

Phil and Tom Ervin, a Nuremberg trial prosecutor, in Moscow, 1991.

meeting. Then their lectures dealt with Iron and Steel, Shooting Stars, as well as Tableaux Vivants, music, and readings.

Now, when I attend, we meet at museums, botanical gardens, Wave Hill, Ellis Island, the Abyssinian Baptist Church (to hear the choir) and we eat soul food at Sylvia's restaurant in Harlem. We emphasize the glories of New York, Old and New. One of my daughters and her husband belong. Being a member of the Thursday Evening Club provides welcome activity with a unique group of friends and is just one more reason why I love New York.

Another meaningful membership for me has been in the Council on Foreign Relations. Sam had been a member forever, but this august body did not admit women until about twenty years ago, and I was not in the first wave of famous women who were tapped. Luckily, thanks to my late friend Hedley Donovan, former head of Time, Inc., and Sam's partners, Francis Plimpton and Rod Perkins, I was elected to the council about fifteen years ago. It has been a great intellectual stimulus and has helped me keep up with developments, both economic and philosophical, all over the world. Especially rewarding has been my membership on two council task forces visiting, first, the Strategic Air Command (SAC) with installations in the western United States and, then, the NATO headquarters in Brussels, with stopovers in Bonn, Berlin, London, and airbases in between.

We were briefed by military heads of SAC out west and the German, American, and British NATO directors in Europe.

The NATO trip was especially fantastic and our brains were bursting with what we had learned. It was my first trip to Berlin. I had no idea how enormous the city was, with its immense geographical spread. The Wall had just begun to come down and we were each given a piece of it mounted on a brass plaque and properly dated and identified. The only frightening experience was a briefing by the head of the NATO air force who was a German general (and I understand he is now the German head of their Joint Chiefs) who sounded just like a NAZI, overbearing and bragging about what the Wehrmacht could have and did actually accomplish under Hitler. I thought Bill Scranton was going to explode with anger, but we managed to leave the conference room having kept our cool. Most of the brilliant members of our group were very young, not old enough to really have an understanding of our horror when we heard this man's arrogant presentation.

One of my most recent excursions was with ten couples from the University Club of New York on an irresistible itinerary which included Vietnam, Cambodia's Angkor Wat, Phnom Penh, and Burma where we sailed up the Ayeyarwady (Irrawaddy) from Rangoon to Mandalay with many stops in between. We also enjoyed Bangkok after which we visited Chiang Mai, the former capital of Thailand in the North. It is fascinating to see the one country which was never colonized in that part of the world. During four restful days at Hong Kong's Ritz Carlton on our way home, we savored the island once more at an historic moment before it was returned to China.

Trips on the Royal Scotsman train to the Scottish Highlands, on the Elbe River from Wittenburg, Germany, through Meissen, Dresden, Prague, and Budapest with a Princeton University group have both been marvelous. Later I was to visit Chile, then round Cape Horn to Argentina and Brazil.

On my own, but still traveling. My cup runneth over!

CHAPTER NINETEEN

Our Family: My Ultimate Pride

*That our sons may be as plants grown up in their youth; that our daughters
may be as corner stones, polished after the similitude of a palace.*
— *Psalms 144:12*

My family has been the principal focus of my adult life from 1943 to
date. That life has had its fulfillments is evidenced by our three daughters
and their husbands, my eight grandchildren (twelve with four spouses),
and my great grandchildren. They enrich my life every day, and I thank
God for every one of them. Our love for one another has sustained us
through anxieties, heartaches, and the daily challenges of stressful times.

Our daughters, Gilda, Sharon, and Kathe, and their families appear
throughout these pages, but I feel eager to devote some small space to
their lives and accomplishments in a chronological order. As has been
noted, they all graduated at 18 years of age from the wonderful Brearley
School of New York City.

Gilda was born in 1943 with weak eye muscles; but after two eye
operations, had perfect focus by the time she entered the third grade at
Brearley School. She sang in star roles in Gilbert and Sullivan operettas
and enjoyed Brearley's exciting extracurricular life. Although she was
not athletically gifted as a child, now in her fifties she is a great "jock"—
a mountain climber, hiker, skier, a very good tennis player, and a lover of
outdoor life. She had inherited her father's and grandfather's love of gardening.

Gilda graduated from Smith College in Northhampton, Massachusetts, her first choice, cum laude. Additionally, on graduation, she won a
two-year fellowship to acquire a master's degree at the Foreign Studies

The Gates' daughters (from left), Kathe, Sharon, and Gilda at their paternal grandparents' 50th wedding anniversary, 1950.

Institute, Columbia University. During her senior year at Smith, Gilda had a few dates with a brilliant young lawyer, Cecil Wray, whom she had met at our house in the following way. One morning during her senior year, Gilda phoned from Smith to say that she and a housemate, Cecili Dillingham from Hawaii, were taking the bus to New York to see us for the weekend. This call came just after breakfast, and I caught Sam's sleeve just as he had rung the elevator button to go to the office. "Are there any young lawyers in your firm whom you would like to invite to lunch Saturday?" I asked. "Gilda and her friend will be here as well as Adolf Berle and Beatrice with their son Peter and his new bride Lila." On his way into the elevator, Sam flashed back, "There are about thirty I'd like to ask, but I'll find a couple for Saturday lunch."

The Berle family came and so did Bevis Longstreth and Cecil Wray, both of whom had been Yale Law Journal stars and had done some work at Debevoise for Sam. He felt they would enjoy very much meeting Adolf, the celebrated FDR braintruster, law professor, and author. The luncheon was great fun after which the Berles left for a matinee and the young men for a squash game at the Yale Club. After receiving thank-you letters from our guests, we never thought much more about the occasion.

About a year later, however, Cecil came into Sam's office and asked his permission to invite his daughter out. Sam reported this to me with the caveat that I was not to tell Gilda as she might get her hopes up, and Cecil might forget about it. I said, "Ridiculous, in the first place, Gilda has lots of beaux, if he should forget, but with such a formal request, I very much doubt that he will." He did not.

Some while after our lunch, my great friend, Helen Leyland Hexter, who had assumed my hostess responsibilities in Georgetown the night I went to the hospital to deliver Gilda, invited us and our three daughters to visit her and Paul in Miami Beach during the 1965 Spring holidays. I hesitated, "Oh, Helen, you don't want all five of us?"

"I not only want all five of you, but I am inviting three young men of your daughters' choice to join us," she replied. "We will be out playing golf, and I do not know any young men for them to be with. I'd prefer to invite dates the girls like for the week. There is a motel directly across the road from our house (they lived right on Biscayne Bay in a lovely Spanish villa). I'll put the boys up in the motel, stock their fridge with breakfast food, and they can have lunch and dinner with us. For a week, we dined exquisitely, served on Helen's best Lowestof and Spode in the garden under a Miami moon, and enjoyed soft balmy breezes fragrant with the perfume of night blooming jasmine. That weekend, Gilda and Cecil became engaged.

The road to romance was not without its potholes, however, put in place by none other than Sam Gates. He was losing his first daughter to a young lawyer in his office which had a strict rule against nepotism. Because of that rule, the firm had not made an offer to Tom Debevoise, the only son of the founding partner, Whitney. Sam felt his firm would not look kindly on offering a partnership to Cecil if he should be married to Gilda, no matter how brilliant he was or how long he had performed in stellar fashion (seven years) before the wedding.

When Gilda and Cecil picked me up at the hairdressers the second full morning we were in Miami, they made their announcement to me. I was seated in the back seat of the car and nearly swooned, as they had been seeing one another for such a short time. Cecil, in his thick Tennessee accent, punctuated their news with, "I wanted to tell you earlier, but I had to speak to Mr. Gates first." My curiosity was killing me wondering what Sam could say that wasn't a resounding "Yes."

Cecil continued, "He said, you have spelled your professional doom." Cecil replied, "Well, if that old firm of yours doesn't make me a partner because I have married your wonderful daughter, there is always Sullivan and Cromwell," (another very prestigious and much older law firm than Debevoise where he had worked one summer). The happy ending is that a year later he was made a partner, in spite of Gilda who was supposedly an albatross! Cecil, in fact, was head of Sam's firm in Paris from 1976-1979 and a senior corporate partner before his retirement.

They have now been married over thirty years. I am so proud of them both, the way they have conducted their lives, their marriage, and their children. Christopher, their son, attended the Bilangue School in Paris, the Buckley School in New York, and Andover Academy in Massachusetts before entering Yale and Yale Law School. He met and married his Yale classmate, Helen Howell of Atlanta immediately after graduation. After law school, he clerked for Federal 4th Circuit Judge Lutig and was an associate of King and Spalding, a large and well-known firm in Atlanta at which our old friend Griffin Bell was head partner. He is presently serving as an Assistant U.S. Attorney in Atlanta, fighting crime both of the regular and white collar variety. Helen, associated with a fund development firm, is busy with their two children, my first great grandchildren, Caroline and Trip (Thomas Cecil Wray III).

Kathleen (Katie), Gilda's and Cecil's daughter, attended Brearley, as her mother and aunts did, interrupted by three years at those marvelous schools, Bilangue and Les Oiseaux in Paris. She graduated summa cum laude from Princeton, earning a Phi Beta Kappa Key. Katie completed her master's degree and the oral exams toward her Ph.D. in medieval studies at Harvard, while her husband, Steve Baughman, her Princeton classmate, finished his law degree at Harvard. Initially, Steve was an associate at Sullivan and Cromwell and, currently, he is with Ropes and Gray in its Washington, D.C., office. Katie enjoys being a high school history teacher at the Garrison Forest School in Baltimore, Maryland, and was honored by having the yearbook dedicated to her. She and Steve are the proud parents of Margaret Malone. Both Wray children have bought nice houses—Katie in Maryland and Christopher in Atlanta.

At this writing, Cecil has just finished a ten-year stint as Senior Warden of St. James Episcopal Church in New York. Gilda has been president of the Charles Hayden Foundation, an organization devoted to educational and community related programs for youth. Having finished their dream house in Keene Valley near their beloved Ausable Club in the Adirondacks, they serve on several museum and worthy community boards associated with their residences in not only Keene Valley, but in Garrison on the lower Hudson, and New York City. Their lives are full and rewarding. It is the best possible luck to have them within two blocks of my apartment when they are living in New York City.

Sharon, born in 1945, entered the world at a time happier than it had been for four years for the war was coming to a close. She was a wonderful smiling, healthy baby. We were so thrilled to have her and know that she was perfect in every way. No eye problems. Sharon has always loved "playing games," cerebral or physical. The only time that was not true was a period of several years when she and her darling friend, Moo Moo Ewing, were partners in tennis tournaments, playing the "fifteen and under," circuit of the Eastern U.S. Lawn Tennis Association. Moo Moo's father, Dr. James Ewing Jr., son of the great doctor of the same name at Memorial Hospital, was obsessed with their winning, or at least playing far above Sharon's level. I often chauffeured them to neighboring clubs for these matches, and they cried all the way home if they had lost, as Dr. Ewing would not be pleased. Often the spectators booed them if they won a point, most of whom were tennis pros, parents of their opponents, and anything but good sports. They did achieve a high seeding and learned to play much better tennis because of these competitions. Sadly, Moo Moo, died within two days of being stricken with spinal meningitis during her early twenties. Sharon, following in the footsteps of her sister Gilda, graduated cum laude from Smith College, majoring in history. The summer between her junior and senior years, she worked in a student exchange program sponsored by the American Economic and Scientific Exchange Committee for the DuPont Company in Geneva. We drove her and Kathe that summer on a great trek through Spain. After graduation, Sharon was hired by Pepsico to edit an in-house magazine dealing with that company's projects and discoveries. She and her Brearley friend, Jeanie Sour, decided to have their own apartment on 83rd Street near 2nd Avenue after their college graduations. The same year the daughter of my law school classmate, Mary K. Bell, was being married in New York, and I offered to have a prenuptial party for her. Her parents, Mary K and Bob, lived in New Canaan, and the young couple's friends were all in Manhattan. As a result of our party, Sharon was included in most of those wedding festivities. The groomsmen were confreres of the groom at Chase Bank. At our party, Richard Stearns, one of the ushers, had to leave early, so I escorted him to the elevator door. I later remarked to Sharon that I thought him especially handsome and engaging. She didn't seem to react one way or the other.

Rick Stearns was just about a perfect object for a young girl's affections. He was tall, athletic, handsome, and from a loving, stable New Hampshire family. He had graduated from Colgate and was an honor student at the Wharton School of Business at the University of Pennsylvania. As a competitive athlete, Sharon had met her match. Rick, having grown up within easy reach of New Hampshire snow country, was an excellent skier, and he would not ask Sharon to marry him until she had climbed up and skied down Mount Washington, the tallest in New Hampshire's White Mountains. She confessed to me later that it was one of the most stressful days of her life. She was so in love with this Adonis and anxious to complete this feat as one of her personal labors of Hercules. She had cramps, a headache, and kept falling down all of the time. They were accompanied by Rick's great friend and tennis partner, Don Roehm. Sharon felt it was important to win Don's approbation as well, knowing that Rick would probably ask him "shall I marry her or not?" Despite everything she passed with flying colors.

Their wedding and its accompanying festivities were jammed with approving friends and family. Hordes of us threw rice as they left their wedding reception in a London cab from New York's Union Club — an appropriate vehicle inasmuch as they were leaving to live in Ireland. Rick was to be Chase's man in Dublin, after a honeymoon at Algarve on the southern tip of Portugal.

As I was helping Sharon pack Rick's things just before the wedding, my eyes happened to land on a bag of golf clubs. Since Sam and I were beginning to be enthusiastic about the game, I ventured, "Sharon, I have an extra set of clubs, why don't you take one of my sets of clubs with you along with your tennis equipment? Ireland is full of splendid golf courses." Rick would never allow Sharon to beat him at tennis, but maybe golf? (Only in the last few years of his life did he go down in defeat on the tennis court at the hands of his son, Owen, quite an ace at the game.)

Sharon and Rick were outstanding parents of three talented children, Owen 29, Hope 26, and Leigh (Lili) 23. After Owen graduated from Milton Academy he took a year off from his studies to work in Boston at "City Year." This is the public-private cooperation program which provided the pattern on which President Clinton's National Service Americorps has been organized. Young people, mostly poor and disadvantaged, because of teenage pregnancy, a drug problem, or a variety of personal handicaps, are given a minimum wage job. They work at cleaning parks, improving their town, and, if they prove themselves a reliable employee, they are each given help ($5,000 a year) toward a college education. Owen was accepted for this program as one of a few private school achievers who furnish leadership within the participating group. After "City Year," Owen enrolled in Amherst, became an All-American squash player, and graduated with honors. He worked in Boston with Monitor, a management consulting and is now heading "City School" in Boston.

Hope graduated cum laude from Kenyon College, Ohio, where she concentrated on studies in the drama department. She tried to survive as a budding thespian and teacher in a family of athletes, but later received her masters degree in education, teaching at the Buckley School in New York, and aiming to be in the theater one way or another. She moved to Iowa to work, study, and teach there where her current beau was in dental school. They were married in the summer of 2000 in Westhampton Beach in our beautiful St. Marks Church and held the reception in our back garden. She is not only beautiful but adorable and a joy to us all. She dedicated her senior play at Kenyon, as its director, to her wonderful father who had died that year of bladder cancer.

Hope's younger sister Lili is pretty and outgoing. She is a fine soccer and basketball player, serving often as captain of those teams at the Brearley School, and co-president of the school's athletic association. She graduated from high school in 1995 and from Carleton College in

Minnesota in 1999. She is now pursuing her masters degree in geology at Ohio State and spends a few months a year in Antarctica. Luckily, I see all three of my Stearns grandchildren quite often as Sharon lives directly across the street from me in Manhattan and owns the two houses in back of our Westhampton house which complete our compound. In New York she can look straight down into my living room (6th floor) from her 14th floor living room, which is rather unsettling.

Throughout his active life, which was all too short, Rick worked and played to win. He struggled to overcome cancer of the bladder, but by the time the doctors had replaced his bladder with an artificial one, the lymph nodes were infected. Chemotherapy, radiation treatments, a macrobiotic diet, and transcendental meditation could not save this handsome young man of fifty-three. When Rick was dying, I told him how much I loved him, and he, for the first time, told me how much he loved me. I said, "I have been so proud that you are Sharon's husband." He whispered in a clear, distinct voice, "I am proud to have been Sharon's husband."

Kathe, our baby, was born in 1947 while Sam was attending an International Air Transport Association general meeting in Brazil. She, who was about a year old when we moved to New York, followed her older sisters in Brearley. When she reached high school, she had a splendid time. The other two girls did not know very many boys during the tenth, eleventh, and twelfth grades, but Kathe did. There was, during Kathe's high school years, a group of boys her age who attended Collegiate School, an old established school in Manhattan. The group with whom Kathe shared a lot of good times included Arthur Rubenstein's son John, who is now a prominent actor and producer on Broadway (*Pippin, Children of a Lesser God*), Michael Leader, and others. That group had a very wholesome and city-type good time with Brearley girls. In the Westhampton summers, there were other boys who attended boarding school with whom Kathe could play tennis, dance at the country club, frolic, and generally hack around with when we were at the beach.

While Kathe's high school credentials should have gained her admittance at Smith, she was not accepted. We were furious! We were told that it was their year to favor public school and black girls. Duke in Durham, North Carolina, was a marvelous and an exciting university in which to study. In any case, she had always wanted to do things a bit differently from her sisters. Duke, at first, seemed to be disappointing to Kathe although she had made good friends there and even had a beau with whom she could share student activities and enjoy being in a co-ed atmosphere for the first time in her life. She decided to give up her major in political science, as she said the professors were boring after a lifetime at our dinner table talks. She, therefore, pursued French and music, both of which she knew quite well before going to Duke.

About the time of her junior year in Durham, Kathe joined our family Fourth of July weekend party in Westhampton. We had given an annual supper for our friends and their children (that time, counting our age group and those of college age and older, we had about sixty at eight separate tables in various rooms of our house). That year John Niehus, a friend of Sharon's, came in with a very handsome young man dressed a bit differently. He did not have on the uniform madras slacks and colorful or navy blazer as was the Long Island preppie dress. Edwin Williamson walked in the front door with knee socks of navy, chino Bermuda walking shorts, and a navy jacket. Kathe was a goner. Cecil, our only son-in-law at that time, came to me during the evening and said, "Mom, look out on the little yellow porch." Cecil, with a wine bottle in each hand, was helping with the wine service. "That guy doesn't have a chance," he said. Kathe was looking adoringly into Edwin's eyes and saying, "Oh, really, how fascinating." As it developed, he did not have a chance! They were married in June 1969 in Westhampton. Theirs was the only country wedding we had, and our family was joined by an entire busload of Edwin's South Carolina relatives, not all of his forty-six cousins from Darlington County, but a good number of them. Just thirty-one years later, Hopie was married in the same back yard. Kathe and Edwin lived for three years (1976-1979) in Belgrave Square in London while he headed the Sullivan and Cromwell office there.

Their first-born was named for my husband, Samuel Gates Williamson. When the family returned from London, he attended St. Bernard's School on East 99th Street in New York City, proceeded to Milton Academy in Massachusetts for his high school years, and following in his mother's footsteps, spent four years at Duke.

During the summers Sam studied Mandarin at Indiana University's Asian Language Center. His passion for Chinese began when he went to Beijing on a Milton Program trip studying at the same school attended by Deng Xiaoping's grandson and living with the school's faculty members who were rewarded with a refrigerator for their housing. He also worked in a New York law firm as a general handyman and library assistant, while

Phil with family members after a tap dance at Christopher and Helen Wray's wedding.

studying Mandarin on the side. Sam graduated from Duke magna cum laude, earned a Phi Beta Kappa, and received a Fulbright Scholarship to continue his studies of Mandarin in Singapore. He had also enjoyed two six-week summer stints in the Marine's Reserve Officers' Training Corps. After this taste of military life, he enlisted, promising his country over three years of his life. He was separated as a lieutenant, after commanding a platoon in the Pacific. With his tour of duty over, he aced his law boards, attended and has just graduated from Harvard Law School and married his extraordinarily gifted Duke classmate Eleanor Fuqua, a graduate of Harvard Business School. They currently work and live in Nashville.

His younger brother, Edwin Williamson, Jr., whom we call Beebo, is the only one of our grandchildren who could take advantage of the public education system. There is near our apartment an experimental public school called the Hunter School (connected at one time with the Education Department of Hunter College). If one is lucky enough to be accepted in the first grade, one STAYS. At least most do, as it saves the family about $20,000 a year in tuition. Beebo had an excellent classroom experience, and I always felt that he and his sidekick, a Puerto Rican child named Felix, could have been dropped into any jungle and come out alive. They were "street smart!"

Hunter School offered little extracurricular activity, however. He had no friends during the Westhampton summers and had to tag along with his older brother. Kathe also complained to me that the third grade Hunter girls were phoning him so often after school that he had no time for homework. Feeling that Beebo needed after-school activities, summer friends, and the discipline such as a private school offered, Kathe moved him to St. Bernard's, with his brother Sam.

That school, so conveniently located next door to their apartment house, was apparently not working out for him, and he was often "sent to the headmaster." One afternoon, I was having tea with Kathe in her kitchen when Beebo walked in, his lower lip quivering. Kathe gave him a hug and said, "Oh Beebo, you didn't get in trouble again, did you?" Immediately, he blurted out, "Yes, I got sent to the headmaster's office, but it WASN'T FAIR! I wasn't doing anything half as bad as the boys behind me in class." When Kathe had given him a glass of milk and a cookie and wiped his face with a warm cloth, she asked him what he had done to be sent to the front office. "Well," he said, "I was just humming. The math was boring."

Beebo, an extraordinarily bright boy, was probably ahead of his class. "What ELSE were you doing besides humming?" Kathe probed further. "Well," he replied, "I was sort of pretending like I was playing a sliding trombone while humming. But mother, I was doing it quietly in my seat, not bothering anybody."

Kathe, of course, explained that whether his gyrations and sounds were muted or not, his silent tromboning WAS disturbing to the class and probably his teachers had acted properly. "But" he continued to protest, "those two guys in back of me were chanting out loud!" "What were they singing?" his mother wanted to know. "Well, that's the worst of it," he said. "They were chanting vagina, vagina, vagina!"

This is the fifth grade! We did our best to keep a straight face. Beebo was right—what they were doing was quite a bit worse than his humming. Why mothers get gray!

Beebo, in his teens became a Chinese scholar and spent some months in 1994 working in a spool factory for an American company in Taiwan, eighty miles from Taipei. He subsequently went via a Middlebury College program (as an undergraduate) to the University of Harbin, way up there next to the Russian border! He completed his studies there and re-

Phil and her daughters as depicted in an original drawing by Al Hirschfeld, whose drawings appear regularly in the New York Times, *with nine Ninas.*

turned speaking and reading Mandarin very well. He graduated from Middlebury in February 1996, skiing, with about sixty others in black caps and gowns, down the Vermont snowy slopes to grab his diploma from the college president! He is a darling and lovable human being and has absorbed much from the remarkable educational opportunities which have come his way. He has finished a premed course at Bryn Mawr, taken his medical school boards, and is now a second year man in medical school at Columbia University. He worked for the Dreyfus Medical Foundation stationed in Capetown covering about eight African countries where the foundation awards medical assistance grants, supervision of which was his job. This was much responsibility for one so young, and we were proud.

Phil celebrates her 80th birthday with family at her Westhampton Beach home, 1998.

The Williamson's youngest, Bess (Sara Elizabeth), is a lovely girl who also attended Brearley. When the family moved to Washington, D.C., she went to the National Cathedral School and later graduated, as did her brother Sam and cousin Owen, from Milton Academy. She attended Pomona College in Claremont, California, for her first two years of higher education and transferred to Brown University after taking a semester off pruning trees for her Uncle Ben at Oaklyn Plantation in Darlington, South Carolina, and touring colonial Mexico with me. She is heavily into the arts, making pottery as well as getting all "A's" in courses in literature, history, and liberal arts. She is writing me the most beautiful letters and poems; occasionally I circulate them so that her cousins and brothers can see how gifted she is. She has continued to do pottery and other media and is at the Penland, N.C. arts program.

The Williamsons moved to Washington some years ago, and bought the Dean Acheson[1] home on "P" Street, N.W. Alice Acheson had lived there for 63 years, a number of them after Dean died. It must have been a terrible wrench for her to leave her home, but my children have lovingly restored it and made it a welcoming, beautiful place which we visit frequently and gather as a family at Easter. I burst with pride at the marvelous job Kathe and Edwin have done as well with their family and their lives. Edwin left Sullivan and Cromwell for a few years to serve as legal adviser to the Department of State under James S. Baker and the Bush administration and has returned to an international practice as a Washington partner of Sullivan and Cromwell. Kathe was a gifted high school Latin and Spanish teacher at Holton-Arms, a private school in nearby Bethesda, Maryland, and now is substitute producer of a PBS news and interview program, "The Diane Rehm Show."

This is my brief description of our "tribe," the real focus of Sam's and my life. We supervised their training and raised them with care. The only extracurricular activity we insisted upon, from the second grade through high school, was the study of piano, explaining that we knew no one over the age of thirty who did not wish he could play the piano. "You can all pick out melodies, so we know you have 'an ear' for tunes. So as long as we can pay for lessons, we will insist that you take them," we said. Kathe, our youngest, benefited most from eleven years of instruction, while the others never seemed to gather much interest or enthusiasm for learning to play, but they all have music in their lives.

They all remember and refer to one routine of their childhood. Mother always emphasized to me, especially when she so often stayed with us when the children were very young, that the last moments before children fall asleep are all important. Mother had taken some courses after Daddy died, not only in public health, but also in child psychiatry. For whatever reason, she was convinced that children should NOT cry themselves to sleep, even though it is often only an attention-getting device. I seldom disagreed. I was so eager to please my mother, as well as to have well-adjusted children, that I tried to follow her example. When we, mostly I, tucked the children into their beds, we sang a lullaby, improvised each night. It began with the phrase, "We have two little girls with blue eyes and one little girl with brown" — then I would go on to sing whatever came into my mind, but usually ending up with, "we have such fun at our house when Wednesday (for example) comes around." They all remember this bedtime routine as a "corny and mushy" family ritual, but they remember it fondly, and maybe they followed suit often as their own children went to bed.

Whatever you believe is the unseen and unprovable power that shapes our lives— call it God, as many do—that power has influenced my psyche. I'm not long on the efficacy of prayer as I am endlessly asking God for things, and not thanking him enough. More than once what I prayed for fervently which I thought vital to my life at the time, he never granted—in other words, it did not happen.

In strange ways, twenty or thirty years later, however, it often becomes abundantly clear that it should not have taken place as I so much desired. If it had, other good things might not have gone as well as they had. So I've settled on "someone up there knows better than I."

Our parents, as well as our God (or whatever the power is), want us to stretch our souls—to try to be as perfect as we can. Many children break down under these pressures from their parents' expectations. If our children, or if we, became the perfect people we were expected to be by God or our parents, we would be unendurable bores. My sympathies are with people who do not have a spiritual home such as St. James has been for me. Since Lent 1949, we have been there, a part of its periodic specials, such as parish parties, spring auctions, and fairs and rehearsed with our children and their friends the all important annual Nativity Play. One parishioner tapped me on the back during that pageant and said, "Phil, without your progeny this show could not take place!" Not true, as it has a cast of thousands, but that one event makes me feel as though I belong in spirit to that group of fellow parishioners.

Our oldest grandson, Christopher Wray, an 8th grader at the time, strode majestically down the aisle during the Nativity Pageant as one of the Magi, followed by two second graders carrying his heavy velvet and gold braid train. As he passed me seated on the aisle so that I would not miss a bit of it, he said in a loud whisper "Goggi, I'm having a horrible time keeping my pages in line!" When I sit waiting for a service to begin, my mind recalls that incident as well as so many more which cause me to smile.

At the joint christening of two of our grandsons—Owen Stearns and Samuel Williamson, there were an inordinate amount of godparents and relatives and friends, accompanied by little noisy, wiggly children. These were racing around the sanctuary making of it general chaos while the rector, blessed now Bishop John Coburn, was trying to organize this joint baptism. He finally said to my husband, a Methodist minister's son obviously disapproving of these goings on, "Sam, there is NO way we can have an orderly christening, let's just get on with it and let them throw the bibles if they want to." They did finally get disciplined by Gilda and Cecil Wray and we proceeded with the ceremony.

Whatever we did, or did not do, our children are now my "friends" as well as my loved ones. Mother said, "The best statues erected to your memory will be those of your children. Be sure they turn out the way you want them to be!" They have, and they make me proud of them every day.

Notes

1. Secretary of State under President Harry S. Truman.

Epilogue

One must wait until the evening
to see how splendid the day has been.
— *Sophocles, 495–406 B.C.*

Too suddenly I have come to the end. Time and distance flash by—so many hours of enjoyment, so many hours of distress, so much unsaid to those I love. What do I want to be or do when I get on with the rest of my life, now that I am a quite healthy eighty-two?

I want to delight in every happy moment left to me. To nourish my friendships, to "be there" for my family, take pride in my behavior and my looks. Lady Duff Cooper told someone about my age, "Don't try to look younger, just try to look better!"

My idol, Eleanor Roosevelt, who had so much to be sad about, said, "No one can make you feel inferior without your consent." I want to be useful—to say to so many causes I believe in, "Use me."

I listen to the whispers of my body when I want to say "yes," but I must say "no" in order to attain that delicate balance between work, play, and commitment.

I want to listen more carefully and respond with compassion and a willingness to help.

What can I share? History has been covered. Anecdotes which make me yearn to live life all over have been recounted. Surely I must not indulge in bad mouthing the present era. We live in this marvelous country where almost every person in the world would like to live, except the French and the English, perhaps.

I've always been so proud to be a member of the legal profession, and especially to have been a member of the team of our firm, Debevoise, Plimpton, Lyons, and Gates. Just this week I attended a gala bash in the firm's headquarters, when the head of the firm, Barry Bryan, announced that *The American Lawyer*'s survey of American law firms had judged the Cravath firm and the Debevoise firm are tops in the country in pure partnership quality and are tops in 10 percent of the firms in total profitability, while keeping a good segment of its lawyers committed to pro bono matters.

Yes, I am still proud of our profession, even though it has suffered from moral and ethical misdeeds. There is still, in small and large firms, a demand for excellence in crafting legal documents and in holding to the highest standards service rendered their clients. In most firms there are one or two senior partners who set these standards. In our firm, as in other New York firms, there are many whose great skills and judgment help the New York community. Indeed, where would the Legal Aid Society, hospitals, museums, parks, and schools be without lawyers who donate their time to them? We read only about the **bad** guys. Yet there are so many who are **good.**

It is all very well to say that the teaching of ethics and morals begins in the home. This was ever the case in my day. Those years at Grandmother Annie's home, and at ours, often rang with the admonitions, "Phil, you know what is right. Just do it." Unfortunately, today with so many single parent households, the teaching of social mores, ethics, and morals is left to single individuals, and the great majority are working females. At the conclusion of a hectic day, today's working mothers can do little more than produce a soup and sandwich or frozen dinner. With that out of the way, "family time" consists of hunkering down in front of a television set, generally cluttered with sex, violence, and game shows. In other words, "instant, tailor-made trash." No time for "right and wrong" discourses. Even families blessed with both parents seem to have little time for "sit down" meals and "talk sessions," or they don't make the effort to be sure such gatherings take place.

It is not surprising that the media are constantly reporting scandal, sex, murder, and mayhem. Those "sell" the products the advertisers pay for. A good majority of today's movies are full of sex, violence, and obscene language, all accessible to teenagers.

Government and corporation scandals seem to flourish. Nice guys, such as the whistle blowers who report corruption in their organizations, often seem to finish last. Breaches of ethics abound at every level, even in academe.

In 1943-1945, I was to serve as a confidential legal assistant to Harlee Branch during his tenure as a member and chairman of the Civil Aeronautics Board, alas now abolished. Before joining FDR's New Deal, he was managing editor of the *Atlanta Constitution*. There was no "beating around the bush" with Mr. Branch. Right was right. Wrong was wrong. And there was no Mr. In-between!

His opening speech to new CAB employees never varied and went something like this:

> You are fortunate to be employed by a branch of the Government of the United States. Our agency, the CAB, is responsible for the regulation of the Civil Aviation Industry. During your employment you will come in contact with many members of the industry it is our duty to regulate. Under no circumstances are you to accept lunch or dinner invitations or gifts of any kind from members of this industry. A candy bar is just as incriminating as a box seat at a Redskin game or a fur coat. You can't be "a little pregnant." Your daily actions and decisions can have enormous influence on the economics of their company, or their own advancement up the corporate ladder. If it comes to my attention that you have violated these guidelines of ethical behavior, it will result in your immediate dismissal.

Take that Messrs. Kennedy, Johnson, Nixon, Reagan, Clinton, Boesky and Milken! Not one of Harlee Branch's employees ever, to my knowledge, violated his standard of ethics.

Perhaps I am naive, but if government heads would follow these same guidelines, private industry would, more than likely, fall in line as well. Even heads of state and captains of finance learn ethics and morals the same as we, at their grandparents' knee, from their father and mother, if they learn them at all.

While I am still atop my soap box, back to the family!

Cloaked in my "domestic personae," that of homemaker, wife and mother, my observations will be even more heartfelt. Principles of ethical and moral conduct played a pivotal role in my life. They guided and served me well through the highs and lows of my formative years. Most importantly, they led this Florida Cracker through one of the happiest and grandest marriages ever created on this good earth!

Recently, marriage is making a dramatic comeback. Marriage and family values are "in" again. And why not? Marriage always has and forever will be the best accepted model on which to build a rewarding life and rear a family. How fortunate I was to have had those forty wonderful shared years with Sam Gates.

For the most part, my generation took "till death do us part" in its strictest interpretation.

To achieve a loving marriage or to become a family, there must be rules. We had them, Sam and I, and here are some of his, corny as they might sound. But remember. Sam was a realist—an honest realist. Consider: Sam's caveats to me after I said "yes."

First: never doubt our priorities. This concerned children. Sam always intended to be the principal wage earner, yet he never begrudged me my own career. This was in the fifties, and Sam was far ahead of his time! However, if my own career was temporarily shelved to stay home with the children, then so be it!

Thus I committed—a practicing member of the bar—to an indefinite number of years, devoted in their entirety to "homemaking" and "child-rearing." They were exhausting and demanding and provided me with the most fulfilling years of my life. Perhaps there is someone out there today who can think of a better way to insure a child's health, good education, and happiness. I did not know of one then, nor do I know of one now.

Second, please don't laugh: Never rush me into dinner. Bless his heart. Early on I was on notice that he would be under stress, wanted to catch his breath and have a cocktail before dinner to unwind, and intended to unburden himself at that time to me of the highs and lows of his day.

Third: Never question his work habits. Sam said they were outrageous and they were. I was forewarned. I never uttered a peep. Well, almost never.

Sam had but three "rules." Naturally, I had to best him, so I had four. I called them my Golden Rules.

First: Keep smiling. (All women are actresses, and most are diplomats intuitively.) Never lay the day's stress and distress on your spouse at the door. I always tried to let Sam relax and talk about his day before I ever aired the litanies of life's unbearable moments of "my" day.

Second: Happiness should always be "coming home." A woman who works to make the house welcome and attractive creates a "home." So far, this has been the woman's responsibility.

Perhaps it should not be, but it is! The wives of four couples interviewed on their Golden wedding anniversaries echoed one another. Each said, "A neat house and good aromas from the kitchen guaranteed a smile on my husband's face when he walked in the door."

Third: Always look as good as you can. Boy, does this seem unfair, especially in light of how he looks around the house.

Well, life is not fair. This may sound antiquated, even Victorian, but nothing can make a man want to come home more than an attractive wife and an inviting home.

Fourth and Last: Alternate household chores. Today's husbands and fathers know that they will be sharing the tasks, and sincerely want to help.

Keep in mind that most of the premier chefs in the world are men. Teach him to take pride in dinner preparations. He can really be excited by cooking if you have taken care of much of the preliminary preparations.

I hope that you will be as fortunate as Sam and I. Our great joy was to find in each other someone who was our very best friend. By doing so, we learned that love, as C. S. Lewis said, "is a deep unity maintained by will and strengthened by habit."

Scenes of a wonderful life race by me. The faces and places no longer blur.

To me it was easy to choose to be a mother and wife. All of the women in my life—mother, grandmother, aunts, and even their friends—emphasized one thing: all men and women may be created equal, but marriage contracts are not. No, these were 75 percent to 25 percent propositions with the wife accepting the lion's share of responsibility for the tone of the relationship, social life, and observances of family "togetherness." Modern career women resent this advice and most refuse to accept it out of hand.

To satisfy my curiosity, I posed statistics to thirty recently married women in the following manner:

> "Am I completely crazy to suggest that my own acceptance of these percentages (75-25) has merit?"

Surprisingly, twenty-eight of the women—all between the ages of thirty and fifty—agreed with the percentages emphatically! Think of that, all but two said in essence, "Your older relatives were right on." That does not mean they thought it was "fair" or should be that way. It had simply worked out that way in their lives if they wanted the marital relationship to succeed.

The reason is, and always will be, quite simple. Women, no matter how liberated or successful in their careers, have far more to lose if the marriage fails. The extra effort on her part—the extra 25 percent—is an investment in herself, and, of course, in her children's future happiness. Cheap at any price!

What does this extra effort entail? Consider Ann Landers' job description—of a housewife—if you will, and in today's world a working wife. She is, and I quote, "wife, mother, friend, confidante, peacemaker, housekeeper, laundress, chauffeur, interior decorator, gardener, veterinarian, manicurist, barber, seamstress, appointment manager, financial planner, bookkeeper, personal secretary, disciplinarian, entertainer, psychoanalyst, nurse, diagnostician, public relations expert, dietitian, nutritionist, baker, chef, fashion coordinator, letter writer for both sides of the family, travel agent, speech therapist, plumber, and automobile maintenance-repair assistant, and, in the marketplace, wage earner. She must be all of the above while still maintaining a cheerful and radiant demeanor. And it goes without saying that she must be ready to jump into bed with fervor at a moment's notice."

Most of today's brides of any age blanch at the above; younger women may balk at the idea of planning to give up any part of their career track when a baby arrives. Should the future groom not see it that way, best iron out the difference of opinion before walking down the aisle. I have handled several divorces resulting from such lack of understanding between the parties. Wearing my matrimonial lawyer hat, I believe that most of the marriages that do not "take" could have had the participants discussed all possible sources of conflict beforehand and committed themselves to the necessary give and take of compromise.

I admit my generation was a pretty square bunch—the Powells, Gates, Ashers, and Browns—when we consider the family sagas of today. Our stories are not lurid, psychotic, or violent enough to make this memoir as popular as the tales on the best seller list of dysfunctional families. Our births, deaths, celebrations, right and wrong directions taken when we came to forks in life's journey are perhaps not hair-raising enough. Lots of mistakes are made, and plenty of pain and suffering is experienced by most families of all eras.

We are a distillation and product of those parents and grandparents who came before us and gave us their hopes, dreams, and rules to live by. One way or another, we worked to keep those traditional observances and celebrations alive because we really love one another. That is not a sappy, mushy statement; in our case, it is true. Lance Morrow, contributing editor of *Civilization,* puts it. "The complex, aching, binding love is the real biological energy of families." We feel this most poignantly when we lose a spouse, a parent, or, as we did recently, a wonderful son-in-law. His inspiring, comforting memorial service is over, but we will continue to mourn and miss him, as we do Sam, my husband, and our own parents. Love has to pull it all together to be a family and abide one another, warts and all.

As Albert Camus, the French writer, said, "There is no substitute for having consideration of others—which is what good manners are all about." I always try to leave the people I love with loving words—I may die before I see them again. If there has been a cross word during the day, forgiveness is the key to your relationship in the future. Home is where we must practice all this because if we don't teach love there, it will be hard to give it or receive it elsewhere. That's why nourishing love and friendship means so much. It is terrible to grow old alone, so to love and be loved will sustain you.

Mother used to admonish me, when my feelings were hurt that, "if someone says something hurtful to you, must behave so that nobody else will believe it." One must be a friend as life has little joy without friends. It doesn't cost anything to be nice. Also, I've spent a lot of time learning that one can get by on charm for only about half an hour. After that you must know something. All my jobs have taught me a lot—accounting, law, fundraising, mothering, and making a home—but I've enjoyed them. Such things I have learned from those endeavors no one can take away from me. For a long time, I have attempted to be the person I want to be, and I'm trying always to look for the best in everyone and never to bore people with my problems. Now that I'm older, I don't have to impress anyone. I believe in an occasional miracle because I have seen several happen.

Perhaps this Florida Cracker has learned a few things about life, and through these pages I've relived it.

Once more with feeling, "Play it Again, Sam."

Index